WORKSHOPS IN COMPUTING
Series edited by C. J. van Rijsbergen

Also in this series

5th Refinement Workshop, Proceedings of the 5th Refinement Workshop, organised by BCS-FACS, London, 8–10 January 1992
Cliff B. Jones, Roger C. Shaw and Tim Denvir (Eds.)

Algebraic Methodology and Software Technology (AMAST'91)
Proceedings of the Second International Conference on Algebraic Methodology and Software Technology, Iowa City, USA, 22–25 May 1991
M. Nivat, C. Rattray, T. Rus and G. Scollo (Eds.)

ALPUK92, Proceedings of the 4th UK Conference on Logic Programming, London, 30 March–1 April 1992
Krysia Broda (Ed.)

Logic Program Synthesis and Transformation
Proceedings of LOPSTR 92, International Workshop on Logic Program Synthesis and Transformation, University of Manchester, 2–3 July 1992
Kung-Kiu Lau and Tim Clement (Eds.)

NAPAW 92, Proceedings of the First North American Process Algebra Workshop, Stony Brook, New York, USA, 28 August 1992
S. Purushothaman and Amy Zwarico (Eds.)

First International Workshop on Larch
Proceedings of the First International Workshop on Larch, Dedham, Massachusetts, USA, 13–15 July 1992
Ursula Martin and Jeannette M. Wing (Eds.)

Persistent Object Systems
Proceedings of the Fifth International Workshop on Persistent Object Systems, San Miniato (Pisa), Italy, 1–4 September 1992
Antonio Albano and Ron Morrison (Eds.)

Formal Methods in Databases and Software Engineering, Proceedings of the Workshop on Formal Methods in Databases and Software Engineering, Montreal, Canada, 15–16 May 1992
V.S. Alagar, Laks V.S. Lakshmanan and F. Sadri (Eds.)

Modelling Database Dynamics
Selected Papers from the Fourth International Workshop on Foundations of Models and Languages for Data and Objects, Volkse, Germany, 19–22 October 1992
Udo W. Lipeck and Bernhard Thalheim (Eds.)

14th Information Retrieval Colloquium
Proceedings of the BCS 14th Information Retrieval Colloquium, University of Lancaster, 13–14 April 1992
Tony McEnery and Chris Paice (Eds.)

Functional Programming, Glasgow 1992
Proceedings of the 1992 Glasgow Workshop on Functional Programming, Ayr, Scotland, 6–8 July 1992
John Launchbury and Patrick Sansom (Eds.)

Z User Workshop, London 1992
Proceedings of the Seventh Annual Z User Meeting, London, 14–15 December 1992
J.P. Bowen and J.E. Nicholls (Eds.)

Interfaces to Database Systems (IDS92)
Proceedings of the First International Workshop on Interfaces to Database Systems, Glasgow, 1–3 July 1992
Richard Cooper (Ed.)

AI and Cognitive Science '92
University of Limerick, 10–11 September 1992
Kevin Ryan and Richard F.E. Sutcliffe (Eds.)

Theory and Formal Methods 1993
Proceedings of the First Imperial College Department of Computing Workshop on Theory and Formal Methods, Isle of Thorns Conference Centre, Chelwood Gate, Sussex, UK, 29–31 March 1993
Geoffrey Burn, Simon Gay and Mark Ryan (Eds.)

Algebraic Methodology and Software Technology (AMAST'93)
Proceedings of the Third International Conference on Algebraic Methodology and Software Technology, University of Twente, Enschede, The Netherlands, 21–25 June 1993
M. Nivat, C. Rattray, T. Rus and G. Scollo (Eds.)

Logic Program Synthesis and Transformation
Proceedings of LOPSTR 93, International Workshop on Logic Program Synthesis and Transformation, Louvain-la-Neuve, Belgium, 7–9 July 1993
Yves Deville (Ed.)

Database Programming Languages (DBPL-4)
Proceedings of the Fourth International Workshop on Database Programming Languages – Object Models and Languages, Manhattan, New York City, USA, 30 August–1 September 1993
Catriel Beeri, Atsushi Ohori and Dennis E. Shasha (Eds.)

continued on back page...

Matt Smith, Alan Smaill and Geraint A. Wiggins (Eds.)

Music Education: An Artificial Intelligence Approach

Proceedings of a Workshop held as part of AI-ED 93, World Conference on Artificial Intelligence in Education, Edinburgh, Scotland, 25 August 1993

BCS

Springer-Verlag Berlin Heidelberg GmbH

Matt Smith, BA, MSc

Department of Computing
King Alfred's College of Higher Education
Sparkford Road, Winchester, SO22 4NR, UK

Alan Smaill, BSc, DPhil
Geraint A. Wiggins, MA, PhD

Department of Artificial Intelligence
University of Edinburgh, 80 South Bridge
Edinburgh, EH1 1HN, Scotland, UK

ISBN 978-3-540-19873-4

British Library Cataloguing in Publication Data
Music Education: Artificial Intelligence Approach – Proceedings of a Workshop Held as Part of AI-ED 93, World Conference on Artificial Intelligence in Education, Edinburgh, Scotland, 25 August 1993. – (Workshops in Computing Series)
I. Smith, Matthew Richard II. Series
006.3
ISBN 978-3-540-19873-4 ISBN 978-1-4471-3571-5 (eBook)
DOI 10.1007/978-1-4471-3571-5

Library of Congress Cataloging-in-Publication Data
Music education, an artificial intelligence approach : proceedings of a workshop held as part of AI-ED 93, World Conference on Artificial Intelligence in Education, Edinburgh, Scotland, 25 August 1993 / Matt Smith, Alan Smaill, and Geraint A. Wiggins, eds.
p. cm.
"Published in collaboration with the British Computer Society."
Includes bibliographical references and index.
ISBN 978-3-540-19873-4

1. Artificial intelligence–Musical applications–Congresses. 2. Music–Instruction and study–Congresses. I. Smith, Matt, 1967–. II. Smaill, Alan. III. Wiggins, Geraint A,, 1962– . IV. World Conference on Artificial Intelligence in Education (1993 : Edinburgh, Scotland) V. British Computer Society. 93–48464
ML73.5.M87 1994 CIP
780'.7–dc20 MN

Originally published by Springer-Verlag Berlin Heidelberg New York in 1994

Typesetting: Camera ready by contributors

34/3830-543210 Printed on acid-free paper

Preface

The research fields of "artificial intelligence and music" and "cognitive musicology" are relative newcomers to the many interdisciplinary groupings based around the centre of AI and cognitive science. They are concerned with the computational study and emulation of human behaviour with respect to music, in many aspects, and with varying degrees of emphasis on psychological plausibility. Recent publications have included work in such diverse areas as rhythm and pitch perception, performance, composition, and formal analysis. Music shares with language the property of giving access to human mental behaviour in a very direct way. As such, it has the potential to be a very useful domain for AI work. Furthermore, in the course of time, AI related work will surely throw light back onto some or all of the fields to which it is applied. Indeed, we are already beginning to feel the benefits of the application of AI techniques to music technology.

It is not surprising, therefore, that one of the first areas of interest for musical AI study is that of music education. There are many ways in which an artificial intelligence or cognitive science approach to music education may be applied – for example, to automate tuition, to explain learning processes, to provide metaphors for human computer interaction, and so on.

This collection of papers, which is intended to give an impression of both the breadth and depth of the field, originated from a workshop entitled "Music Education: An Artificial Intelligence Approach". The workshop took place in Edinburgh, Scotland, on Wednesday 25th August 1993 as part of AI-ED 93, the World Conference on Artificial Intelligence in Education. Although the workshop was part of an AI and education conference, the aim was less a specific dissemination of AI education work for music theories and tasks, than a focus for workers in related disciplines to meet, present and discuss work of interest at various levels.

It is particularly appropriate that this collection appears at a time when a community of AI/music researchers is becoming internationally established. Even so, the researchers represented in this volume come from a variety of backgrounds. The diagram below summarises one view of the overlaps and relationships between their work, and highlights the breadth of interaction and cross-fertilisation which can take place in this field.

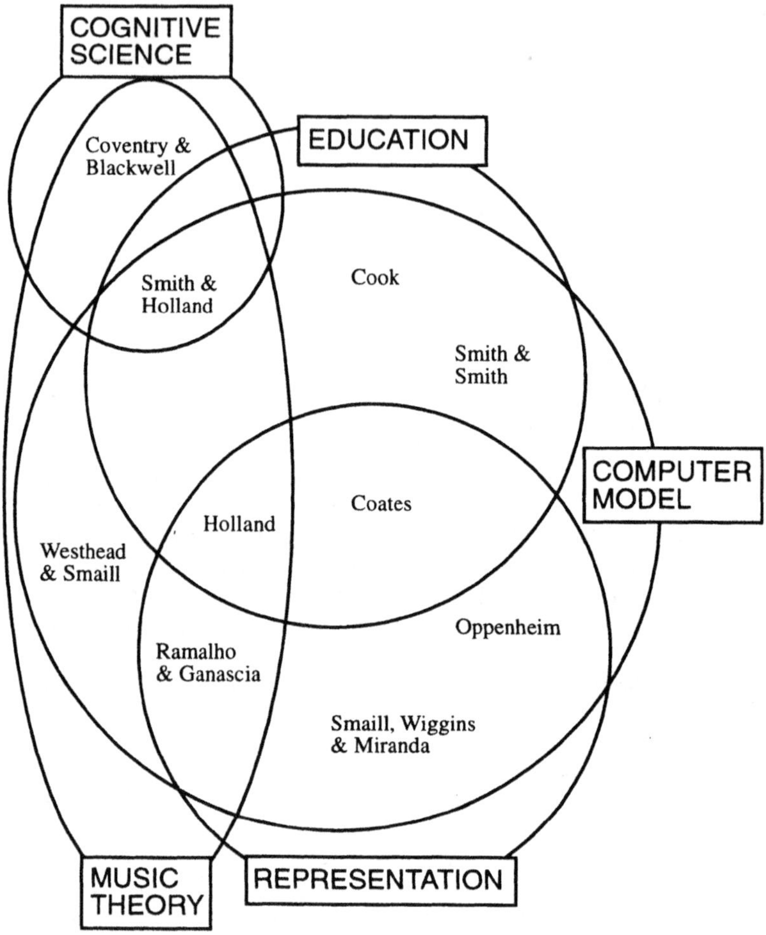

The book has been organised in three sections, representing the three themes used to organise the workshop. It is intended as a communication of current research in these related fields. In the section on **Music Education**, various aspects of the design of musical education systems are discussed. John Cook specifies a multi-level architecture for an intelligent learning environment, using agent reflection to reason about the learning process; Simon Holland and Matt Smith present psychologically motivated systems for tutoring in the composition of tonal harmony and melody, respectively; and Brian Smith and William Smith compare cognitive modelling tactics for representing musical experts' thought processes.

In the second section, **Representation of Musical Knowledge**, Daran Coates discusses architectures and representations for systems dealing with problems of tonal harmonisation; Daniel Oppenheim presents a metaphor for user/computer interaction, and demonstrates its application in a music processing system; and Alan Smaill, Geraint Wiggins and Eduardo Miranda suggest that abstraction is important for representation in music education and user modelling, and propose an appropriate approach.

Finally, in **Music Theory and Computational Models**, Kenny Coventry and Tim Blackwell compare pragmatic issues in music with those already understood from the study of linguistics; Geber Ramalho and Jean-Gabriel Ganascia describe a "musical memory" based approach to the modelling of composition tasks; and Martin Westhead and Alan Smaill describe a statistical method for analysis of music with reference to motivic "fingerprints" of particular composers.

The editors would like to thank the following researchers who acted as reviewers for this publication:

Bernard Bel, GRTC-CNRS Marseille, France;
Antonio Camurri, University of Genova, Italy;
Kenny Coventry, University of Plymouth, England;
Mitch Harris, University of Edinburgh, Scotland;
Simon Holland, Open University, England;
Alan Marsden, Queen's University, Belfast, Northern Ireland.

Thanks are also due to the authors for their efficiency during editing, without which the task might have been much more onerous than it was.

Milton Keynes; Edinburgh
October 1993

Matt Smith
Alan Smaill
Geraint A. Wiggins

Contents

Section I: Music Education

Section II: Representation of Musical Knowledge

Section III: Music Theory and Computational Models

Section I: Music Education

Agent Reflection in an Intelligent Learning Environment Architecture for Musical Composition

John Cook
School of Technology and Information Studies
Thames Valley University
Ealing, London W5 5RF, England
st0038@uk.ac.tvu.e.pa

Abstract

The goal of the research described in this paper is to develop an Intelligent Learning Environment (ILE) that is reflective about its own teaching. The ILE will aim to engage a learner in some goal-directed, problem-seeking activity in the open-ended domain of musical composition. This paper describes a theoretical framework we have developed for describing the teaching-learning processes in musical composition. The 'Intelligent Learning Environment Architecture' (ILEA) will provide a framework for a critical comparison of what different Teaching Interventions can contribute to the learning of reflective thinking skills and abilities in open-ended domains like musical composition. We claim that an emphasis on problem seeking is crucial if ILEs are to be extended to open-ended domains like musical composition where there is no right or wrong answer. We make a clear distinction between the reflective and non-reflective processes carried out by a composer, by a learner and by a teacher. Further, we assert that ILEs should shift their emphasis from encouraging a learner to be reflective about domain knowledge to include fostering a learner's ability to be reflective about their own learning.

1 Introduction

In this paper, we discuss how a theoretical framework can describe the teaching and learning of "higher-order" thinking in the context of musical composition. Higher-order thinking can include problem solving, decision making, critical thinking, logical reasoning and creative thinking. The theoretical framework we present has two purposes. First, it will be used to identify a categorisation for future empirical work (*e.g.*, protocol analysis). Second, the framework will help to determine which areas of formal Artificial Intelligence (AI) can be applied to the computational modelling of what we call reflective teaching. We are not claiming that our framework, or any planned computational instantiation of the framework, describes or models higher-order thinking. Rather, the framework will provide a meta-level description of the teaching-learning processes in musical composition. By meta-level we mean that the framework is interested in describing the management of its own resources and the monitoring, evaluation and improvement of its own performance. This distinction can be best illustrated by highlighting the fact that the framework is not a description of creative cognition. Instead, it is a meta-level description of how teaching interventions could foster creativity in a learner.

The first question to examine is: does learning involve more than the acquisition of knowledge? Western societies' traditional view of an educated person is of someone who is 'knowledgeable', *i.e.*, someone who is perceived as having learnt many facts. However, knowledge can quickly become obsolete, and what we believe to be true may be incorrect or inappropriate. In a response to these issues the philosopher Matthew Lipman [Lipman 91a, Lipman 91b] has proposed that we must stipulate that education should include reasoning and judgement about knowledge. Education in the Lipman sense of the word is not "simply" learning, it is a teacher-guided community of inquiry. Lipman calls this "the reflective model of education practice" or the "reflective paradigm" [Lipman 91a]. A major influence on Lipman has been John Dewey's examination (at the beginning of this century) of scientific inquiry (summarised in [OEC91]). What makes Lipman's approach relevant to the research reported here is that he has developed Dewey's reflective, problem solving approach to education in a way that takes full account of aesthetics, creativity and democratic participation. Lipman is also concerned with the role of teachers and the circumstances for fostering effective thinking. Lipman's work is of further importance, from the perspective of this research, in four respects.

- First, it defines the objectives of our "educational theory", *i.e.*, our framework. Our educational objectives are to foster in a student reflective composing (the primary objective) and reflective learning. These objectives are explained in section 4.

- Second, it indicates which approaches to educational psychology are appropriate for our educational theory. By this we mean that educational psychology provides the methods and models of how to fulfil educational objectives. Specifically, the origin of Lipman's communities of inquiry is attributed to the work of L. S. Vygotsky [Vygotsky 62] who compared children doing intellectual work cooperatively with those working in competition. Cooperative learning is therefore seen as being compatible with our own educational objectives.

- The third aspect of Lipman's work important to this research is that we view Lipman's educational philosophy as being harmonious with that of the music education philosopher Bennett Reimer [Reimer 89]. Reimer insists that music education "exists first and foremost to develop every person's natural responsiveness to the power of the art of music."

- Fourth, Lipman gives us a clear understanding of why "problem seeking" is appropriate to education in domains such as musical composition where there is no "correct" answer (see section 3 for a full discussion of problem seeking).

Additionally, there is now an increasing focus by researchers such as John Self [Self 93] on the design of Intelligent Learning Environments (ILEs). The ILEs proposed by Self emphasise the role of higher-order thinking by engaging the student in some goal-directed, problem solving activity that a computer-based system *knows* something about – "knows" in the sense of "believe to be correct. Emphasis in an ILE is placed on 'learning by reflection'. Furthermore, there is a research trend that recognises that, if an ILE is to make any kind of teaching intervention to promote a student's activities, the system must, in some way, be able to justify its decision [Elsom-Cook 93]. As we shall see, the above premises present the designer of an ILE with many technical and epistemological challenges.

2 Context and objectives of research

Composition is taught in all university music departments in the UK, and 90% (in 1989) of these use computer technology to enhance training standards [CTI92]. Computers are typically used to aid learning in musical skills such as basic harmony and counterpoint. There have been several attempts to apply Artificial Intelligence and Cognitive Science research to musical composition education [Thomas 85, Desain & Honing 86, Fenton 89, Holland 89]. None of these systems have attempted explicitly to teach higher-order thinking as we have outlined it above.

Educational researchers claim to show that many aspects of thinking can be developed or strengthened by appropriate teaching [OEC91]. Whatever the claims, the crucial question is: what is appropriate teaching? The research reported in this paper is part of a larger project that addresses a key issue for studies involving music composition education [Webster 89]: what roles do different types of *teacher intervention* play in fostering successful *creative thinking*? In our research this issue takes the form of the following questions. Do Teaching Interventions encourage in a learner some reflective cognitive processes? Can we measure the outcomes of these cognitive processes by observing any resultant creative activities (what we call problem seeking activities)? These research questions are shown diagrammatically below in Figure 1. The arrows show relationships between the variables and constructs under investigation.

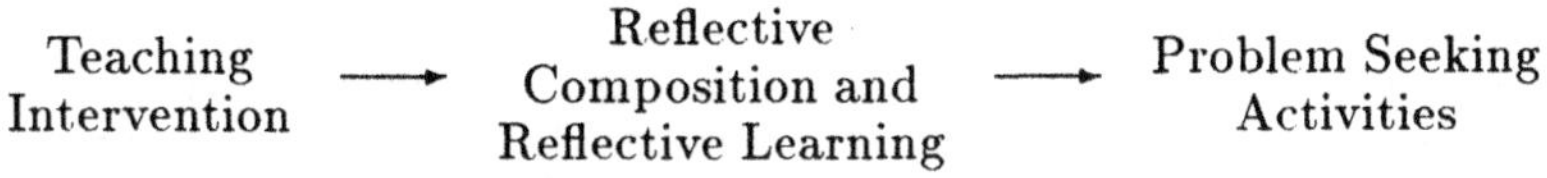

Figure 1: Relationships between research questions.

The goal of our research is, therefore, to develop an ILE that is reflective about its own teaching.

When discussing teaching knowledge it is important to be clear about the different meanings attached to the terminology used by researchers in the field. Mark Elsom-Cook [Elsom-Cook 91, p. 71] uses the term "strategy" to suggest a model that is able to derive variants of and reason about Teaching Styles. A Teaching Style in Elsom-Cook's sense is a rule-based approach to teaching such as cognitive apprenticeship or discovery learning. In the MEMOLAB and ETOILE systems [Dillenbourg *et al* 93] the term Teaching Style is used as a broad term that includes five 'sealed' tutors (which are also referred to as styles and which are similar to Elsom-Cook's Teaching Styles) whose interaction give the 'look and feel' of learner-system interaction. In ETOILE however a Teaching Style also encompasses a Teaching Strategy, which is taken to mean the same as in Instructional Design. In Instructional Design a teaching strategy is based on some taxonomy of domain objects (chapters, concepts, units, topics, etc.) which are used to describe a curriculum. These objects in Instructional Design are used as variables by instructional planning and presentation rules (*i.e.*, the teaching strategy). In this paper we use the broad term of Teaching Method to include a Teaching Style (which is the same as Elsom-Cook's Teaching Style and Dillenbourg et al.'s five tutors) plus a Teaching Intervention. We define a Teaching Intervention as the form, content and justification of the intervention. The emphasis in our research is on developing a ILE that can reason about the goals and intentions of Teaching Interventions and not on modelling cognitive learning strategies. We would describe a ILE with the previously outlined abilities as a reflective teacher.

The general thrust of our approach is that the proposed framework, which we will refer to as the Intelligent Learning Environment Architecture (ILEA), should act as an aid to creativity. By this we mean that the ILEA will not attempt to produce as an output a creative artefact (a composition). It will, however, computationally model reflective activities. The ILEA should be viewed as having a general goal of fostering creativity in a learner by engaging them in reflection about what we call *problem seeking goals.* We regard the emphasis on problem seeking as crucial if ILEs are to be extended to open-ended domains like musical composition where there is no right or wrong answer. What we mean by problem seeking is examined in detail below.

3 Problem seeking

In arguing for an increased emphasis in education on thinking, which is implicit in Lipman's reflective paradigm and Self's approach to Intelligent Learning Environments (ILEs), many sources of disagreement about the nature of thinking emerge. To ask the fundamental question "Can thinking be taught?" is to ask whether particular kinds of teaching can improve particular kinds of thinking. Many are sceptical about the idea, in some cases because they regard thinking as an activity which comes naturally. The term "thinking" is an imprecise term that embraces cerebral activities that can range from philosophical speculation to putting on a pair of shoes. The particular type of thinking we are focusing on in this paper is higher-order or strategic thinking (as outlined in section 1). For example, one basic premise of Self's ILEs is that a student will be engaged in some problem solving thinking. One question that arises is "Can we fruitfully use standard problem solving techniques as an approach to teaching musical composition?". In an attempt to answer this question, we will examine one disagreement that emerges when we begin to explore what we must do to shift the focus of education from learning to include thinking, and which has been summarised by Lipman [Lipman 91a, p. 175]:

> The conception of thinking as primarily *problem solving*
>
> *versus*
>
> The conception of thinking as primarily *problem seeking*

In the above summary, Lipman is highlighting the difference between education in the sciences and education in the humanities (and hence musical composition education). Science text-books have a tendency to treat scientific knowledge as settled. A student learns standard approaches to problem solving. The student is then given problems that vary from the paradigm to see if they are able to extrapolate from that model of how things should be done to solve the problem in hand. In the humanities, however, the subject matter itself is treated as essentially *problematic.* That is to say, students would be encouraged to look for new problems of interpretation or conceptualisation. For example, a problem involving the completion of a section of a musical composition may be interpreted as one of how best to set up tension and create release. The problem could have quite reasonably been interpreted in many other ways. The view that problem *solving* may account for some of the processing involved in musical composition is supported by various researchers [Kratus 85, Sloboda 85, Davidson & Welsh 88, Colley *et al* 92]. John Sloboda [Sloboda 85] warns, however, that the general account of heuristics for solution-generation and verification may have its limitations in the open-ended, creative domain of musical composition. Sloboda's warning seems to suggest that standard problem solving approaches (as outlined above) may be of limited use when teaching thinking in open-ended domains like musical composition. [Lipman 91a, p. 182] makes a related point about his own approach, which places a heavy emphasis on critical thinking:

> "It ... [the reflective, critical thinking movement] runs a danger if it identifies itself too closely with the devising of problem-solving recipes while ignoring the value-laden contexts in which problems occur."

Very little is known about the cognitive processes that composers use when composing. [Sloboda 85] suggests that cognitive plans or "superordinate structures" are used as the basis for making judgements on the form and direction of a composition. These superordinate structures can be viewed as forming the basis for reflective exploration of a composition on a global and note-by-note basis. Further, Sloboda identifies criteria testing of trial solutions as important. By developing Sloboda's last point we propose that problem seeking is governed by contrasting criteria. The phrase "governed by" is used to suggest coercion. We are using the term criteria in the sense of values (matters of importance) that need "satisficing" (sic), *i.e.*, all values can not be satisfied therefore we should satisfy as many as we can. Satisficing can also be taken to mean that it is acceptable to go only part of the way towards satisfying a given value.

An emerging feature our discussion seems to be that any approach to teaching higher-order thinking in the domain of musical composition needs to be rich enough to incorporate issues surrounding value systems, particularly where criteria are concerned. Below is a brief definition of what we shall term **problem seeking goals**, followed by a more detailed statement. The definition is drawn from the above discussion and the definition of creativity of [Lipman 91a]. Problem seeking is defined as being

- conducive to judgement
- governed by context

- self-transcending
- governed by contrasting criteria.

3.1 Conducive to judgement

For problem seeking to have the goal of being conducive to judgement for a group of jazz composers, for example, it should be more concerned with

> "a community of judgements whose internal communications with one another contains the thinking we try to grasp in the form of aesthetic 'meaning.' " [Lipman 91a, p. 138]

That is to say, in such a community, dialogue is of paramount importance when making judgements about the art of musical composition. Judgements, in this context, therefore appraise or pronounce upon relationships, but are governed by criteria. If we asserted that the horn solo was louder than the flute solo, our criterion is loudness (making more or less emphatic music), but the relationship which the judgement expresses is *is louder than*. [Reimer 89, p.141] warns that "judgements should not interfere with [the] immediate, open-minded experiences of music" but that they can help one to "reflect ... about [the] music one is composing".

3.2 Governed by context

Problem seeking is governed by context in terms of the holistic nature of the problem seeking inquiry. Thus, for a composition to have what is called a "dramatic shape", *e.g.,* a good climax, attention must be paid to the composition as a whole. Dramatic shape in a composition is concerned with moving from a beginning towards a climax and is not tied to a particular style of music. For example, a composer may decide that a climax is needed at a certain point. One approach that could be taken is called "prolonging the climax". This is how Matthew Fields (unpublished) describes it:

> "1) make sure the music just before the climax strongly suggests that the climax is coming;
>
> "2) write and insert more of it – possibly a lot more of it. In classical music, this is accomplished by such technicalities as dominant pedals, deceptive cadences ... My favorite example from pop music is one almost everybody has heard: Lennon/McCartney's 'Hey Jude'. It works up to a frenzy, then spends about half the cut repeating the frenzied verse over and over. Two minutes later, the industry-standard fade-out is applied. When this single was released, the crowd went wild ...
>
> "Now, this suggestion [prolongation] doesn't guarantee a fix. If you're expecting a solo flute playing in its lowest octave to sound climactic during a symphony band piece, you may need to rethink other aspects of the piece. However, it works so remarkably well so much of the time that it's worth trying, at least part of the time."

In the above example the low octave flute solo is *governed by the context* of the band climax and the composition as a whole. In another arrangement or a different composition a low octave flute solo may be appropriate, but not in the suggested context of a symphony band climax where all instruments are accompanying the solo.

3.3 Self-transcending

Problem seeking has the goal of being self-transcending in that it monitors itself with the aim of going beyond itself. By this we mean that a composer will attempt to monitor his or her own compositional activities and then make generalisations from that analysis in an attempt to achieve some goal. This could be interpreted as developing a new compositional method or improving on an existing one. Problem solving, on the other hand, tends to be concerned with what is believed to be 'true', and is therefore interested in avoiding error and falsehood. Of course problem seeking is concerned with truth, but not solely what is believed to be true. Indeed, for some composers an error could be taken as the start of an interesting new direction. Rather, in an open-ended domain such as musical composition, problem seeking is also concerned with attitudinal states [Kiss 89]. By this we mean that a musical composer will have the ability to adopt various attitudes to their own music and to that of others, and that it is through their handling of these attitudes that the composer is capable of achieving some goal.

3.4 Governed by contrasting criteria

Finally, problem seeking is governed by contrasting criteria, *i.e.*, the ability to identify the most appropriate ideas by referring to criteria.

> "Anything can be a criterion that functions decisively as the inquiry process moves toward the making of a judgement."
>
> [Lipman 91a, p. 132].

For example, the judgement that "music helps to relax you" *is governed by* the criterion of the ideal value of relaxation and the criterion of the actual value of music; the judgement *expresses* the therapeutic relationship between these two values. [Reimer 89, p. 140] proposes that the four criteria of "craftsmanship, sensitivity, imagination, and authenticity" can provide useful guidelines in music education for both the teacher and the learner.

To conclude this section we propose that problem seeking maximises the opportunities for creativity by 'satisficing' problem seeking goals. Below we describe how our understanding of problem seeking fits into our proposed framework: the Intelligent Learning Environment Architecture.

4 Intelligent Learning Environment Architecture

The Intelligent Learning Environment Architecture (ILEA) is our proposed framework for describing the teaching-learning processes in open-ended domains such as musical composition. We assert that in domains where there is no correct answer, like musical composition, the goal should be to engage learners and teachers in reflection about what we have defined as problem seeking goals. We further claim that it is our emphasis on Teaching Methods that encourage learners to be reflective about problem seeking that differentiates the ILEA form Intelligent Tutoring Systems (ITSs).

We took as a starting point for our framework John Self's proposed architecture for ILEs [Self 93]. The previous document is an internal report from Lancaster University describing the foundations of the SMILE (Student Modelling in Intelligent Learning Environments) project. The SMILE project has empirical, computational and theoretical aspects to it, much of which has not yet been published. At a recent SMILE Workshop[1], the project was described as follows:

> "The theoretical work is concerned with trying to apply various areas of formal AI (belief logics, metareasoning, diagnosis, dialogue games) to aspects of student modelling for intelligent learning environments ...
>
> "The computational work is concerned with developing specific instantiations (such as SciLab, AlgebraLab and MemoLab ...) of the theoretical framework. These systems serve the dual purpose of validating (to some extent) the underlying theory and of providing a means of gathering relevant empirical data ...
>
> "The empirical work involves gathering data, both from students using ILEs or solving problems on paper, to clarify aspects of the theoretical frameworks ... ".

John Self has referred[2] to his four level theoretical framework as "DORMORBILE" (Domain Reasoning Monitoring Reflection Basis for Intelligent Learning Environments). DORMORBILE makes the distinction between an *object level*, which reasons about the problem, and a *meta level*, which reasons about the object level. However, beyond this distinction many issues regarding DORMORBILE remain unresolved. Current debate about DORMORBILE centres on the function of each level and the degree of access one level should be allowed to the other levels.

Below we describe our interpretation of the different levels, which is significantly different to that proposed by Self. In our proposed framework, the ILEA, a clear distinction has been made between a learner's reflections about their own learning, and a learner's reflection about their own domain expertise. We have also isolated what we regard to be the processes involved in reflective teaching. (Note: an agent is a human learner or a computer-based teacher. We will use "it" to refer to agents.)

4.1 General description of the ILEA

Within the ILEA, a Learning agent will engage in some goal-directed, problem seeking activity. One teaching goal of ILEA could be, for example, to foster reflection on the concept of melodic motive (a musical pattern). This goal is supported by the claim of [Davidson & Welsh 88] that melodic motive can act

[1] Ambleside, September 29th to October 1st, 1993, unpublished.

[2] In personal communication.

as an aid to structural unity in a composition and an ability to think in larger structural chunks. Four levels are proposed for the ILEA. Each level takes the levels below it as data and provides results for those lower levels.

By drawing on Lipman's reflective paradigm we are claiming that ILEs should shift their emphasis in the following manner. A Learning agent should not only be reflective about the domain being learned – musical composition for example. Our claim is that a second objective should be for a Learning agent to be reflective about their own learning. We view this as an important distinction if we are to avoid vague discussions of the function of each level. (The distinction will also have implication for the transfer of learning to other areas, which is not discussed here.) In summary then, there are two overall teaching objectives for the Teaching agent in the ILEA. The first, and primary, objective is to foster reflective composition in a Learning agent. The second is to encourage reflective learning.

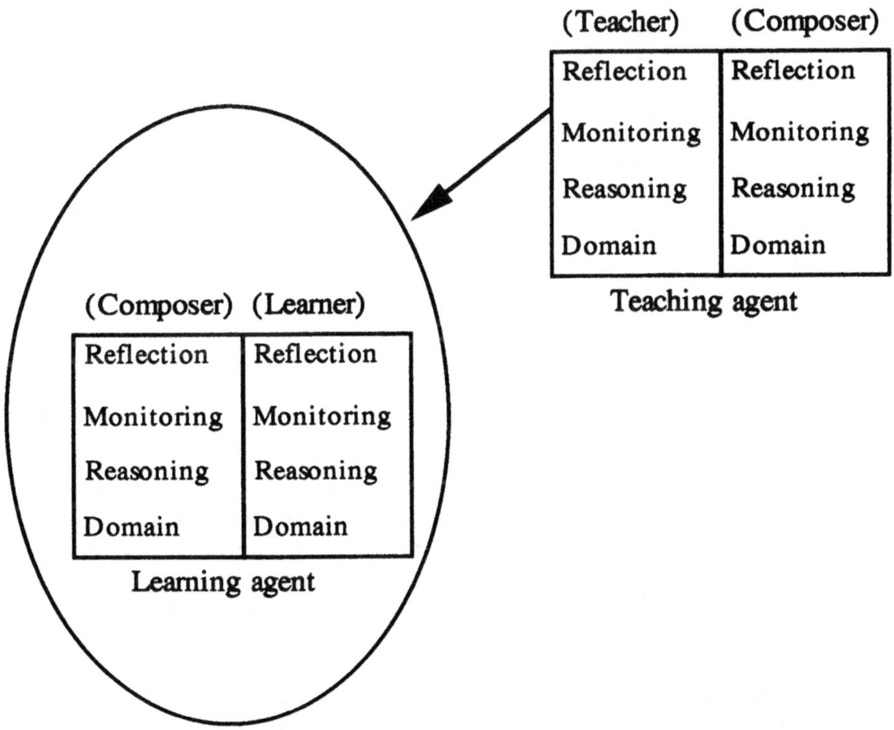

Figure 2: Reflective Agents in the ILEA

Figure 2 shows the organisation of the two reflective agents in the ILEA. There are two components to a Learning agent: a Composer and a Learner. (We will use the convention of stating the agent type followed by the specific component in parenthesis.) The Teaching agent also has two components. These are Teaching agent (teacher) and Teaching agent (composer). Teaching agent (teacher) takes the whole of the Learning agent as its domain. That is to say, Teaching agent (teacher) is interested in all four levels of the rounded, self-directed Learning agent (learner), a human student, as well as all four levels of Learning agent (composer), a human composer. Teaching agent (composer) is similar to Learning agent (composer), the main difference being that Teaching agent (composer) is a reflective composer, whereas Learning agent (composer) may not yet have become a reflective composer. What we actually mean by reflective composing, learning and teaching agents is discussed below and is illustrated in Figure 3.

level: \ agent:	Learning agent (composer)	Learning agent (learner)	Teaching agent (teacher)
Rf	Can I generalise? Can I justify a new method?	Change approach? Add a new method?	Justify introduction of new teaching style? Can I generalise?
	←	(judgements about problem seeking goals)	→
M	Is that good? Did that sound OK? What could I do next?	Which learning method shall I use next? Did I learn that OK?	Did that work? Should I change the teaching intervention?
R	Compositional Methods e.g. use of melodic motive or dramatic shape	Learning Methods e.g. induction, analogy, by example (listening etc.)	Teaching Methods i.e. teaching interventions and teaching styles. Detect & repair learner slips or bugs
D	Harmony, rhythm melody, etc. Dialogue with other composers	Teaching interaction Dialogue with other learners Learning agent (composer)	Learning agent (composer) Learning agent (learner)

Key. Rf = Reflection level; M = Monitoring level; R = Reasoning level; D = Domain level

Figure 3: The concerns of each Reflective Agent at the four levels of the ILEA

Figure 3 shows the concerns of each agent at each of the four levels in the ILEA. Teaching agent (composer) is not shown in Figure 3 because, as we pointed out above, all the activities at all four levels of Teaching agent (composer) are the same as those for Learning agent (composer). The concerns of the levels of the Teaching agent are very different to those of the Learning agent. It is important to note that any agent's activity below the shaded line in Figure 3 would be termed non-reflective, *i.e.*, agent activity at the Domain (D) level and the Reasoning (R) level only. The arrow indicates that judgements about problem seeking goals are carried out at the Monitoring (M) level for all agents. Rf is the Reflection level. Below we examine the concerns of each agent shown in Figure 3. We will illustrate each agent's activities with examples. However, as we have already pointed out, what actually goes at the different levels is the subject of a debate.

4.2 Learning agent (composer)

Learning agent (composer) at the Domain (D) level in Figure 3 will provide a vocabulary for discussing problems relevant to the domain of music composition. Learning agent (composer) at the D level does not specify how to compose. Learning agent (composer)'s domain knowledge will be a subset of what is "known" about the domain of music composition (due to space constraints we intend to side-step the whole issue of agent beliefs in this paper). The Learning agent (composer) at the D level could, for example, know about techniques related to harmony, rhythm and melody. Dialogue with a community of composers will be stored at this level for use by other levels (*e.g.*, to use as the basis for judgements at the Learning agent (composer) M level).

Learning agent (composer) at the Reasoning (R) level will represent knowledge about the possible circumstances in which knowledge at Learning agent (composer) D level could be used. By this we mean that Learning agent (composer) R represents knowledge of possible Compositional Methods, *e.g.*, the use of dramatic shape or melodic motive to aid compositional form. We are using the term Compositional Method in a very broad way and define it as the use of concepts, devices and techniques within the context of a framework. Unlike the proposal of [Self 93], this level *does* indicate when to use the knowledge it represents. By this we refer to the disposition of some cultures towards 'accepted' approaches to writing a composition. The jazz form AABA (verse, verse, chorus, verse) is one example of this tendency. Simply accepting and using this normative composition method can happen at Learning agent (composer) R level. If Learning agent (composer) was to operate only at the bottom two levels of the ILEA (D and R) then it would be termed a non-reflective composer. The example in section 4.2.1 will expand upon this.

Learning agent (composer) at the Monitoring (M) level in Figure 3 will examine the two levels below it (D an R). It asks such questions as: Does that sound right? Should I have done that? At the M level judgements about the lower level activities will take place. As we saw earlier, for a problem seeking activity these judgements have to be made against some problem seeking goals. For example, some governing criterion (a problem seeking goal) could be anything from "beauty" to keeping the composition down to three minutes for a pop song. The ability to make judgements about problem seeking goals will provide an evolving, local plan for the composition.

Learning agent (composer) at the Reflection (Rf) level will examine the next three levels below it to decide if generalisation can be made. This level will also be concerned with planning, but of a more global nature. For example, a decision could be made here, based on data provided by the R and M levels, to introduce an additional Compositional Method, to use its own generalisations to invent a modified or new Compositional Method, and so on. The Rf level is the engine behind much of what is happening in the ILEA. It can examine all the other levels, it can create new generalisations at its own level, and it can decide to push these new generalisations into either the D level (*e.g.*, a new scale), the R level (*e.g.*, a new Compositional Method) or the M level (*e.g.*, new problem seeking goals in the form of new criteria). However, to perform any of the previously outlined operations Learning agent (composer) at the Rf level must be able to justify its reasons for doing so.

4.2.1 Example of Learning agent (composer) using melodic motive

This example assumes learners are at the beginning of their first year on a performance course at a conservatory. The Domain (D) level of Learning agent (composer) could represent melodic motive knowledge in the form:

> "The features of a motive are intervals and rhythms, combined to produce a memorable shape or contour which usually implies an inherent harmony." [Schoenberg 43].

Domain knowledge related to 'intervals' and 'rhythm' could also be represented at Learning agent (composer) D level.

As has already been pointed out, [Davidson & Welsh 88] claim that melodic motive can act as an aid to structural unity in a composition. A composition method at the R level being used by Learning agent (composer) could be called 'Motive Aids Structural Unity' (MASU). In further support of MASU as a Compositional Method we draw on Arnold Schoenberg's [Schoenberg 43] approach to teaching composition using motive as a basic building block and his assertion that, when consciously used "the motive should produce [in a composition] unity, relationship, coherence, logic, comprehensibility and fluency." Part of MASU could represent "acceptable" methods of manipulating a motive. John Kratus [Kratus 91] has identified certain "successful" strategies associated with children composing songs (*i.e.*, the judges in the experiments found certain characteristics of compositions to be "acceptable"). MASU may therefore represent the heuristic: "If a motive seems 'boring' introducing rhythmic variation may help."

At the M level, Learning agent (composer) could examine the introduction of rhythmic variation to a motive and make a judgement as to whether it fitted certain problem seeking goals in the form of criteria that are being used to evolve the composition. One criterion might be to write a motive that links the verse and the chorus smoothly. The activities at the M level would be very much concerned with making judgements about the activities at the R level against its criterion, namely of a smooth transition from verse to chorus.

Learning agent (composer) at the Rf level will examine the M and R levels and perhaps make generalisations about the use of motives in an attempt to develop its own "style" of composition. Such generalisations could be pushed back down to the R level as part of the MASU Compositional Method, provided such a move could be justified. In this sense the Rf level can produce changes in the other levels, which may themselves be subjected to change at a later date. (This will introduce problems of "consistency", common in self-improving agents, an issue that is not dealt with in this paper.)

The reflective Learning agent (composer) at the M level may be developing as a problem seeking goal (of being conducive to judgement) the ability to be able to predict how the use and development of a melodic motive will act as an aid to the coherence of a composition. 'Expert' or accomplished composers seem to be able to make these predictions in their 'head', *i.e.*, they are able to plan the use of motives without playing a single note. This is an advanced form of reflection and it highlights the fact that, to a certain extent, we have simplified our discussion of melodic motive. [Davidson & Welsh 88] found that a detailed knowledge of how scale degrees function (which are, for example, helpful in planning key modulations) was necessary for advanced forms of reflection about tonal compositions. (Scale degree 1 in C major is C, 2 is D, etc.) The point we are making is that, even when operating at the Rf level, to make some generalisation about the use of melodic motive there is still a requirement to communicate with the bottom level: access to the D level is required for knowledge about scale degree functions. Once the Learning agent (composer) has achieved this advanced form of reflection about melodic motive, this whole approach may be pushed down to the R level as part of the MASU compositional method. (We do not intend to imply that non-musicians can not be reflective composers.)

4.3 Learning agent (learner)

In section 4.1 the educational objectives of Teaching agent (teacher) were defined as fostering a reflective composer and a reflective learner. Above we examined the reflective composer. The reflective learning agent or Learning agent (learner) shown in Figure 3 will, arguably, take at least three sources (stimuli to learning) as its domain knowledge (D level).

- First, any teaching interaction it has been exposed to. An example could be an approach to examining musical phrase boundaries given by Teaching agent (teacher). A teaching interaction in this context will include Learning agent (learner)'s response to a Teaching Intervention.
- The second source for Learning agent (learner) at the D level will potentially be all four levels of Learning agent (composer), *i.e.*, the learning agent's representation of its own internal state or understanding of how to compose at a particular point.
- Third, Learning agent (learner) could, in certain circumstances, take dialogue with other learning agents as a stimulus to learning at the D level. From another perspective such dialogue could be viewed as a Learning Method. However, dialogue with other learners brings in the idea of a community of inquiry which, Lipman claims, is how the ability to make judgements can be learned. Therefore, experience of dialogue with other learners may yield valuable domain knowledge, *e.g.*, an analogy and its possible circumstances for use that was not made available by any other source.

Learning agent (learner) at the R level can use different Learning Methods. If the teacher gives an example it is taken from the D level and used here by a Learning Method. Stephan Schwanauer [Schwanauer 93] has described six Learning Methods that are a subset of those possible for compositional learning. They are learning by rote, from instruction, from failure, from examples, by analogy, and from discovery. Each Learning Method will represent the appropriate context for its own use. For example, learning by analogy implies the transformation of old rules into new rules and presupposes the ability to recognise similar situations. Such learning assumes cross-contextual reference is possible and is widely used in jazz composition (where it is called quoting or stylistic derivation). A good example of the use of analogy is provided by Charlie Mingus, who took what Duke Ellington had already achieved with New Orleans and swing-style and successfully applied it to the more rigid and complex language of bebop [Priestley 82].

The M level contains problem seeking goals that help Learning agent (learner) decide such things as: Was the learning successful? Which Learning Method shall I use next? The M level performs local planning by evaluating the problem seeking goals in its learning system. For example, Teaching agent (teacher) may have said (at Learning agent (learner)'s D level) "how could we develop the motive in your Latin composition in a way that helps the structure?" Learning agent (learner) at the M level will access the different Learning Methods at the R level. The Learning agent (learner) M may then ask: Which Learning Method shall I apply to this particular situation? Learning agent (learner) may decide to use learning by analogy by first taking the melodic motive from Mingus' "Goodbye Pork Pie Hat" (from the D level) and by then looking for possible transformations of it to the Latin motive under construction. Learning agent (learner) M may then make a judgement as to whether analogy worked as a Learning Method (by reference to a 'governed by context' goal) and pass this information up to the Rf level.

At the Rf level Learning agent (learner) may ask: Can I think of a new way of learning next time? Should I have used a different Learning Method here? Should I change what I'm trying to get out of the learning (as defined by the current values of the problem seeking goals at the M level)? Details of successful and unsuccessful approaches to learning are retained at this level. The latter may include details of the contexts in which analogy works and does not work. It is as soon as Learning agent (learner) starts to operate at the top two levels (M and Rf) that it starts to take control of its own education and would therefore be described as a reflective learner.

4.4 Teaching agent (teacher)

Figure 3 shows that the D level for Teaching agent (teacher) is the learner, *i.e.*, all four levels of Learning agent (learner) and Learning agent (composer). The R level is concerned with Teaching Methods, which will have two components: Teaching Interventions and Teaching Styles. A Teaching Intervention encompasses the justification for the intervention, as well as the format and content of the intervention. A "justification" will be arrived at from the Teaching Method involved and the problem seeking goals used at the M level. A Teaching Style is based on some psychological theory, *e.g.*, cognitive apprenticeship or cooperative learning (the latter is also a Learning Method, however Teaching agent (teacher) may decide to create the appropriate conditions for such learning). The ILEA uses Teaching Styles in a domain specific manner, unlike ETOILE of [Dillenbourg *et al* 93], which makes use of domain independent teaching agents. ETOILE is described as "an experimental toolbox for creating interactive learning environments". Like ETOILE, ILEA will send out a signal of "pedagogical drift", *i.e.*, an indication that a particular Learning agent is moving away from the current Teaching Style. In the case of the ILEA the message will go to the level above (the M level).

At the M level Teaching agent (teacher) evaluates the success of a Teaching Style in a different way to ETOILE's "coach". ETOILE's coach guides the switching between Teaching Styles primarily on the basis of its assessment of a Learning agent's need for increased or decreased interventions. In the ILEA, judgements about goals for fostering problem seeking activities at the M level will influence the justification for a Teaching Intervention at the R level. This is different to ETOILE, where approaches to problem solving are built into separate "expert" agents, with whom a Learning agent is engaged in dialogue. Another difference between ETOILE and ILEA is that ETOILE will tend to swap Teaching Styles more often than ILEA.

If a particular Teaching Style is not working Teaching agent (teacher) at the Rf level will always be informed of this. Details of successful or unsuccessful attempts by the M level at adjusting the Teaching Interventions will be stored at the Rf level. If the M level is unsuccessful then it may pass temporary control to a new Teaching Method call 'Detect and Repair'. Detect and Repair will attempt to detect and repair learner "failures" in a way similar to those suggested by Sarah Douglas [Douglas 91]. Douglas found that teachers tend to stick to the same teaching style and try to repair what she calls slips and bugs. Failures are classified into performance failures called *slips*, or reasoning failures called *bugs*. Douglas suggests that we should concentrate our efforts on detecting and repairing trouble as indicated in the *form* of communication. Concentrating on the form gives us hints about what is misunderstood by the learner and how. Once Detect and Repair has completed its task the Teaching Method that was previously active will regain control. Detect and Repair should therefore be regarded as an interrupt and not a switch in Teaching Style.

Ultimately, the Rf level may decide to introduce a new Teaching Style (or Teaching Method), but only if it can justify its decision. At the Rf level, Teaching agent (teacher) examines the circumstances under which its Teaching Methods do and do not work. On the basis of the outcome of the previous examination and other data the Rf level may attempt to make generalisations from its analysis. The Rf level may then decide to modify the problem seeking goals at the M level or to insert new knowledge into a Teaching Style. For example, Teaching agent (teacher) at the Rf level could decide to update the musical examples that are appropriate in a cooperative learning exercise. When Teaching agent (teacher) begins to operate at the M and Rf levels it is described as a reflective teacher.

4.4.1 Example for Teaching agent (teacher)

[Kratus 85, pp. 232-233] has suggested the following Teaching Method which Teaching agent (teacher) could use at the R level and which could be called 'Repeating Motives':

> "... students could be asked to compose a song lasting less than one minute using the patterns E-D-C at least three times. Such a task would focus students' attention on how repeating melodic motives work in music. This could be followed by listening and studying selected songs from the class and other music that uses repeating melodic patterns."

Figure 4 illustrates how the ILEA would make use of the Teaching Method called Repeating Motive (step 1 in Figure 4). (Note that to simplify the diagram Learning agent (composer) has been omitted as have all Learning agent (learner)'s processes.) Teaching objectives would be stored as part of the Teaching Method. The teaching objective could be to 'encourage Learning agent (learner) to reflect on the use of motive within a composition'. The latter, we claim, is closely linked to our previously outlined Composition Method (MASU), and is therefore appealing to a plausible cognitive model of how composers perceive tonality when composing. Step 2 in Figure 4 shows a Teaching Intervention in the form of the one minute exercise suggested above by Kratus being made concerning Learning agent (learner). Learning agent (learner)'s response (step 3) is picked up by Teaching agent (teacher) at the M level where it asks at step 4: did that Teaching Intervention work? The latter will be a judgement made against some problem seeking goals.

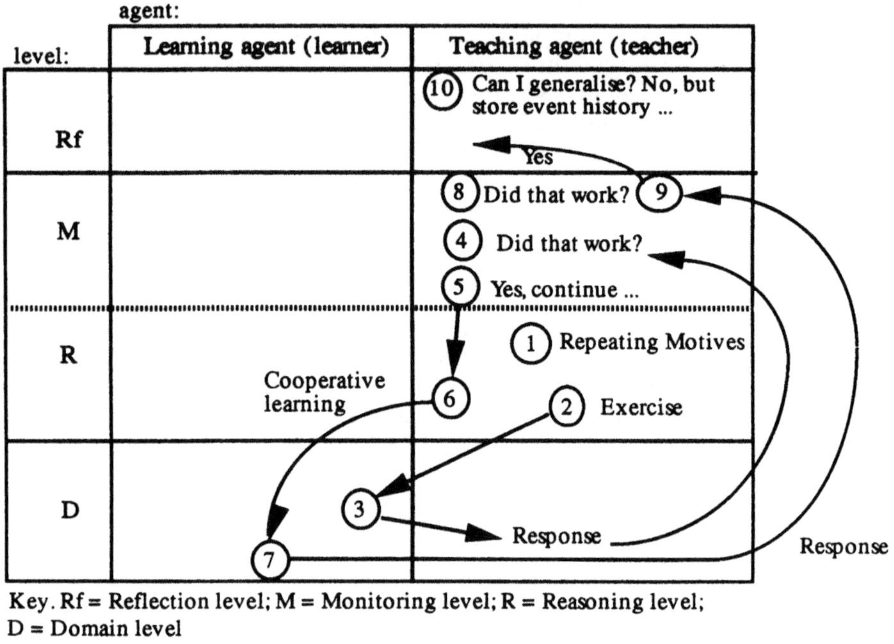

Figure 4: Example of Teaching agent and Learning agent interaction

In this exercise the composition will, it is hoped, 'be governed by the context' of being one minute long. Additionally, the motive will be governed by the criteria of being used three times within the time period allowed. Step 5 judges that the exercise was successfully completed, step 6 calls up the Teaching Style of Cooperative Learning; *i.e.*, getting two learners to discuss their one minute compositions with each other. The justification for such an intervention is partly based on the success of the Learning agent (learner) and on an implicit compatibility of this Teaching Style with the desire to fostering a community of inquiry. The response from Learning agent (learner) is fed into Teaching agent (teacher) and step 8 makes a judgement about the success of the Cooperative Learning session against such a problem seeking goal as: was it conducive to judgement? Step 9 shows the answer "Yes" being fed up to the Rf level where step 10 decides that no generalisations can be drawn at the moment, but that the event history should be stored for future reference. Had the answer to step 9 been "No" then the M level would have attempted to detect and repair any slips or bugs by temporarily giving control to the Teaching Method called Detect and Repair at the R level.

5 Future work

As a result of exploring the teaching-learning interactions within the theoretical framework of the ILEA, six areas for future work have become apparent.

- First, the categories for gathering empirical data (*e.g.*, protocol analysis) of reflective activities can be taken from the ILEA structure. Three categories have emerged. These are composers as they reflect on their work, learners as they reflect on how they are being taught composition and teachers as they reflect on how to teach composition. Some protocols taken of composers as they reflect on their work already exist (*e.g.*, [Sloboda 85] and could be applied to the ILEA. To date no studies of sufficient detail to guide the building of Teaching Interventions in the ILEA has been found for the latter two categories. To fulfil the requirement for detailed data of reflective teaching and learning a protocol study is in preparation.

- Second, some work has already been done on self-improving tutors, the 'can I generalise?' question in the ILEA, and should be examined (*e.g.*, [Dillenbourg 89].

- Third, theories of reflective agents, agent values and agents with attitudinal states would seem to be relevant to the ILEA (*e.g.*, [Doyle 88, Kiss 89, Blandford 91].

- Fourth, bugs and slips, gaps, misconceptions and self-explanations are all promising areas of research that have relevance to the ILEA [Douglas 91, VanLehn 93]. A lot of work has been carried out on metacognition (there are many definition of metacognition, a simple one is thinking about thinking). Sharon Derry's [Derry 92] work on metacognition in a Vygotskian Cognitive Mentor System (CMS) is germane to the ILEA.

- Finally, meta-level and multi-layered architectures research could be examined (*e.g.*, [Kaelbling 86, Downs & Reichgelt 91].

6 Summary and conclusion

In this paper we have:

- claimed that an emphasis on problem seeking is crucial if Intelligent Learning Environments (ILEs) are to be extended to open-ended domains like musical composition, where there is no right or wrong answer.

- claimed that our emphasis on Teaching Methods for problem seeking differentiates our proposed framework (ILEA) form Intelligent Tutoring Systems (ITSs).

- made a clear distinction between the reflective and non-reflective processes carried out by a composer, by a learner and by a teacher.

- asserted that ILEs should shift their emphasis from encouraging a learner to be reflective about domain knowledge to include fostering a learner's ability to be reflective about their own learning.

- claimed that our proposed Teaching Method, called Repeating Motive, is appealing to a plausible cognitive model of how composers perceive tonality when composing. We have called this cognitive model Motive Aids Structural Unity (MASU).

We are not proposing that all of the agent activities outlined in the ILEA will be modelled computationally in our research. The goal of our research is to develop an ILE that is reflective about its own teaching. The emphasis for any prototype based on the ILEA and any protocols gathered will be on those aspects of teacher-guidance (Teaching agent (teacher)) that are "appropriate" to computer-based systems. A learning agent model would be "simulated", *i.e.*, the appropriate parameters would be submitted to Teaching agent (teacher) at the Domain level by a human observer. [Reimer 89] has described the application of computers to inexpensive keyboards as "the birth of mass composition opportunities". We would view the research reported in this paper as an important aspect of the education of such an infant.

7 Acknowledgements

This project is being undertaken through part-time registration for a Ph.D. at The Open University. Thanks to Mark Elsom-Cook (my external supervisor), this paper owes much to his dialogue and guidance. Matt Smith, Simon Holland (my internal supervisor) and Mike Dobson of The Open University all helped me a lot with their critical comments of earlier drafts.

References

[Blandford 91] A. Blandford. *Design, Decisions and Dialogue.* Unpublished PhD thesis, IET, The Open University, UK, 1991.

[Colley *et al* 92] A. Colley, L. Banton, J. Down, and A. Pither. An expert-novice comparison in musical composition. *Psychology of Music*, 20(1):124–137, 1992.

[CTI92] Computers in university teaching: Core tools for core activities. Technical report, CTISS Publications, University of Oxford, 13 Banbury Road, Oxford OX2 6NN, 1992.

[Davidson & Welsh 88] L. Davidson and P. Welsh. From collections to structure: the developmental path of tonal thinking. In J. Sloboda, editor, *Generative Processes in Music: The Psychology of Performance, Improvisation, and Composition.* Oxford University Press, New York, 1988.

[Derry 92] S. Derry. Metacognitive models of learning and instructional systems design. In M. Jones and P. Winne, editors, *Adaptive Learning Environments: foundations and frontiers.* Springer-Verlag, Hamburg, 1992.

[Desain & Honing 86] P. Desain and H. Honing. Loco: Composition microworlds in logo. In *Proceedings of the International Computer Music Conference*, The Hague, 1986.

[Dillenbourg 89] P. Dillenbourg. Designing a self-improving tutor: Proto-teg. *Instructional Science*, 18:193–216, 1989.

[Dillenbourg *et al* 93] P. Dillenbourg, P. Mendelsohn, M. Hilario, D. Schneider, and B. Borcic. Representing domain-independent teaching styles. Technical report, TECFA, Faculté de Psychologie et des Sciences de l'Education, Université de Genève, 1993.

[Douglas 91] S. Douglas. Tutoring as interaction: detecting and repairing tutoring failures. In P. Goodyear, editor, *Teaching Knowledge and Intelligent Tutoring*. Ablex, 1991.

[Downs & Reichgelt 91] J. Downs and H. Reichgelt. Integrating classical and reactive planning within an architecture for autonomous agents. In *Proceedings of the European Workshop on Scheduling and Planning*. Springer-Verlag, 1991.

[Doyle 88] J. Doyle. Artificial intelligence and rational self-government. Technical Report CMU-CS-88-124, Carnegie Mellon University, PA, 1988.

[Elsom-Cook 91] M. T. Elsom-Cook. Dialogue and teaching styles. In P. Goodyear, editor, *Teaching Knowledge and Intelligent Tutoring*. Ablex, 1991.

[Elsom-Cook 93] M. T. Elsom-Cook. Environment design and teaching intervention. In Towme, Munro, and DeDong, editors, *Experiential Learning*. Springer-Verlag, 1993.

[Fenton 89] A. Fenton. The design of an intelligent tutoring system for music. *Musicus*, 1(ii):125–143, 1989.

[Holland 89] S. Holland. *Artificial Intelligence, Education and Music*. Unpublished PhD thesis, The Open University, UK, 1989. (Report No. 88).

[Kaelbling 86] L. Kaelbling. An architecture for intelligent reactive systems. Technical Report 400, SRI International, Menlo Park, 1986.

[Kiss 89] G. Kiss. Some aspects of agent theory. In *Proceedings of International Joint Conference on Artificial Intelligence*, Detroit, MI, 1989.

[Kratus 85] J. Kratus. *Rhythm, Melody, Motive, and Phrase Characteristics of Original Songs by Children Aged Five to Thirteen*. Unpublished PhD thesis, Northwestern University, USA, 1985.

[Kratus 91] J. Kratus. Characterization of the compositional strategies used by children to compose a melody. *Canadian Journal of Research in Music Education*, 33:95–103, 1991. (Special ISME Research Edition).

[Lipman 91a] M. Lipman. Strengthening reasoning and judgement through philosophy. In S. Maclure and P. Davies, editors, *Learning to Think. Thinking to Learn.* Pergamon Press, 1991. (Proceedings of the 1989 OECD Conference.).

[Lipman 91b] M. Lipman. *Thinking in Education.* Cambridge University Press, 1991.

[OEC91] Background report: The key issues and literature reviewed. In S. Maclure and P. Davies, editors, *Learning to Think. Thinking to Learn.* Pergamon Press, 1991. By the Secretariat, Centre for Educational Research and Innovation (Proceedings of the 1989 OECD Conference.).

[Priestley 82] B. Priestley. *Mingus: A Critical Biography.* Granada Publishing, 1982.

[Reimer 89] B. Reimer. *A Philosophy of Music Education.* Prentice-Hall, 1989.

[Schoenberg 43] A. Schoenberg. *Models for Beginners in Composition.* Schirmer, New York, 1943.

[Schwanauer 93] S. M. Schwanauer. A learning machine for tonal composition. In S. M. Schwanauer and D. A. Levitt, editors, *Machine Models of Music.* MIT Press, 1993.

[Self 93] J. Self. The foundations of smile. Technical report, Department of Computing, Lancaster University, 1993.

[Sloboda 85] J. Sloboda. *The Musical Mind : The cognitive psychology of music.* Oxford University Press, 1985.

[Thomas 85] M. T. Thomas. Vivace: rule-based ai system for composition. In *Proceedings of the International Computer Music Conference*, Vancouver, Canada, 1985.

[VanLehn 93] K. VanLehn. Cascade: A simulation of human learning and its applications. In *Proceedings of World Conference on Artificial Intelligence in Education*, Edinburgh, Scotland, 1993.

[Vygotsky 62] L. S. Vygotsky. *Thought and Language.* MIT Press, 1962. Edited and translated by E. Haufmann & F. Vakar.

[Webster 89] P. Webster. Composition software and issues surrounding its use in research settings with children. *Psychomusicology*, 8(2):163–9, 1989.

Learning about harmony with Harmony Space: an overview

Simon Holland
Department of Computing
Faculty of Mathematics and Computing
Open University, Milton Keynes, England
s.holland@open.ac.uk

Abstract

Recent developments are presented in the evolution of Harmony Space, an interface that exploits theories of tonal harmony. In particular the design of the interface draws on Balzano's and Longuet-Higgins' theories of tonal harmony. The interface allows entities of interest (notes, chords, chord progressions, key areas, modulations) to be manipulated via direct manipulation techniques using a single principled spatial metaphor to make a wide range of musical tasks accessible for novices to perform. The interface can also be used by experienced musicians to make a range of expert tasks more tractable than by using conventional tools and notations. The interface is highly interactive and multi-modal, using two pointing devices and spatial, aural and kinaesthetic cues that all map uniformly into the underlying representation. Some recent implementations of Harmony Space are discussed, together with some of the musical tasks which they make tractable for beginners and experienced musicians. Aspects of the simple, consistent, principled framework behind the interface are outlined.

1 Introduction

Harmony Space is a highly interactive interface for exploring harmony and learning to compose music. The interface draws on two cognitive theories of harmony. It exploits artificial intelligence and human computer interaction methodologies to help beginners learn about and make use of tonal harmony. The interface was originally inspired by Longuet-Higgins' [Longuet-Higgins 62a] theory of the perception of harmony, and some current versions of the interface still strongly reflect this influence. However, for many purposes, it has turned out to be more appropriate to use Balzano's [Balzano 80] group theoretic characterisation of the perception of harmony as a grounding for the interface. In this paper we will focus on the use of the interface for tonal and modal harmony: most versions of the interface employ a 12-fold equal-tempered division of the octave, though other implemented versions [Holland 89] employ just intonation in order to facilitate the exploration of harmonic ideas using this tuning (especially modulatory ideas). Versions of the interface have also been constructed for 6-fold, 20-fold 30-fold and 42-fold divisions of the octave, to facilitate musical investigation of microtonal scales that Balzano's theory predicts may be particularly interesting musically. We do not consider here possible applications to atonal music, since the most commonly used configurations of the interface tend to relate harmonic structures to the diatonic and related scales (*e.g.*, the pentatonic and harmonic minor), or to hypothesised microtonal analogues of the diatonic scale. The convention used in this paper for notating chord sequences is described in an appendix.

2 Balzano's theory

To better understand the interface, it is useful to outline informally the key result of Balzano's theory. For fuller accounts of the derivation, see [Balzano 80] and [Holland 89]. The basic idea behind Balzano's theory can be summarised as follows. Balzano's theory identifies the 12-fold western pitch set (more or less irrespective of tuning) as being isomorphic with C_{12}, the cyclic group of order 12. This identification arises because the notes of the scale have a natural ordering (their pitch) which is circular (under octave equivalence). The subgroups and group theoretic properties of C_{12} turn out to characterise many of the harmonic properties of the pitch-set very parsimoniously. Loosely speaking, the key result is that most of the central relationships of tonal harmony can be expressed economically as simple, spatially expressible relationships in an array (Figure 1) in which notes of the chromatic scale are arranged as follows:

- 4 semitones (major thirds) on one axis,
- 3 semitones (minor thirds) on the other axis.

There is some evidence that this representation (the "thirds space" representation) is intimately connected with the way in which people perceive and process tonal harmony. Of course, there are other competing accounts; for example, see [Watkins & Dyson 85], [Krumhansl 91], [Barucha & Krumhansl 83], [Rais 92] and others.

3 Uniqueness of the spatial representation

This section outlines some theoretical reasons for considering the spatial representation used by Harmony Space to be uniquely privileged in a sense to be explained below. The reader wishing to gain an initial overview of this paper, or interested in more practical aspects, may with to skip this section. Longuet-Higgins' theory was the principal initial inspiration for the interface, and many interface features have grown out of detailed consideration of aspects of Balzano's and Longuet-Higgins' theories, but no claim in this paper hinges on the psychological accuracy or otherwise of either theory. However, it is *not* the case that any arbitrary spatial representation of the scale would serve our purposes equally well. Irrespective of the psychological worth of Balzano's theory, if we choose to characterise the pitch set as a set of 12 objects with circular ordering (due to octave equivalence), then Balzano's result *proves* that the third spaces provides a uniquely economical co-ordinate space for this pitch set, in a sense explored below. Let us now explore the result a little further.

Balzano's theory may be viewed as resulting from a special case of a general strategy that is very common in the physical sciences. According to this

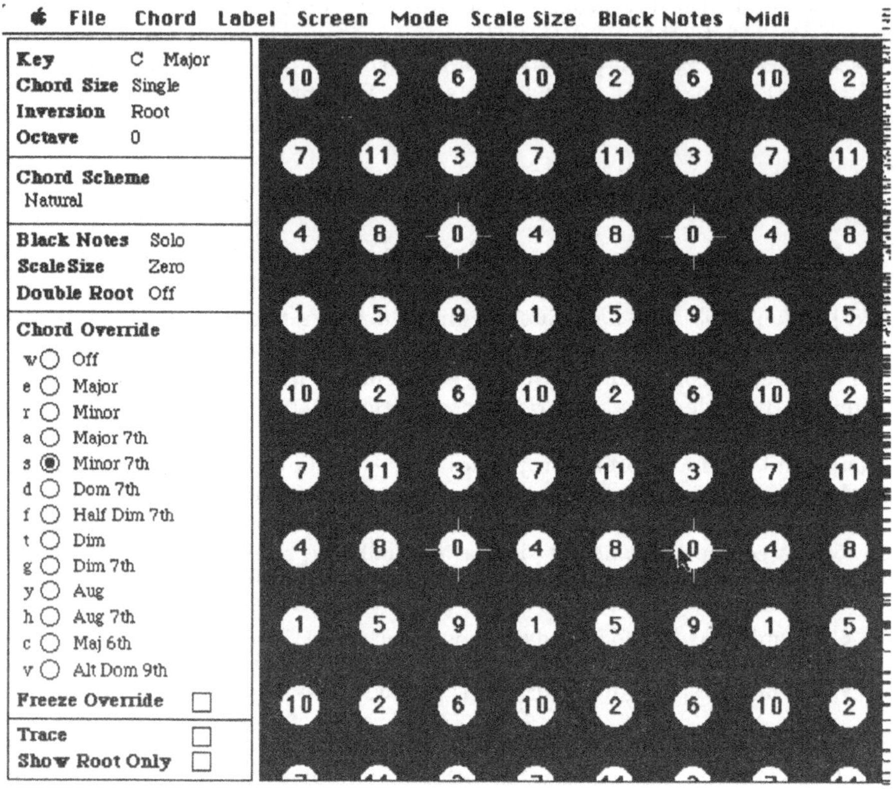

Figure 1: A very simple Harmony Space display. The labelling 0-11 refers to the 12 notes of the chromatic scale.

strategy, whatever objects are under consideration (notes, intervals etc.), a *complete, well-defined* co-ordinate system is sought to span the objects. *Complete* means here that all objects being considered must be specifiable using that co-ordinate system. *Well-defined* means here that in any particular co-ordinate system, no object must be describable by more than one set of distinct co-ordinates.

It is not hard to see that these are reasonable properties to demand of a co-ordinate system: for example, a candidate co-ordinate system for the Euclidean plane would seem lacking in some way if it could not be used to specify certain points on the plane, or if several distinct co-ordinates were found equally able to specify a single point. Now, recall that we have chosen to characterise the tonal pitch set as a set of 12 objects with a circular ordering (under octave equivalence). This is not the only possible characterisation, but it is a perfectly reasonable one. From the viewpoint of seeking out complete, well-defined co-ordinate systems, Balzano's proof simply demonstrates that for such a pitch set, the following three structures:

- the chromatic ordering,
- the circle of fifths,
- and the two-dimensional thirds space,

correspond to three *complete* co-ordinate systems; and furthermore that these three co-ordinate systems are the *only* ones that provide *unique* co-ordinates for each note. This result is quite strong, since it turns out that it applies not only to all possible 1- and 2- dimensional co-ordinate systems, but also to all possible n-dimensional systems for any integer n. Hence the result establishes that these three co-ordinate systems are especially privileged, compared with all other possible co-ordinate systems for describing relationships among a circularly ordered set of 12 notes. Let us now consider some of the characteristics that distinguish the three co-ordinate systems among each other.

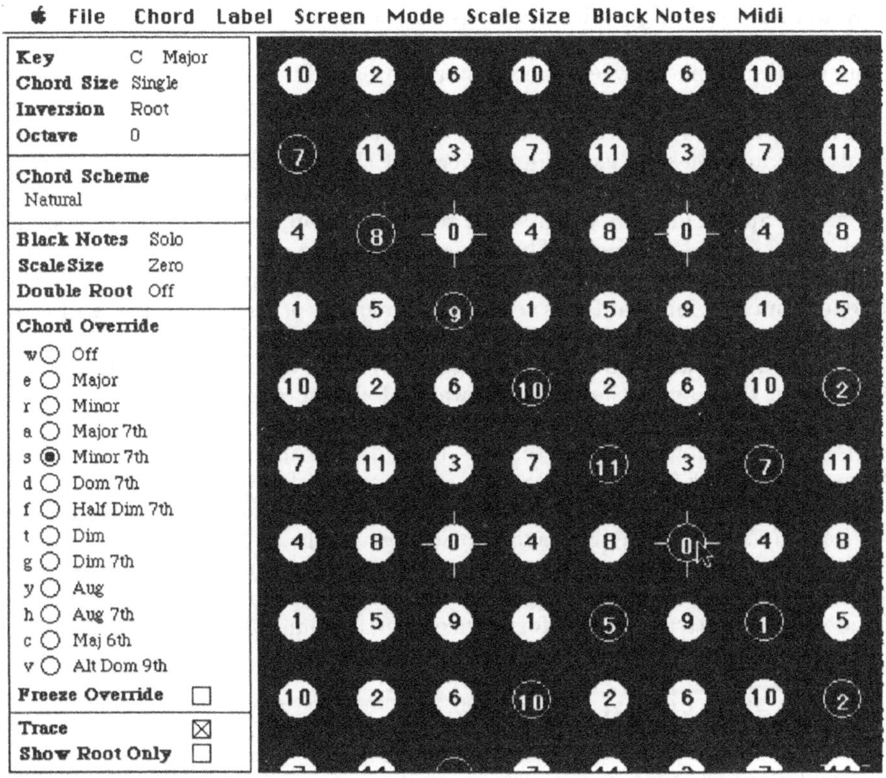

Figure 2: A Harmony Space display with notes labelled by semitone numbers. Two diagonal axes, which correspond to the chromatic scale and the circle of fifths are highlighted.

Of the three co-ordinate systems identified by Balzano, the chromatic ordering seems particularly well-suited to representing melodic closeness (roughly speaking). The circle of fifths ordering is particularly well-suited to representing aspects of relationships between keys and certain common harmonic progressions. However, as we will see later on, the thirds space representation actually turns out to subsume the other two representations, since the chromatic scale and the circle of fifths appear as its diagonal axes (Figure 2). This is not to say that we are claiming that the thirds space is superior to all other representations of pitch for all purposes. This would be to neglect other factors that can be important. Indeed, other spatial representations may be viewed as combining two or more axes in ways especially suited to particular musical activities. For example, Common Music Notation may be viewed as combining, roughly speaking and amongst other things, a chromatic, melodic-related axis with a time axis. The guitar fretboard may be viewed as combining a chromatic, melodic-related axis with a fourths (or inverted fifths) axis, for reasons to do with harmonic relationships and constraints on finger span. These 'representations' (*i.e.*, music notation and the guitar fretboard) may be viewed as reflecting ingenious compromises between competing demands of harmony, melody, time, and human physiology. The thirds space, on the other hand, may be viewed as using two dimensions solely to display harmonic relationships (*i.e.*, simultaneous relationships between one or more notes). Thus it is not surprising that the thirds space appears to be uniquely powerful for exploring harmonic relationships. Other representations may be better suited to other purposes - *e.g.*, analysing melodies, or exploring aspects of the interplay between melody and harmony. Of course, to encourage development of a rounded musical viewpoint, Harmony Space, like any other single representation, needs to be complemented with other representations. The foregoing theoretical arguments can be illustrated at length with concrete examples. A detailed analysis of various musical phenomena and musical tasks seen from the point of view of a variety of spatial representation systems (including common music notation, pianoroll notation, the guitar fretboard and Longuet-Higgins' space) can be found in [Holland 89]. Of course, there are other possible ways of characterising the chromatic scale than as a set of 12 objects with a circular ordering: in some cases, other characterisations yield other complete, well-defined co-ordinate systems. For example [Longuet-Higgins 62a] and [Longuet-Higgins 62b] define the pitch set in terms of overtone theory, yielding a different co-ordinate system intimately related to Balzano's. Different characterisations of pitch, and their co-ordinate systems tend to emphasise different aspects of tonal harmony. For an argument that that Balzano's characterisation focuses particularly closely on aspects of immediate practical concern for novices, see [Holland 89].

4 Basics of the interface

We will now examine the interface itself. Let us start with the most basic version of the display from the current Macintosh version (Figure 1). Notes of the chromatic scale are numbered from 0-11 in ascending pitch order. Each circle represents a note. Clicking on the circle with the mouse pointer causes that circle to darken and the corresponding note to sound via an external MIDI synthesiser. The horizontal and vertical axes of the grid correspond to movements in semitone step sizes 3 and 4, as motivated by the theoretical reasons noted above. The diagonal axes both turn out to have interesting

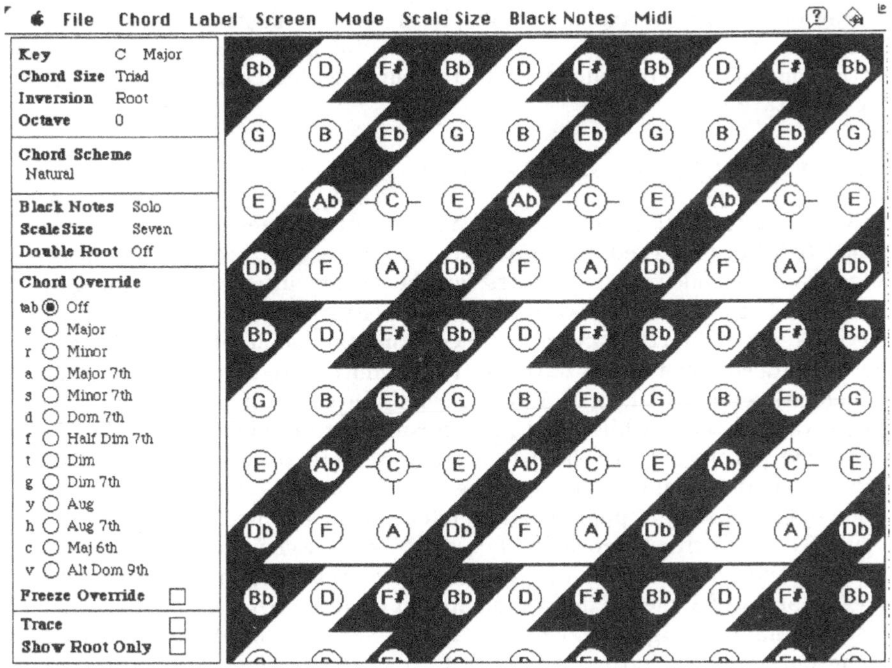

Figure 3: A Harmony Space display with the system in the key of C major.

properties. The NW axis yields a regular semitone ordering, as seen in Figures 2 and 3. The NE axis corresponds to the circle of fifths, visible in Figures 2 and 6. From an educational point of view, these are two important dimensions that western musicians constantly make use of (and novices need to learn about). They have simple physical, spatial interpretations in the interface. The NW axis is important since, for example, motion along it is much used in melodies, and relates to the notion of melodic 'closeness', as noted previously. The NE axis (*i.e.*, the circle of fifths, based on regular semitone steps of size seven) is also very important in tonal music, for example being fundamental to the movement of commonplace bass lines, chord sequences, and key progressions. Alphabetical, semitone, roman numeral and various other forms of labelling are available, as illustrated in Figures 2, 4 and 6. Due to limitations of screen space in the version shown, the note F♯/G♭, for example, is labelled F♯, but this notational point is addressed in later versions. With the interface in its simplest state, all of the notes on the screen, when played as roots, normally sound in the same octave. This means that there are only really 12 distinguishable notes on the screen. The pattern of 12 notes has been propagated, like a wallpaper pattern, to allow certain other patterns, some of which we will examine in a moment, to strike the eye more easily. Notes can be shifted up or down one or more octaves interactively, using alternative mouse buttons (on a SparcStation) or alphanumeric keys (on the Macintosh). To make changes in octave height visible as well as audible, the note circles are illuminated in different shades of gray depending on any octave displacement, as illustrated in Figure 5. A data glove or high precision multiple-touch touchscreen might make a much better controller than a mouse, but any such refinements must wait for later implementations.

4.1 The diatonic scale and other scales

By accessing the scale menu, it is possible to cause diagonal slices of any length from 1 to 12 to be picked out in white. This corresponds to picking out certain notes from the full set of 12 notes for special attention, *i.e.*, forming scales. Diagonal slices on the NE axis are by no means the only way to form scales, but they are of particular importance from the point of view of Balzano's theory. Indeed, such scales have particular musical significance. For example, a diagonal section of length 5 taken from the circle of fifths corresponds to the pentatonic scale, while length 6 corresponds to the medieval scale, Guido's hexachord [Grove 40]. By far the most important scale is the slice of length 7 the familiar diatonic scale, as shown in Figures 3-7. With a scale of size 7, the diagonal slice appears visually folded alongside itself (for example as in Figure 3), producing a repeating box shape with a chunk cut out. To make it easier for the eye to distinguish positions in the repeating pattern, the interface gives an option for the shading to be broken up by horizontal breaks, which can be seen in all of the figures except 5, 1 and 2. Notes in the white area correspond to the notes of the diatonic scale, and notes in the black area correspond to notes outside the diatonic scale. Note that in the special case when the system is in the key of C major, these areas correspond to the white notes and black notes on the piano respectively. We will refer to the pattern of white notes (the visible shape of the diatonic scale in the interface) as the 'key window'.

4.2 Key areas and modulation

Using the arrow keys on the alphanumeric keypad, we can move the key window (*i.e.*, the white diatonic enclosure) around over the fixed grid of notes. This action corresponds to modulation. For example, if we slide the window up the diagonal cycle of fifths axis starting from the key of C, this corresponds to modulating to the dominant (Figure 4). The key one 'notch' below our starting point on the diagonal axis is the subdominant (Figure 5). There are 12 distinguishable positions for the key window: *i.e.*, 12 major keys are distinguished. In general, keys that are musically closely related are nearby, and more remote keys are further away. We can use the interface as it stands to play simple melodies changing octave using mouse buttons or control keys as required. Note that if we run the mouse down the SE axis with the mouse button depressed, we will hear the chromatic scale (Figure 2). If we run down the same axis but play only the notes in the key window, which is easily arranged by setting all the notes in the dark area to respond with silence, we will hear the diatonic scale (Figure 3).

4.3 Chord construction

So far we have discussed only the playing of single notes. The interface allows the user to change the number of notes that will normally be played in response

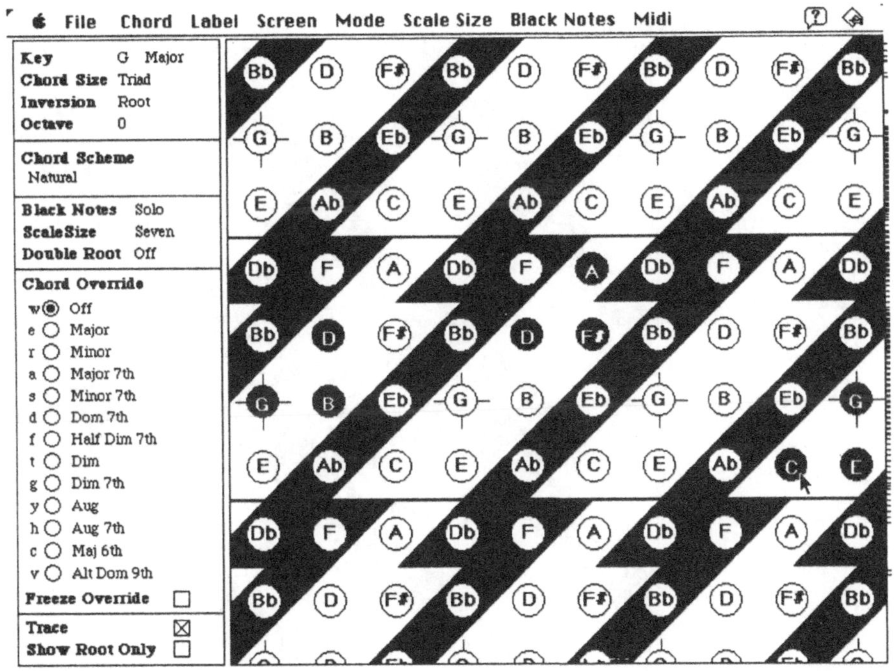

Figure 4: Three major triads in root position in the key of G. Normally, it would be convenient to play representatives of these triads closer together (*e.g.*, all in a single key window). The triads have been triggered and displayed widely apart here for clarity of display on the printed page.

to a single mouse click, *i.e.*, to play in triads, sevenths, ninths, etc., at any time by using a menu or control key (Figures 4 and 5). The interface can help beginners study the way that scale tone diads, triads, sevenths, ninths etc. build up forming different intervals on different degrees of the scale, independently of key transpositions. The rule for building chords on any degree of the scale is easy to appreciate visually. The rule is simply that the chord must expand along and up, and must fit into the key window. Intuitively speaking, the notes 'bounce upwards'. The visual behaviour gives the beginner a simple rationale for understanding why different degrees of the scale are associated with different heard chord qualities; namely, they conform to fit the shape of the key window: *i.e.*, the diatonic scale.

4.4 Inversions, voicing and altered chords

In the simplest setting of the interface, all of the notes in a natural chord are sounded in root inversion in close position. In implementations with more than one mouse button the different mouse buttons allow root, first and second inversions to be played respectively (Figure 5). Visually, in accordance with the metaphor for octave height already noted above, notes played in different

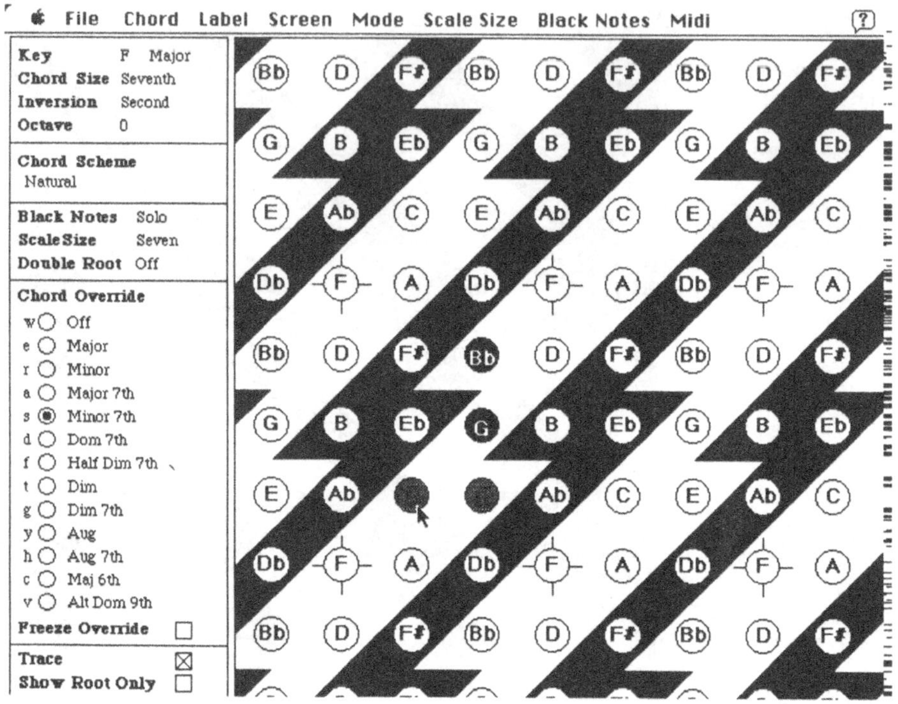

Figure 5: A C dominant 7th chord in second inversion in the key of F major. The fact that two notes at the bottom of the chord are grey (*i.e.*, displaced up an octave) identifies that the chord is in second inversion. A slight variant of the display is illustrated (key windows are not shown as separated).

octaves from their root are shaded accordingly to show their displacement in the z-plane (Figure 5). Amongst other things, this allows similar 'least move' considerations to be taken into account when moving between inversions as apply, for example, on a piano keyboard. In addition to the moment-by-moment manual control of inversions, a chord editor can be used to pre-prepare families of chords voiced in any way desired: *i.e.*, to displace particular notes by one or more octaves, double notes, suppress notes, etc. This allows appropriately voiced chords of whatever size (triad, seventh, etc.) to be associated systematically with given degrees of the scale, or played individually on demand. So, for example, one can create and store a favourite Ravel or Debussy piano voicing scheme. Such schemes can be arranged to give good "least move" voice leading more or less automatically. Yet more complex voicing can be played by shifting dynamically between pre-prepared voicing schemes. The same chord editing mechanism that can be used to set up appropriate voicings can also be used to set up entire new chord scales, for example, scales that involve altered chords, or minor or modal variants.

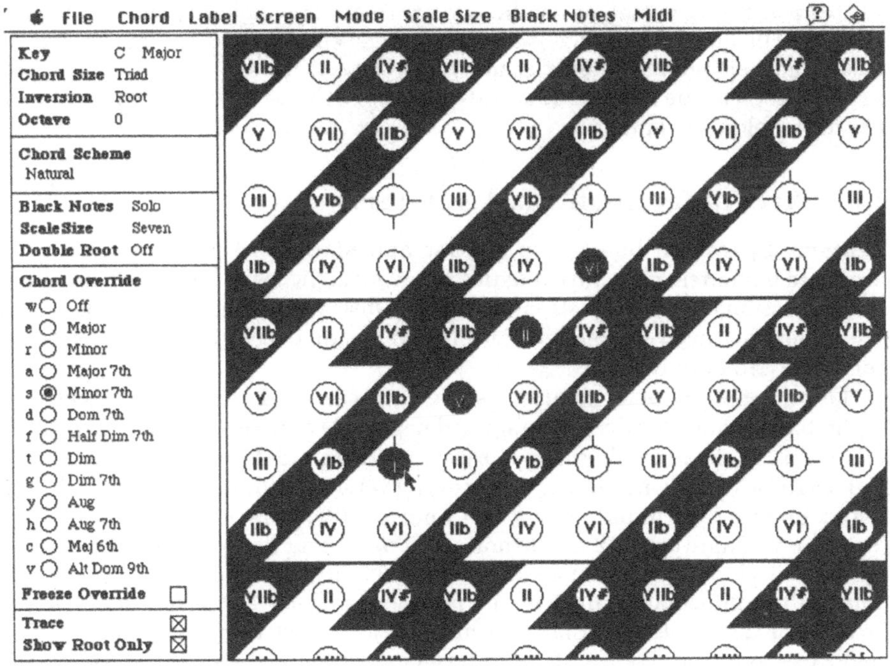

Figure 6: A Harmony Space display where notes are labelled with Roman numerals. The numerals move in step with the key window for modulations and changes of mode. The roots of a VI II V I progression are shown.

4.5 Triads and tonal centres

In Harmony Space, there is a one-to-one mapping between chord quality and visual chord shape, independently of key. Triads can be identified as the maximally compact three element shapes, *i.e.*, shapes packed as closely together as possible, that will fit into the diatonic scale (Figure 4). There can be seen to be exactly three chords of the first such shape (the major triads), and exactly three chords of the second such shape (the minor chords). There is only one chord of the third shape, (the diminished chord). Both major and minor chords are laid out in groups of three with a clearly visible central major chord and a clearly visible minor chord. The existence and location of the major and minor tonal centres are thus visually highlighted in a pedagogically useful way. This spatial metaphor for the two tonal centres reflects a hypothesis by Wilding-White [Wilding-White 61], as follows. Balzano [Balzano 80] notes that before three note harmonic textures became the norm, six of the seven possible notes in the diatonic scale were extensively used as central notes. At about the time when triadic textures became the norm, this modal system of harmony (with no especially privileged 'centres') collapsed to be replaced by a system in which just two centres (major and minor) came to predominate as stable starting and finishing points. Balzano speculates that the emergence of two structural tonal centres and the adoption of triadic textures were mutually dependent. Balzano [Balzano 80] quotes Wilding-White [Wilding-White 61] to the effect that the central notion behind a tonic is not a central note, but a central triad. Harmony Space can be used to illustrate this hypothesis in a way which is easily demonstrable to beginners.

4.6 Accompaniment and analysis

Harmony Space can be used to analyse and play chord progressions. Indeed complete beginners can start making music straight away ignoring the theoretical discussions we have just entertained. Observations in this section, except where noted otherwise, refer to an informal pilot evaluation with novices, reported in [Holland 89].

For the first pilot evaluation, screening was used to select subjects with negligible previous musical training and negligible demonstrable musical ability: as a result of the screening, five subjects aged from 8-37 were chosen. Subjects had single sessions with an early prototype version of Harmony Space. Sessions lasted between 30 minutes and two and a half hours. Sessions were video-taped and audio-taped. The author acted as instructor. A range of tasks were taught individually including simple accompaniment and compositional tasks. Some of the informal findings of the pilot evaluation were as follows. The pilot evaluation demonstrated that non-musically trained users (including a child) could use and make sense of the interface given initial guidance. Most of the users could be taught in a few minutes to play accompaniments to pieces in the major or minor mode in any key using typical two, three and four chord patterns. Some subjects were able to remember and find the location of tonal centres. More extended 'classical harmonic' chord sequences could be played after a few minutes by most of the subjects, as diads, triads, sevenths or ninths. Such 'classical harmonic' chord sequences can be played by establishing a tonal centre, jumping to some non-tonic triad and then moving back to the tonic in a straight line through all intermediate triads along the cycle of fifths axis. This corresponds in Harmony Space to making single vertical straight line gestures (Figure 6).

Some harmonically rich forms of tonal music typically use complex progressions that make use of moving targets (i.e modulations) in systematic ways. Harmony Space offers the opportunity of understanding such harmonic patterns strategically, in a series of trajectories, rather than just at chord-by-chord level. For example, the chord sequence for John Coltrane's 'Giant Steps', which modulates every two chords or so, is typically considered hard to play and to memorise. The Harmony Space trace reveals this piece to be based on a very ingenious but essentially simple sequence of V I and II V I chords, *i.e.*, straight lines, modulating 'westwards' down in major thirds every two or three chords (Figure 7). The sequence makes use of the "pun" that four such steps bring you back to the original key.

In a more recent and as yet unpublished pilot evaluation, for which data are currently being analysed, twelve year old volunteers from a comprehensive school in Milton Keynes received individual tuition from the author and others in Harmony Space after school. One interesting preliminary result was an informal demonstration that, given initial familiarisation with the interface, at least one child with minimal keyboard skills could be taught to play the chord sequences for 'Giant Steps' in Harmony Space in a minute or two. Interestingly, in the case of musically educated adults using Harmony Space to analyse Giant Steps [Coates 92], once the basic harmonic trick used in this piece has been grasped, Harmony Space allows such users to explore what simple or radical variants on the basic idea might also work musically. For example, what happens if the V I's modulate consistently up a major third, or up a minor third, or down a tone? Harmony Space makes it very easy to explore. Each idea presents problems to the ear, which then have to be solved, producing new potential pieces.

Contrasting uses of Harmony Space include ingenious harmonisation games devised recently by Dr Pat Howard of the Open University, as part of the second pilot evaluation [Howard 93]. These games are playable by total novices to teach them to harmonise material such as Bach chorales. Note that as currently designed, novices require guidance in the use of Harmony Space - there is no claim that simple exposure to Harmony Space without guidance would by itself teach novices.

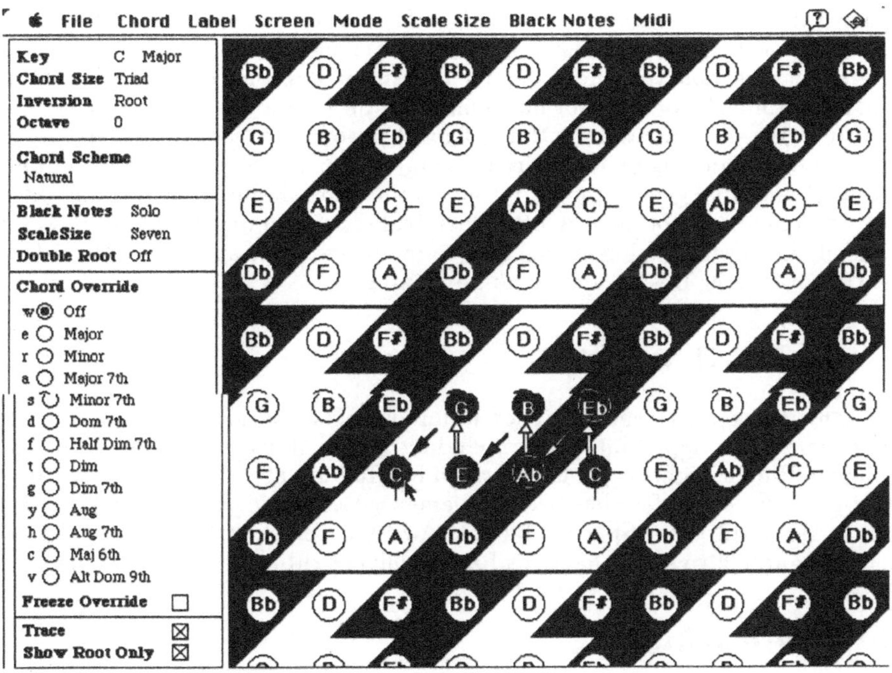

Figure 7: A simplified version of the sequence of chord roots for 'Giant Steps'.

Figure 7 depicts a simplified version of the sequence of chord roots on which 'Giant Steps' is based, as seen in Harmony Space (shown transposed into C major). The sequence modulates rapidly in such a way (not shown in this diagram) that it constitutes a series of V I chords, each in a new key. The full chord sequence has elaborations that include II V I sequences and modulations both up and down a major third. Each chord is a major or dominant ninth.

All simplifications have been made to aid clarity on the printed page.

5 Some educational uses of Harmony Space

Harmony Space has at least six general uses; musical instrument, particularly for sketching chord sequences; tool for musical analysis; tool for learning basic harmonisation; learning tool for exploring the theory of tonal music; discovery learning tool for composing and modifying chord sequences; and notation for aspects of chord sequences not obvious in conventional notations. Discussions of examples of each of these activities, as carried out by novices, can be found in in [Holland 89].

6 Implementations of Harmony Space, and some variants

A family of variants of the interface have been implemented in prototype on the SparcStation. Each variant is specialised for various musical tasks. The basic implemented variants include: a microtonal version; a just intonation version; a version switchable to either Longuet-Higgins or Balzano configuration; a version for graphically performing harmonic analysis by graphical best fit; a version able to drive melodic and rhythmic figural patterns; a version as a recursive programming language able to drive the interface; a version designed to integrate with an intelligent tutor for music composition. Many other variants have been designed, prototyped or otherwise realised, including a human-powered performance-event version staged as a co-operative game at the Utrecht School of Art with Peter Desain and Henkjan Honing.

7 Related work

In many respects, Harmony Space is unique. Its relationship to various independently developed interfaces including Music Mouse, Harmony Grid, and Longuet-Higgins light organ is described in [Holland 89]. A complete declarative model of the interface has been implemented as a logic program [Buchan 91], which allows Harmony Space to be linked with a constraint-based musical planner [Holland 89] to form the core of an intelligent tutor for music composition.

8 Limitations

There are some aspects of harmony that the current version of Harmony Space does not represent well, for example, voice-leading and the visualisation and control of harmony in a metrical and rhythmic context. Harmony Space emphasises vertical aspects of harmony at the expense of horizontal aspects (using these terms as they are conventionally used in harmony - not with reference to the spatial layout of Harmony Space). Despite this, the Sparc version of Harmony Space can demonstrate several aspects of voice leading reasonably well using techniques sketched in [Holland 86]. The current implementations of Harmony Space would benefit from various simple refinements including the following. On the current Macintosh version, though less so the Sparc version, melodic and rhythmic context is not provided by any built-in features; rhythmic playing is hampered somewhat by response speed; only three or four levels of z-displacement are currently visible; the constituent notes of chords are not independently manipulable while sounding; mode changing, key changing, and label changing cause slight delays; inversions, voicings and non-standard chord scales should be more easily changeable. Other required facilities include: a simple visual record playback facility, a MIDI-IN facility, more flexible ways of using the notes of a chord (*e.g.*, via Alberti patterns, arpeggiation patterns and finer manual control).

9 Further work

Around sixty further work projects related to Harmony Space are itemised in [Holland 89]. We will note two or three of particular current interest. Harmony Space is based on theories that reconceptualise the domain in question, *i.e.*, harmony. The reconceptualisations call for and give an opportunity to make radical changes to the curriculum and teaching approaches in this area. The developing of new curricula and teaching methods to take advantage of Harmony Space's theoretical basis has begun, but needs much more work. Various technical improvements are required. Various major variants of the interface await resources to implement, such as the full graphical analysis tool, and full associated discovery based composition tutors, currently only partly implemented.

10 Conclusions

AI and Education researchers have long been interested in taking AI theories (of particular domains, ways of learning, and styles of teaching) and of finding ways to exploit them for educational purposes. One less advertised way of doing this is to dispense with a teaching component, an expert component, or a student model, and to use something like the following strategy.

- Investigate as deeply as possible any cognitive theories or AI theories of the domain in question and gather computational models.
- Taking into account the best current HCI practice, try to devise an interface that represents abstract domain concepts in perceptually concrete, interactive, manipulable ways.
- Try to make concepts and relationships perceptually salient which should be conceptually important.
- Reduce cognitive load by representing explicitly and uniformly relationships that would otherwise have to be learned or calculated.

The ideas presented in this paper can be seen as example of this approach. We have outlined how cognitive theories of harmony can be used to design and build an interface that allows objects and processes of interest in harmony (*e.g.*, notes, chords, chord progressions, key areas, modulations) to be manipulated directly using a single principled spatial metaphor to make a wide range of musical tasks accessible for novices. We have also sketched ways in which the interface makes certain expert tasks more tractable than using more orthodox tools and notations. We have shown how the two pointing devices together with visual and sound output are used to give rise to spatial, aural and kinaesthetic cues that all map uniformly into an underlying theory. Some recent implementations of Harmony Space have been discussed, together with some of the musical tasks which it facilitates.

11 Acknowledgements

This work has been assisted by grants from the University of Aberdeen Research Committee and the Open University Research Committee. Thanks to Mark Elsom-Cook, Tim O'Shea and Mark Steedman for help early on. Thanks to Colin Watson, Fiona Houston, Matt Smith, James Bissett, Jim Buchan and Andrew Mayo for more recent work on various implementations. Thanks to Pat Howard, Daran Coates, Matt Smith and Nigel Morgan for recent useful discussions and work on evaluations. Thanks to two anonymous reviewers for helping to improve this paper.

12 Appendix

The convention used to notate chords is that of [Mehegan 59], where full details of the notation can be found. The key points are summarised below. This notation is particularly well suited to describing and reasoning about chord sequences in the context of Harmony Space. In the Mehegan system, chords are described using roman numerals, though this does not imply that the rules of classical functional harmony necessarily apply. A sequence of numerals is taken to consist of triads, unless the texture of the sequence as a whole is specified to be otherwise, and except for any individual chords annotated differently. A sequence of numerals as a whole may be declared to refer to sevenths or ninths or diads (again, excepting any individually annotated chords). Upper case roman numerals are used throughout the system: the case (*i.e.*, upper case or lower case) of a roman numeral does not imply anything about chord quality. Unless a roman numeral is explicitly annotated to indicate additions, alterations or a specific quality, the corresponding chord is understood to be of 'scale-tone chord quality', a term which is explained below. Chords of scale tone quality are constructed by stacking thirds upwards from the root so as to stay inside the prevailing key or mode. Note that in the case of major and harmonic minor scales, and in modes that share the same notes as these scales, this is a well-defined method of chord construction. Annotations for inversions, altered qualities, etc. exist in this system but are not described here as they are not used in this paper.

References

[Balzano 80] G. J. Balzano. The group-theoretic description of 12-fold and microtonal pitch systems. *Computer*

Music Journal, 4(4), 1980.

[Barucha & Krumhansl 83] J.J. Barucha and C.L. Krumhansl. The representation of harmonic structure in music: hierarchies of stability as a function of context. *Cognition*, 13:63–102, 1983.

[Buchan 91] J. Buchan. *Initial steps in the design of an ITS for Music Composition (Unpublished MSc thesis)*. Unpublished PhD thesis, Department of Computing Science, University of Aberdeen, Scotland, 1991.

[Coates 92] D. Coates, 1992. Personal communication about analysis and recomposition of 'Giant Steps' in Harmony Space, in the Department of Computing Science at the University of Aberdeen. Coates harmonically analysed Giant Steps using Harmony Space, and Holland performed various recompositions.

[Grove 40] G. Grove. Grove's dictionary of music and musicians (4th edition), 1940.

[Holland 86] S. Holland. Design considerations for a human-computer interface using 12-tone three dimensional harmony space to aid novices to learn aspects of harmony and composition. Technical Report CITE Report No. 7, Open University, Milton Keynes, United Kingdom, 1986.

[Holland 89] S. Holland. *Artificial Intelligence, Education and Music*. Unpublished PhD thesis, published internally as OU IET CITE Report No. 88, July 1989, 1989.

[Howard 93] P. Howard, 1993. Personal communication about harmonisation games devised by Dr. Howard and played in a pilot evaluation at a local school in Milton Keynes in June 1993.

[Krumhansl 91] C.L. Krumhansl. Memory for musical surface. *Memory and Cognition*, 19,4:401–411, 1991.

[Longuet-Higgins 62a] H.C. Longuet-Higgins. Letter to a musical friend. *Music Review*, pages 244–248, 1962.

[Longuet-Higgins 62b] H.C. Longuet-Higgins. Second letter to a musical friend. *Music Review*, pages 271–280, 1962.

[Mehegan 59] J. Mehegan. *Jazz Improvisation I: Tonal and Rhythmic Principles*. Watson-Guptil Publications, New York, 1959.

[Rais 92] M. Rais. Jaan Soonvald and his musical system. *Leonardo Music Journal*, Vol 2, No 1:45–47, 1992.

[Watkins & Dyson 85] J. Watkins and Mary C. Dyson. On the perception of tone sequences and melodies. In Peter Howell, Ian Cross, and Robert West, editors, *Musical Structure and Cognition*. Academic Press, London, 1985.

[Wilding-White 61] R. Wilding-White. Tonality and scale theory. *Journal of Music Theory*, 5:275–286, 1961.

– MOTIVE –
The development of an AI tool for beginning melody composers

Matt Smith & Simon Holland
Department of Computing
Faculty of Mathematics and Computing
Open University, Milton Keynes, England
m.r.smith@open.ac.uk; s.holland@open.ac.uk

Abstract

The goal of the research described in this paper is to find ways of using artificial intelligence to encourage and facilitate melody composition by musical novices. The first stage of the research is the formalisation of an analytical theory of melody, Eugene Narmour's Implication-Realisation Model. This hypothetical theory offers an explanation of how listeners of music break-up a melody into "chunks", and hear some notes as more important than others. The formalisation process involves the implementation of a declarative parser in Prolog, and then comparison of Narmour's published analyses with those of the parser. With such results it will be possible to present a critical evaluation of Narmour's theory, and the parser.
Around the parser a constraint-generation tool (called MOTIVE) is being built. This paper presents the features of the tool and a possible design for an iconic interface, and we suggest a number of ways in which MOTIVE may facilitate the development of melody composition skills in an educational context.

1 Introduction

The aim of our research is the development of an AI tool to aid novice composers of melody. Our thesis is that such a tool can be developed using constraint-based extensions of a computational model of the Narmour's Implication-Realisation model [Narmour 90]. The tool (MOTIVE) is aimed at musical novices with a simple understanding of metre, harmony and common music notation, but with no experience of composition, and little of analysis.

The research involves two programming stages, the first being the implementation of a computational model of the Implication-Realisation Model - an analytical theory of melody. The computational model (a musical parser) generates hierarchical analyses of melodies, and is (to the authors' knowledge) the first substantial, symbolic computer model of Narmour's theory. The second programming stage extends the parser using constraint techniques, to allow the generation of melodies. This means that with a single computer model a user will be able to analyse a given melody, modify a melody in musically sensible ways by changing constraints at various hierarchical levels, generate new melodies and finish partially completed melodies.

Presented in this paper are:

- an introduction to those aspects of Narmour's theory reified in the computational model,
- a description of the computational model,
- an outline of the additions to the model to allow generation of melodies using constraint techniques, examples of a possible interface for MOTIVE,
- a discussion of potential educational uses of MOTIVE.

2 Narmour's theory

Narmour [Narmour 90] proposes a theory of how a listener "processes" a melody that results in hierarchical analyses of given melodies, the theory he names the "Implication-Realisation Model". He describes a procedure for a combination of bottom-up and top-down "parsing" of melodies. As Smoliar [Smoliar 91] points out, Narmour proposes an almost natural language processing approach to melodic analysis.

Although there are hierarchical aspects to Narmour's theory, their "bottom-up" nature distinguishes his theory from others, such as the reductionist theories of Heinrich Schenker [Schenker 79] and more recently Lerdahl and Jackendoff [Lerdhal & Jackendoff 83].

Narmour's theory takes into account how stylistic learning can affect a listener's expectations, from the top down, as opposed to the low level, bottom-up hypotheses of continuation and reversal. Narmour considers style from two points of view: the extra-opus style a listener builds up by listening to a corpus of melodies in a tonal tradition (*e.g.*, Western Tonal Music), and the intra-opus style of each melody, where repeated figures and their variations are quickly recognised (and so expectations effected) at later points in a melody. It is the bottom-up aspects of Narmour's theory which have been formalised in MOTIVE.

Narmour's theory is based on two hypotheses which predict the moment-by-moment, low level implications a listener has of the properties of future melodic events (such as contour, interval size and duration). He uses the term "implication" rather than "expectation" to emphasise that such activities are going on at a low, subconscious perceptual level.

The two hypotheses are called "continuation" and "reversal". The hypothesis of continuation, based on the Gestalt school of psychology, states that when a listener hears a small interval ("small" is determined by a parametric scale - see below) then the listener will expect the next interval to have similar properties to that of the generating interval, for example ascending contour followed by ascending contour, small interval followed by small interval. The hypothesis of reversal is based upon Narmour's own musical intuitions, and similar ideas can be found in others theories, for example Meyer [Meyer 56]. Reversal is when a listener expects melodic parameters to change - such expectations are usually initiated by a large interval and in such situations the listener normally expects a large interval to be followed by small, and contour to change direction.

Parametric scales form a fundamental base for the Implication-Realisation model. The scales (for example of interval and registral direction (contour)), define when melodic parameters are similar or different (thus whether the hypothesis of continuation or reversal should be applied). Each scale contains four regions (although sometimes a region is empty), they are: **sameness, similarity, threshold, differentiation.**

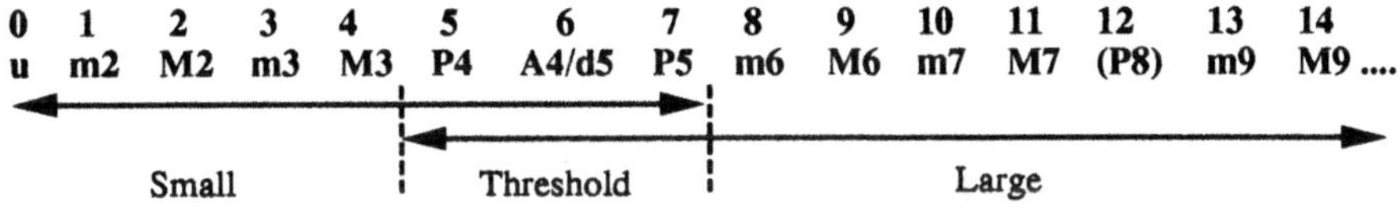

Figure 1: Narmour's parametric scale for interval.

For example, the parametric scale for interval is shown in Figure 1, where the intervals in each of the four categories above are:

sameness	u
similarity	m2, M2, m3, M3
threshold	P4, A4/d5, P5
differentiation	m6, M6, m7, M7, (P8), m9, M9, ...

Narmour describes a set of "structures" (resulting from the hypotheses of continuation and reversal), these structures group together contiguous notes in a melody which realise and deny the same expectations. Note that the structure list is exhaustive, *i.e.*, all notes in a melody will be a member of one of the given structures. The two hypotheses lead to two classes of structures: continuation structures are either "Iterative" (where pitches or intervals are repeated) or "Processive" (where initial contour and interval size are continued). There is only one category of reversal structures.

Figure 2: Some examples of melodic structures.

Figure 2 illustrates the following structures:

- P - Process, small intervals, all contours the same,
- IP - Intervallic Process, small intervals, but contour changes,
- VP - registral Process, not all intervals small (but first is), contours the same,

- D - Duplication, all notes the same,
- R - Reversal, initial interval large, followed by small interval and change of contour.

Since one needs two notes to create a "generating interval", and a third note to determine realisation or denial of implications, the smallest category for most structures is three notes. In cases where closure is very strong, implication may be stopped before three notes (of a new structure) have been heard, in which case one of two special structures occurs: dyads (closure (see below) after two notes), and monads (closure on a single note).

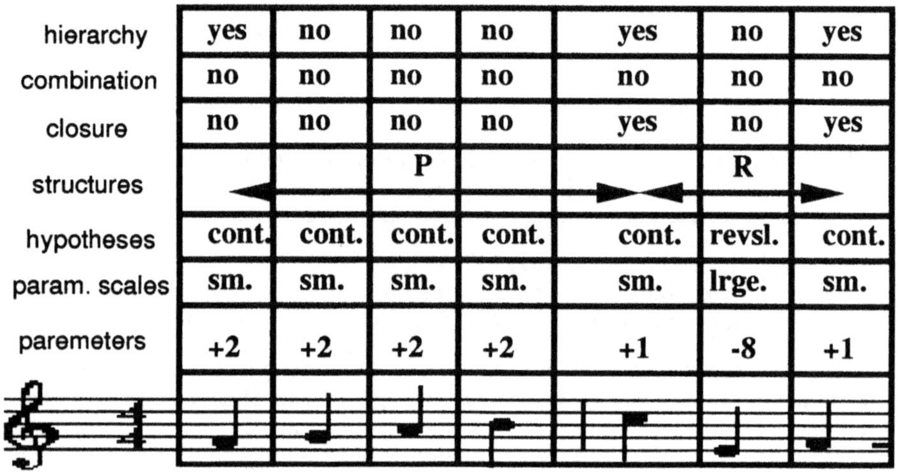

Figure 3: Combination of elements of Implication-Realisation model.

A key concept of the implication-realisation model is that of "closure". Narmour uses the term in a general sense, where closure varies in degree of strength, occurring throughout a melody, as well as at points when a number of melodic parameters combine in a manner indicating a summarisation. Strong closure causes structures to terminate, and if closure on a note is strong enough the note is promoted to the next hierarchical level of the analysis. Formalising when a combination of closure from different melodic parameters is sufficient for termination of a structure and hierarchical promotion is one of the tasks in the development of the computational model. Closure is caused by melodic parameters (such as short to long durations of notes), and also from other musical parameters, such as metre (weak beat to strong beat) and harmony (dissonance to consonance). Another form of closure (which Narmour calls "stopping"), and which always terminates a structure, is when a new note is heard which implies and realises melodic parameters in a different way to the ongoing structure (for example a change of contour during a processive structure). If closure is weak, structures may combine in a number of ways, such as sharing a note (the last note of one structure being the first of another), or the sharing of two notes (for example the last two notes of a reversal becoming the first two notes of a processive structure). Examples of structure combination can be found in Figure 6, an example of a generated melody.

Figure 3 illustrates how the different elements of Narmour's theory combine to result in a hierarchical analysis of a melody (for parsing one should work from the bottom of the diagram, upwards).

3 The Computational Model

Although the parser is not based upon a strict grammar like some natural language programs, it does exhibit some of the behaviour of such parsers. Structures in Narmour's theory can be "processive", where the expectations are matched with forthcoming notes, or "retrospective" where the listener comes to re-interpret some past notes and revises a previous structure. These retrospective structures are analogous to "garden path" sentences in natural language (*e.g.*, [Markus 80]):

the old man the boats,

is such a sentence. Garden path sentences can be understood from this example if we consider the simple grammer re-write rules, and two possible ways to parse the sentence illustrated in Figure 4.

A parser using naive backtracking would first parse "the old man" as a noun phrase, before getting stuck since "the boats" fails as a verb phrase. The parser would then backtrack and find that "old" can also be a collective noun, and proceeds to successfully parse the sentence as shown in Figure 4.

The melodic parser looks at each note of the melody in chronological order, and processes it with a number of steps:

1. Check note attributes (pitch, onset time, duration).
2. Calculate attributes of interval between new note and previous note (interval size in semitones, contour).
3. Check whether in the current context the interval is considered large or small according to the implication-realisation model (small intervals initiate continuation expectations, while large ones initiate reversal).
4. Check if stylistic knowledge matches with the current events and if so, generate expectations according to a style structure (not yet implemented).
5. If there is an existing structure see if the new note causes closure or whether the structure should be extended to include the new note, or possibly whether the old structure should be abandoned and a retrospective one created. If there was no existing structure, initiate one.
6. Run an intra-opus learning program (not yet implemented).
7. If closure has occurred, see if it is strong enough to promote the new note to the next higher hierarchical level. If so, go through steps 1-7 for the notes and structures at the next hierarchical level.

Grammar

sentence = noun_phrase, verb_phrase
noun_phrase = determiner, adjective, noun
noun_phrase = determiner, noun
noun_phrase = adjective, noun
verb_phrase = verb, noun_phrase
noun = singular_noun
noun = plural_noun
noun = collective_noun

Lexicon

determiner(the)
adjective(old)
singular_noun(man)
plural_noun(boats)
collective_noun(old)
verb(man)

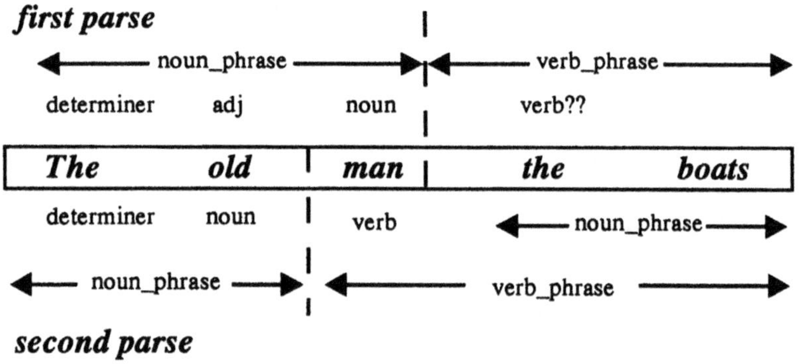

Figure 4: Grammar and parser for example garden path sentence.

As the program moves through the melody it will build up structures at a number of hierarchical levels, and will exhibit the re-structuring of past notes when it encounters situations of retrospective structures. Although a more efficient parser could be written, working on a complete melody in one go, it would have the limitations of not being able to show the intermediate structures before retrospective structures are identified, and could only work on complete melodies. The note-by-note parser described in steps 1-7 above has neither of these limitations.

The development of the computational model has taken the form of four main activities:

- The representation in declarative form of aspects of Narmour's theory (from his publications); for example part of the representation of a processive structure definition becomes the following Prolog fragment:

```
struct_class(process, 'P',
             implications(continuation, small, [Contour]))
```

- The modelling of aspects of music analysis Narmour takes for granted (*e.g.*, strong/weak beats, harmonic consonance dissonance); for example a model of Longuet-Higgins and Lee's [Longuet-Higgins & Lee 84] approach for inference of metre has been implemented as part of MOTIVE's metric closure module.
- The inference of aspects of Narmour's theory he doesn't make explicit (such as how closure from different parameters combines, and when it is strong enough for termination of structures and hierarchical promotion).
- Development of additional program code to automate the procedural aspects of parsing which 'human' music analysts perform, such as choice of next note to consider, action to take on next note (does it start a new structure, has an ongoing structure been terminated, if a note is to be promoted it should be considered for membership of ongoing structures in higher hierarchical levels etc.).

4 The Constraint-Based Generator

Melodies can be generated by applying harmonic and metric constraints to notes occurring in particular levels of the hierarchy. Such constraints might be very restricting at high levels, and weakened for each lower level. For example, harmonic constraints could take the form of movement through Lerdahl's [Lerdahl 88] "Pitch Spaces", a set of spaces which contain pitch classes of increasing harmonic importance. There is also the built-in constraint that a note appearing in a particular hierarchical level must generate sufficient closure in the next lower level, to justify its place in the hierarchy.

The metric and harmonic constraints for an example of constrained melody generation are described below. The example is shown graphically in Figure 6 the first hierarchical level is H4, working down to the music surface at H1. The example can be thought of as both a bottom-up, analysis of the melody, and a top-down, hierarchical construction. The difference being that analyses for existing melodies would not have explicit constraints for the hierarchical levels (a constraint inference module is under development).

Figure 5 shows the themeThe example in Figure 6 shows how the theme in Figure 5 can be generated using a small number of constraints and Namrour-structures, in a 4-level, top-down method.

Figure 5: The principal theme from Tchaikovsky's *Swan Lake.*

Figure 6 is a constrained generation (*i.e.*, the notes in higher levels were generated first, each subsequent level being an "embellishment" of its parent level).

Initial decisions for the generation were a time signature of 4/4, and the key of A minor.

The metric constraints below show how the onset times on notes were highly constrained at the higher levels (H4, H3 only notes on bar boundaries, then half bar boundaries are allowed). As one moves down the hierarchy the constraints are relaxed (so that at levels H1 and H2, notes are allowed on eighth bar boundaries).

4.1 Metric Constraints

(Time signature = 2/4)

```
H4: notes on bar boundaries
| O           | O           | O           |
H3: notes on half bar boundaries
| O     O     | O     O     | O     O     |
H1 and H2: notes on eighth bar boundaries
|  OOOO OOOO  |  OOOO OOOO  |  OOOO OOOO  |
```

The harmonic constraints are relaxed in a similar way as one moves down the hierarchy. Initially (H4) only notes in Open Fifth Space are allowed (the second highest of Lerdahl's pitch spaces). At each level down, notes from less consonant pitch spaces are permitted, ending with any non-chromatic note (Diatonic Space) being allowed for the lowest levels (H1 and H2).

4.2 Lerdahl's Pitch Spaces

(From [Lerdahl 88], numbers in brackets indicate degree of scale, the spaces are in order of decreasing consonance)

Tonic Space	1
Open Fifth Space	1, 5
Triadic Space	1, 3, 4
Diatonic Space	1, 2, 3, 4, 5, 6, 7
Chromatic Space	any note

The lowest two levels of the constrained generation (H1 and H2) are closely linked. H1 can be thought of as a correcting level, where notes (such as the two E's in bar 2) which didn't have sufficient closure for hierarchical promotion are given extra closure by the shortening of following notes (*i.e.*, the shortening of the two C's in bar 2). In this way any over-simplifications due to hierarchical constraints are countered.

4.3 Harmonic Constraints

(Based on the above pitch spaces from [Lerdahl 88])

(Key = Am)	
H4	A, E
H3	A, C, E
H1 and H2	A, B, C, D, E, F, G

The constraint satisfaction process is driven by the logic programming language Prolog. Using Prolog's backtracking and automatic instantiation (reversible assignment) of variables, the same rules and facts that test for certain properties of a melodic sequence can also be used to assign properties to variables. In such a way the program to analyse a melody and generate an implication-realisation model hierarchy can be used with extensions to generate notes for the musical surface of a melody that satisfy the structures and constraints at higher hierarchical levels. The extensions take the form of heuristics for the appropriate application of constraints at given hierarchical levels. These constraints and the heuristics for their application are, in effect, compiled stylistic knowledge.

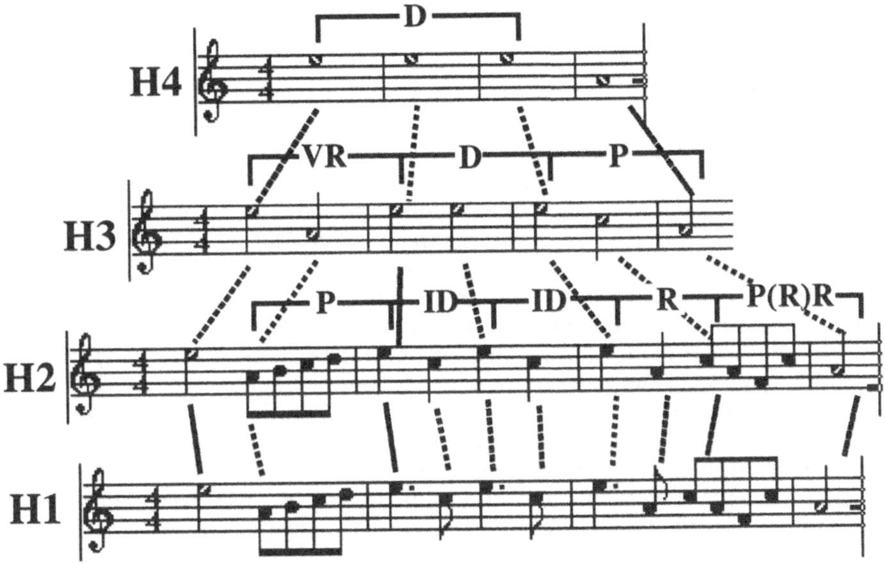

Figure 6: An example of a MOTIVE constrained generation.

5 An interface for MOTIVE

Narmour's one or two letter mnemonics for structures (P, VR, (IP) etc.), while a useful aid for music analysts using his theory, are not a particularly intuitive aid for novices using MOTIVE. For the tool to be easily used and understood, a more graphical representation could be developed, whereby the symbol (icon) referring to each structure contained elements representing the distinguishing characteristics of the structure. For example the icons in Figure 7 show how interval size and contour can be represented in a single icon (a double line means a large interval).

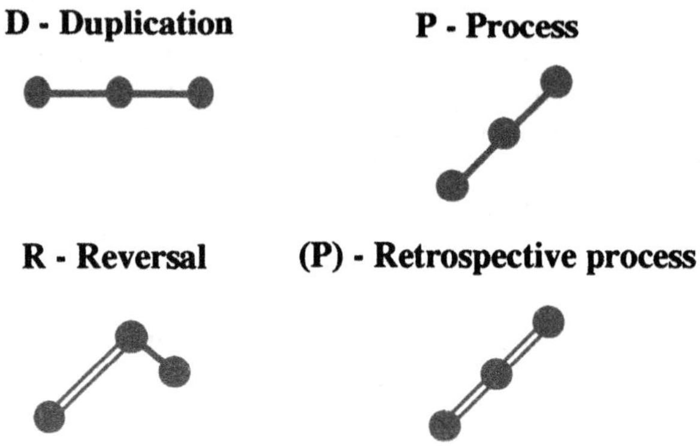

Figure 7: Four examples of a visual representation for Narmour's melodic *structures*.

Such ideas, along with more standard toolbox and menu-based approaches could be combined to form such an interface as that illustrated in figure 8. The top of the figure shows icons for the nine structure classes, and one for creating retrospective structures. In the example the icon for a process structure - P in Narmour's notation - is highlighted, referring to the process structure highlighted in the lowest level of the hierarchical generation. By choosing a different structure the student could get MOTIVE to re-generate the melody (also the number of notes in the structure is a choice the student would have to make, unless it is pre-determined by the constraints). Two other icons allow a student to view (and change) the metric and harmonic constraints.

It is intended that MOTIVE be used in conjunction with tools for rhythm and harmony (for example Holland's [Holland 89] Harmony Space), so that reasonably sophisticated constraints can be be chosen for MOTIVE to generate within. For example, a harmony tool could generate a chord sequence (perhaps including a modulation), this "horizontal" sequence of chords would become contraints for the "vertical" levels above each chord - *i.e.*, if bars 3 - 5 had the chord C major, then the Lerdahl pitch spaces for the hierachical levels of bars 3 - 5 would refer to C major.

6 The educational uses of MOTIVE

The driving motivation behind the development of MOTIVE was to create an educational tool (rather than to formalise Narmour's theory, although it is a worthwhile spin-off). MOTIVE has been designed to allow a novice composer to easily perform a number of tasks:

- analysing an existing melody (partial or complete),

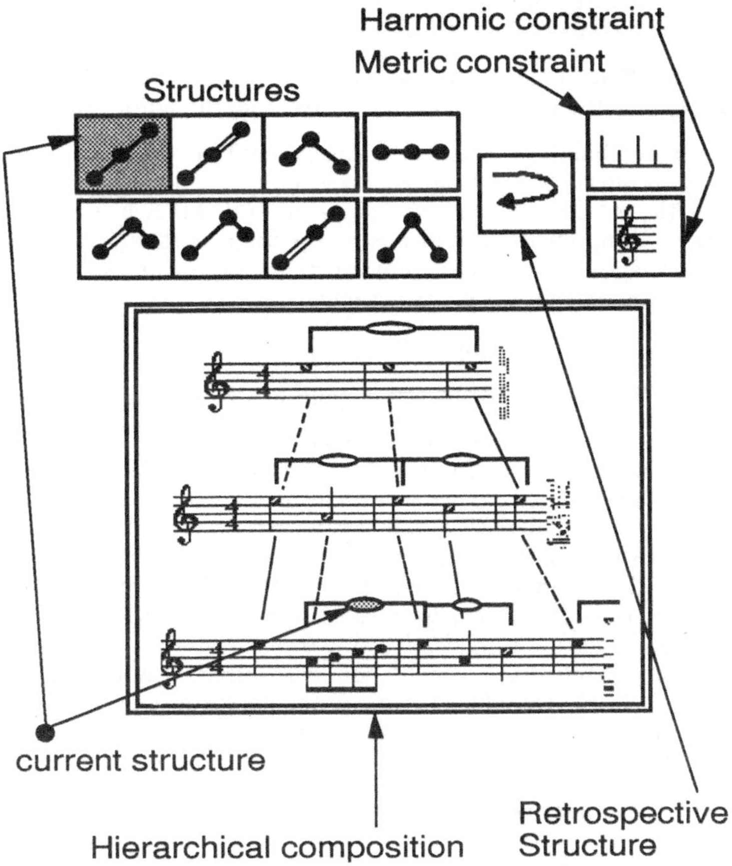

Figure 8: An example of a melody created from top-down constraints

- generating a melody given a constrained analysis,
- completing a partially-finished melody,
- building a complete melody around fragments (*e.g.*, phrases or motives),
- learning Narmour's Implication-Realisation model.

The tool has a number of strengths over pen and paper based composition for novices:

- no instrumental skills are needed (melodies can be heard from a MIDI source),
- few decisions for a novice, but task can be made less and less constrained,

- allows (more developed) critical ability of students to guide their choice of generated (partial or whole) melodies,
- can use "Paul Simon" method [Holland 89] of starting with an existing melody and then reworking it to create something different.

With the combination of analysis and generation a student is introduced to the cycle of initial composition, analysis and then a reworking of the piece (perhaps with certain parts to be unchanged). MOTIVE will allow such constraints as insisting on the use of melodic phrases (although the student will be able to transpose and vary the phrase, and compose around it).

MOTIVE does requires that the student:

- know traditional music notation,
- learn about Narmour's structures (and other parts of his theory).

The interface design described previously in this paper attempts to reduce the workload of learning the Implication-Realisation Model.

Perhaps the two most important educational claims of MOTIVE are: first, that the tasks performed by the student can start at a simple level and be made more sophisticated (by slowly increasing the number of decisions the student must make, and so reduce their reliance on MOTIVE's simplified constraints), and secondly, that MOTIVE allows the student to practice a critical ability (by making decisions about multiple generations from the tool), by initially reducing the amount of composition decisions required. It aims to help students overcome the initial stumbling block of starting with a massively underconstrainted creative task - a blank piece of paper.

7 Further work

A number of future research projects have been identified, based around the MOTIVE software:

7.1 Proposals for empirical educational evaluation of MOTIVE

Perhaps the most useful method for testing educational claims made for an AI tool is by evaluation involving real leaners (such as in a classroom environment). The evaluation results are useful, not only to support research claims, but also to generate criticisms of the tool, and (hopefully) point to ways the tool can be imporoved.

Informal evaluation of MOTIVE has begun (using "dry-running" pen and paper techniques), and once the computational parser and constraint extensions are completed MOTIVE will be tested in a more formal way. The educational evaluation will take the form of pre- and post-tests (to test musical knowledge and competence at simple compositional tasks), and analysis of protocols recorded from students using MOTIVE. Initially the evaluation will be formative, *i.e.*, evaluation while the tool is still being developed, so that the most important areas (from the point of view of students using MOTIVE) can be addressed early on. The use of "talk aloud" protocols and interviewing of students will be used.

After initial formative evaluation and improvement of MOTIVE, summative and comparative evaluation can be performed (perhaps comparing the use of MOTIVE with more traditional music teaching, and other computer tools).

7.2 Testing and formalisation of Narmour's theory

As Smoliar [Smoliar 91, p. 47] states in his review of [Narmour 90]:

> "If one is to consider the 'cognition of basic melodic structures,' one must do so in terms of what we currently know about cognition. Artificial Intelligence and cognitive science have recently provided us with powerful intellectual tools. As the philosopher John Pollock has observed regarding the study of epistemology [Pollock 89], the availability of these tools implies that we can no longer be content to speculate about cognition from the comfort of an armchair."

MOTIVE can be used to investigate Narmour's theory (*i.e.*, to make theory more formal, and to search for inconsistencies). For example, by having music analysts indicate when harmonic closure occurs, and asking them to explain why (in terms of the harmonic representations used in MOTIVE), the sophistication of the parser will increase, and more of Narmour's theory will have been unambiguously represented. One of the problems found when developing the computational model was how to decide when closure (from different melodic parameters) is sufficient to terminate a structure and cause hierarchical promotion. By analysing Narmour's own published examples, and using such interactive techniques as described for harmonic closure, MOTIVE can be used to infer and represent in a symbolic form rules about the Implication-Realisation Model. Such rules can then be shown to music analysts for criticism (perhaps seeing when rules are too general or specific).

7.3 Corpus analysis

A large corpus of melodies could be analysed, then one could investigate the frequency and hierarchical level of occurrence of each of the classes of melodic structure. From such analysis higher level constraints may come to light, which could then be compiled into heuristics to guide student's use of MOTIVE for top-down composition.

8 Conclusions

This paper describes research leading to the formalisation of an analytical theory of melody, and through the principled application of hierarchical harmonic and metric constraints the development of a constraint-based tool for the generation of melodies, for use by musical novices. It describes (to the author's knowledge) the first, large-scale, symbolic implementation of Narmour's implication-realisation model.

Of the work described in this paper, a large proportion has been implemented (in LPA MacProlog). The parser is complete (although its concept of harmonic closure is rather simplistic), and many of the routines for constraint-based generation are in place.

The work shows how a constraint-based AI approach can solve the apparent mismatch between the choice of an analytical theory of melody for the development of an aid for composition. MOTIVE has been designed so as to make the task of analysis and generation of simple melodies a progressive task (*i.e.*, by the gradual removal of default constraints and decisions, thus slowly more of the compositional task falls onto the student). The planned empirical evaluation will bring to light the strengths and weakness of such an approach.

9 Acknowledgements

This research was funded by a SERC PhD studentship. Special thanks to Daran Coates and Jon Oliver at the OU, for useful comments on drafts of this paper, and much appreciated assistance with paper formatting. Thanks also to our paper reviewers for their useful suggestions and criticisms.

References

[Holland 89] S. Holland. *Artificial Intelligence, Education and Music.* Unpublished PhD thesis, IET, Open University, UK, 1989.

[Lerdahl 88] F. Lerdahl. Tonal pitch space. *Music Perception,* 5 (3):315–350, 1988.

[Lerdhal & Jackendoff 83] F. Lerdhal and R. Jackendoff. *A Generative Theory of Tonal Music.* The MIT Press, Massachusetts, 1983.

[Longuet-Higgins & Lee 84] H. Longuet-Higgins and C. Lee. The rhythmic interpretation of monophonic music. *Music Perception,* 1:424–441, 1984.

[Markus 80] M. Markus. *Theory of Syntactic Recognition for Natural Language.* MIT Press, Cambridge, MA, USA, 1980.

[Meyer 56] L. B. Meyer. *Emotion and Meaning in Music.* University of Chicago Press, Chicago, USA, 1956.

[Narmour 90] E. Narmour. *The Analysis and Cognition of Basic Melodic Structures: The Implication-Realisation Model.* University of Chicago Press, Chicago, USA, 1990.

[Pollock 89] J. Pollock. *How to Build a Person: a Prolegomenon.* MIT Press, Cambridge, MA, 1989.

[Schenker 79] H. Schenker. *Free Composition.* Longmans, 1979. English translation of Der Freie Satz (1935).

[Smoliar 91] S. Smoliar. Review of: The analysis and cognition of basic melodic structures: The implication-realisation model. *In Theory Only*, 12, Numbers 1-2:43–56, 1991.

Uncovering Cognitive Processes in Music Composition: Educational and Computational Approaches

Brian K. Smith
Institute for the Learning Sciences
Northwestern University
Evanston, Illinois 60201, United States
bsmith@ils.nwu.edu

William H. Smith, Jr.
Department of Music
Radford University
Radford, Virginia 24142, United States
whsmith@ruacad.ac.runet.edu

Abstract

We present the initial results of a combined music education and artificial intelligence (AI) study on the cognitive processes underlying music composition. The examination of a body of protocol data collected in an earlier study by Younker & Smith led to the development of two models of compositional behavior. One is embodied as a production system emphasizing the high-level actions of novice and expert composers. A hypermedia system has been implemented allowing one to "experience" this model both visually and aurally. In addition, we present some initial unimplemented thoughts regarding the composition task which examine opportunism and memory and their relationship with the final musical product. Both formulations are motivated by the assumption that understanding musical processes and the intermediate products generated during a composer's work may help to increase our perspective on music cognition. As well, we discuss these two models in terms of educational applications and the construction of learning environments based in part on the work described here.

The understanding of music composition has long been approached from a product-centered perspective. That is, the final musical artifact becomes the object of study through the theoretical analysis of form and stylistic constraints. Much can be learned about the structure of a piece in this way, but it explains little about the thought processes of the composer, about the mental acts that led to the complete work.

In many domains, it is important that a practitioner have an understanding of some process, for instance the ways in which a recursive Lisp program returns its values or the steps one takes in performing a Fourier transform on a function. In other words, there is an understanding of the relationships between solution steps occurring over time. It has been argued that making intermediate products explicit can facilitate a deeper understanding of a domain [Merrill *et al* 92]. We believe there is truth to this and that the same logic can be applied to musical pursuits. Since most composers go through long processes of refinement and goal alteration during the musical activity, we presume that there is something to be learned from these process steps that are typically ignored in composition training.

Otto Laske uses the term *compositional theory* to refer to a new generation of empirical research in compositional processes [Laske 89]. The term empirical alludes to data collected from observations of composers at work, data used to study both the cognitive processes involved in composition as well as the end product (see also [Sloboda 85]). Laske's view is that the composer is an expert in *possible music*, **not** existing music. Thus a complete theory of music is dependent on an awareness of music *as it is being composed.*

If we believe Laske's claim, then the notion of process and its representation becomes crucial in understanding the composing mind and guiding its development in educational settings. Many musical models have foundations in representations of theory and product forms and are adequate for describing musical artifacts. In the same way, we feel that an analysis of process models may give us a new outlook on musical creativity. We argue that the control strategies used by composers are central to an increased perspective on music cognition.

The unfortunate difficulty is the lack of explicit data relating to composition. Unlike domains such as physics, geometry, and computer programming, extensive studies have not been conducted into the cognitive nature of the task. We were fortunate to have access to a body of verbal and musical protocol data and a preliminary cognitive model collected by Younker and Smith in an earlier study [Younker & Smith 92]. In particular, their work examined the strategies and goal structures used by composers when solving a specific problem: writing a melody that modulates.

Our work describes a collaborative effort between two camps — music education and artificial intelligence (AI) — to examine research efforts in creative problem-solving and teaching and learning in music composition. From a music education standpoint, we examine the potential of process analysis as a means of presenting the composition task to students and educators. The hope here is that by making internalized processes explicit, one will gain a deeper understanding of what it means to compose. The AI work involves an examination of the data in order to construct a computational theory of composition grounded in an understanding of the role of process. It is our belief that the eventual implementation of such a theory[1] could be used to further refine our understanding of compositional behavior. As well, we hope that such a model could lead to a foundation for the construction of learning environments congruent with well-formed cognitive and pedagogical views.

1 Protocol and product as mirror of process

In a previous study by [Younker & Smith 92], four subjects — an adult expert (music composition doctoral student), an adult novice (public school music

[1] We are currently beginning a computer implementation of the theoretical ideas.

teacher), a high school expert, and a high school novice — were tape recorded as they spoke aloud their thoughts while composing a fourteen-measure melody which was to begin in C major, modulate to A major, and end back in C major. This research method was based on an earlier study which involved the examination of process, working style, and product of ten university students, five first-year and five advanced performers, in a similar composition task [Davidson & Welsh 88]. A rhythmic "shell" was presented to the subjects in both studies, using values found in the opening fourteen bars of a march by Schubert, Op. 27 No. 1. Subjects were given a pen and manuscript paper with the rhythmic values on the first line. They were instructed to continually talk about what they were thinking as they composed the melody and not to cross out any work on the "score". Results indicated that there may be a hierarchy of knowledge necessary for expert level attainment, and that experience as a performer does not necessarily transfer to compositional expertise.

In the more recent study, MIDI pitch data were captured using a sequencing program and both the verbal protocols and the music productions were transcribed. These data were analyzed qualitatively, and the results were used to build two interrelated cognitive models. The first model was based on a conglomerate of the expressed thoughts of all four subjects in a graphic, input-processing-output design. This design illustrates the multiple modalities (*i.e.*, aural, visual, kinesthetic) employed by subjects, constructed in a circular fashion. This scheme alludes to relationships between "composer-initiated" and "composition-initiated" thought as the subjects consider elements of craftsmanship, sensitivity, and imagination [Reimer 89b, p. 62]. The second model, constructed solely on the data generated by the adult expert, incorporates principles of human information processing and is structured as a production system [Anderson 83].

The construction of this second, production system model was developed by those researchers from gleaning relationships between the expert's verbal protocol textlines; the snippets of music sang, hummed, played on the keyboard, or notated as the product was being developed; and the implied nested-goal structure of the composer's thinking made explicit through those behaviors.

For example, the adult expert begins the task by stating:

> Well, since you said to write a piece, a tonal melody, the first thing I'm thinking is that I'm not really being creative in the way I usually am, because that's not the kind of music I write ... So I just start thinking, I look at this, what I'm given ... how many bars is this ... 1, 2, 3, ... 12, 13, 14 ... So I think the first thing I'll do ... is this, is this turned on, the E-max? [Younker & Smith 92, p. A1].

The composer's own words from this protocol are transferred (in bold) into the production system model as [Younker & Smith 92, p. 14]:

Set macrogoal: **Write Piece**

- BAR COUNTING = 0; CHANTING = 0; MODULATORY THOUGHT = 0; PONDERING (ON NOTATION) = 0; MELODIC VERIFICATION = 0

  Set goal: **Write Tonal Melody**

  - IF MODULATORY THOUGHT = 6 THEN LOOK AT GIVEN;

GO TO "LEARN RHYTHM OF GIVEN"
- IF BAR COUNTING = 1 THEN **Access E-Max**
  IF E-MAX = ON THEN PLAY C MAJOR ARPEGGIO;
  GO TO "LEARN RHYTHM OF GIVEN"
- DO INSULATE RESULTS: **not creative**, exercise, academic
- **Look At Given:** GO TO "ESTABLISH FORM"

⋮

Set subgoal: Establish Form
Set microgoal: Determine Length Of Given
- Count Given Bars:
  BAR COUNTING = BAR COUNTING + 1

⋮

2 The planning problem and composition

Music composition can be viewed as an AI planning task. From some initial state, a compositional system seeks to apply operators to visit other states in hopes of finally reaching a desired goal. The selection of a definite goal is followed by the selection of a problem space defining the sets of possible states and operators that can be used to achieve the goal. This view of planning is appropriate for strongly-defined, goal-directed tasks, but unfortunately, in creative domains, such as music composition and performance, this reasoning is difficult to apply [Johnson-Laird 88] since:

- Creative tasks are non-deterministic. At any point in solving a creative problem, there are an enormous amount of possible options to take.
- Creative tasks lack well-defined goals. There is a general impression of what is to be accomplished, but this impression tends to be fairly vague.
- Because these tasks lack well-defined goals, there is no clear point for termination. The criteria used for judging completion and validity (*e.g.*, aesthetics) are just as unclear as the goal itself.

Analysis of the protocol data collected in the previous study [Younker & Smith 92] clearly shows that composition adheres to these three points. Therefore, typical planning approaches would be difficult, if not impossible, to apply to the domain.

This is not meant to be a treatise on the failures of classical planning, but we need to consider a key problem when thinking about music. Many AI planners involve very little, if any, reasoning *during* the execution phase; the plan specification determines the exact behavior of the plan executive. If the plan should fail, the executive terminates and returns control to the planning module. This produces systems that are inflexible in problem spaces characterized by unpredictable events, systems lacking reactive behavior. The need to store a set of plans produced under these conditions is questionable since they will no longer be applicable if slight changes occur in the world. Hence, most traditional planners generate, execute and discard; more will be said about this later. And, as one would imagine, because all of the actions must be encoded in the specification, the required detail for the representation of real world tasks would be phenomenal, never mind the potential computational tractability problems [Agre & Chapman 90].

The protocol data accumulated by [Younker & Smith 92] provide some insight into the processes used by composers. Indeed, in the protocol, there is very little to indicate that composition is a straightforward problem-solving domain, in the sense that, say, mathematics or physics are. This implication suggests a shift to another view of compositional processes. What follows is a preliminary sketch of concepts which we believe are embedded in compositional behavior. Indeed, behavior may prove to be the operative word, as our theory is centered around the notion that the cognitive workings of a composer are greatly influenced by the musical activity itself. In other words, the view of composition as planning must be intertwined with the activity, the execution of the plan.

3 An aesthetic viewpoint

Since we are speaking of the creation of art, it is useful to consult the literature on aesthetics in thinking of plausible cognitive/computational approaches to music composition. Consider what artists have written on the subject, for instance, Aaron Copland's statement:

> "Every composer keeps in mind the possible metamorphoses of his succession of notes. First he tries to find its essential nature, and then he tries to find what might be done with it — how that essential nature may momentarily be changed." [Copland 57, p. 25]

Or Roger Sessions' proposal:

> "[The composer] is not so much conscious of his ideas as possessed by them. Very often he is unaware of his exact processes of thought till he is through with them; extremely often the completed work is incomprehensible to him immediately after it is finished. Why? Because his experience in creating the work is incalculably more intense than any later experience he can have from it; because the finished product is, so to speak, the goal of that experience, and not in any sense a repetition of it." (cited in [Sloboda 85, p. 115])

There appears to be more to the creative process than simply generating a plan and executing it. Copland and Sessions lead us to believe that the composer's experience *while* composing is inextricably linked to the final product. While this seems intuitively plausible, it should force us to consider, at least metaphorically, a different way of thinking about the cognitive processes involved in music composition, and certainly how they can be modeled computationally. Perhaps the most convincing view of creativity, from the aesthetic sense, comes from Bennett Reimer, who states

> "So as the artist works on the material, the material immediately *works on the artist*, and the artist, with her sensitivity and imagination and craftsmanship, responds and decides and carries the act forward. An intimate, reciprocal relationship is established

> between artist and material. The art work grows and develops through the guidance of the artist's sensitivity to the feelings she recognizes, and imagination of their further potentials, and craftsmanly shaping of the material in which the expressive encounter is embodied." [Reimer 89b, p. 61–62]

As mystical as this may sound, it does provide some evidence that music composition is an extremely different task than those which fit neatly into the problem-solving framework. Indeed, as we shall see, composition is closely related to real world activity in which we seek *opportunities* and act upon them. Reimer's feedback loop between artist and artifact prompts us to take a more situated approach to understanding compositional processes. Our goal is to see if there is a psychological means of expressing his philosophical notion. As well, because we take the viewpoint that computer models of cognitive theories are an acceptable means of validation [Anderson 87], we will delve into issues underlying the implementation of accurate simulations of creative behavior.

4 Agency and composition

We adopt the term *agency* from Hammond et al. [Hammond *et al* 90] to refer to the activation of goals, plan selection and construction, and the execution of activity. Given a theory of agency, we can begin to discuss properties required to function in a dynamic environment. Before discussing the required components of such a theory for musical composition, we introduce some of the factors influencing our formulation.

4.1 Distributed cognition

An emerging paradigm in the psychological literature is the idea of distributed cognition [Solomon 93]. The claim is that our social, cultural, and artifactual surrounds influence our intelligence by actively helping us to shape our activities. In this view, cognition no longer resides completely in the head; it is distributed amongst other individuals and affordances. So, for instance, there is no need to think about computing square roots by hand anymore since we now have the calculator to do it for us. A segment of our mathematical intelligence is thus distributed within the computational artifact.

Reimer's statement "the artist works on the medium and the medium works on the artist" [Reimer 89b, p. 62] can be understood through this theory of distributed cognition: that we react in an intelligent manner by manipulating the environment in appropriate ways. Just as the proper set of tools enables us to perform a task more efficiently, so does an unfolding musical piece influence the composer's experience and progressive activity. The constant interaction between artist and musical residue, the reactive behavior displayed during the activity, is an important part of the compositional process and of creative processes in general.

Younker & Smith make explicit the distributed aspect of composition in their research [Younker & Smith 92]. Their production system and input-output models of behavior take multiple modalities into account. From their protocol data, they extract a taxonomy of tasks founded on tactile, visual, and aural sensory modes. Each subject in their experiments differed in how they moved between modalities, showing the individualistic nature of compositional processes. In situated terms, it appears that differences in the competence of the composers influence the way in which they manipulate the affordances at their disposal. For example, we note from the protocol that the novice composers tend to focus their discussions on "low-level" harmonic concepts as opposed to the experts who show a greater awareness of form and stylistic development.

The essence of distributed cognition lies in the principle that we, as intelligent agents, adapt to changes in our environment in order to accomplish our goals. The note above on modalities is one exemplar of this. An optimal cognitive simulation would somehow incorporate these sorts of functional elements into its behavior. For instance, just as a system like POLYA [McDougal 93] makes use of visual cues while solving geometry proofs, we would like to have ours model equivalent tasks that composers perform, *e.g.*, humming, singing, *etc.*

Yet for this stage of the research, we will focus only on the creation of the musical product. Encompassed in the theory is the premise of composition as a task involving the **generation of an environment**, namely the piece of music itself. So it is true that the multiple modalities involved in composing constitute a distributed intelligence, but at the same time, the interaction between composer and aural stimulation can also be thought of as a distributed system, just as Reimer proposes. Given that relationship, it seems fair to propose a theory of compositional processes based upon a notion of activity and control of the musical environment.

4.2 Planning

Earlier, we discussed traditional planning/problem-solving methods saying that they were too restrictive to model creative processes such as musical composition. The most tenuous of the assumptions made in the former view is the separation of planning and execution tasks. In most domains, composition included, it is unlikely that exhaustive pre-planning will yield a successful plan, since it is unfair to assume complete knowledge of the task environment or goal omniscience on the part of the planner. Typically, we presume that plan failures are the key elements of incorrect planners, but we must also consider opportunities for learning from unanticipated plan success [Hammond *et al* 93].

The integration of planning and execution tasks seems to be a viable approach to the problem of composition. The use of reactive systems, autonomous agents that respond intelligently in complex, dynamic environments, has been particularly effective in representing idiosyncratic behavior [Blythe & Reilly 93, Agre & Chapman 90], the sort that is displayed in the compositional task. In terms of a computational model of compositional processes, the goal is to unify elements of planning, action, and learning in a single architecture.

To begin, we should consider aspects of human planning that may be relevant to our specification of machine behavior. [Hayes-Roth & Hayes-Roth 79] presented the view that a planner should be able to shift between planning strategies. In their study of students planning a day's errands, the following four points were derived from a protocol analysis:

- World knowledge is used to assign salience to plan steps.

- Bottom-up processing is occurring; planning is often driven by what seems to be directly attainable.
- Top-down processing is occurring; goals are often incorporated into high-level, abstract plans.
- Planning is opportunistic.

Their implementation consisted of a blackboard architecture and plan specialists which made decisions about differing aspects of the plan under construction, *e.g.*, suggestion of high-level abstractions by some specialists while others mainly provided detailed action sequences. The blackboard architecture is well suited for this sort of planning task since it is, in theory, inherently opportunistic and capable of dealing with multiple representations efficiently [Englemore *et al* 88].

Some purport that Hayes-Roth and Hayes-Roth lack a clean specification for combined planning and execution [Hammond *et al* 93, Palatano *et al* 93], yet we believe that their concept of "mental simulation" — mentally executing the plan in one's head, subsequently influencing further planning — is certainly adequate for our purposes. However, we must make some extensions to their view, since, as Palatano et al. point out [Palatano *et al* 93], there is no notion of memory in the Hayes-Roths' model of planning. The literature generally agrees that our understanding of music is based around the fulfillment and denial of expectations (for example, see [Narmour 90, Dowling & Harwood 86, Sloboda 85, Meyer 56]). Expectation-based processing is highly dependent on the existence of a structured memory [Schank 82]. Our view of compositional processes combines situated activity with remindings of previous musical encounters, therefore requiring a vocabulary to express and retrieve musical cases from an indexed memory.

Before we discuss memory, we must say more about opportunity. An intelligent agent must be able to effectively generate and modify knowledge primitives. Perhaps more important though is the need to decide when it is appropriate to actually perform a given task. In other words, the ability to alter control of cognitive behavior is a hallmark of an intelligent system. Much of the existing work in AI is built upon simple control mechanisms, choosing instead to focus on knowledge representation and heuristics. In this research, we felt it necessary to emphasize the elements of control in composition. It is apparent that some competence knowledge is being used; we see that familiarity with tonal harmony is a large part of composing. The statements made in the protocol data seem to indicate that the composer is commanding a set of plans in order to achieve musical goals. It is clear that human composers do not act as machine plan executives do. They seem to be taking advantage of opportunities when they arise — decisions about further development are based on an assessment of the current state of the piece, presumably through some aesthetic judgment.

Plans and goals seem to play a key role in human plan execution and opportunism. Intelligent agents recognize opportunity based on currently active goals and goals suspended in the past. Consider the following excerpt from the expert composer's protocol:

> "Ah, but now I have to start thinking about going to A. OK? So, I have to think about how I'm going to get to A here ... So I've

> introduced G sharp. That's all I really need to do is introduce the G sharp. That would be good." [Younker & Smith 92, pp. A2–A3]

Here is the explicit statement of an active compositional subgoal, making the modulation to A. The plan to achieve this goal is encoded in the statement concerning the G sharp. The same can be said in the following passage:

> "... C sharp ... A ... Ah. A nice leap up to G natural, that'll be perfect. Because I'm getting too low in the register anyway, I don't want to go much below middle C, I want to use the G natural ... now if I leap to it — that'll be perfect, that'll emphasize the ... the key change, uh, the tonicization." [Younker & Smith 92, p. A8]

Again, there is the statement of a plan to achieve a musical goal, this time including a justification of the act. What's also interesting here is the beginning of the passage where the composer is calling out notes. There appears to be a realization that the G natural will satisfy the goal of emphasizing the key change. The presumption is that this may well be an instance of opportunism: the key change goal was suddenly activated by the progression of notes ending on A.

Often in the course of planning, we take advantage of the organization of the environment. For instance, if you are writing a paper, you may need access to a dictionary that sits on your bookshelf. The fact that the dictionary is *stabilized* in its location [Hammond *et al* 92] reduces the amount of inference and search needed to carry out the paper writing plans. Of course, one must enforce stability by ensuring that the dictionary is put back in its proper place after use. Stabilization of location (and, indeed, of schedule, resource availability, plan use, satisfaction, *etc.*) is something that we take for granted, yet these constraints are important in everyday decision making. The planning agent is able to use the environment to its advantage, but also, it is able to reorganize the environment in ways congruent with its goals.

Stability provides a greater reuse of plans and reduces the amount of information-gathering one must perform. To make use of this property, a planner should enforce as many stabilization constraints as possible. The tacit knowledge of musical styles that a composer possesses is very much like these constraints. [Meyer 89] discusses "universals" which assist in the perception and cognition of musical events; repetition of musical structures, revisiting previously presented patterns to strengthen closure, and preference for regular patterns are amongst some of these. A composer (as well as listeners and performers, in their own ways) will generally attempt to ensure that such things are present in a piece. For instance, the expert composer makes statements like the following:

> "Well since, you said to write a piece, a tonal melody, the first thing I'm thinking about is that I'm not really being creative in the way I usually am, because that's not the kind of music I write ... I guess, because of the last note, and so I wonder how many, whether I should make this some kind of Classical phrase like antecedent-consequent ... " [Younker & Smith 92, p. A1]

Although he ordinarily works in other forms, he seems to be establishing a set of working constraints based on a knowledge of Western musical forms. As he states that he ordinarily does not write tonal music, he seems to be establishing a new set of constraints for himself. He is using the boundaries of tonality to assist him in the planning process.

4.3 Memory

Integrating a memory component into our theory is important if the goal is to remain faithful to human cognitive mechanisms. Unlike some AI work grounded in situated action, (for instance, [Brooks 91]), we make the presumption that memory and internalized representations have an integral role in the composition task. We will explain in this section the need for a structure that allows for musical remindings and their use while composing.

Schank proposed a model of memory in which we make extensive use of remindings in everyday tasks [Schank 82]. The view is that new, novel situations are typically understood by recalling previous, similar events and making adaptations to fit the current requirements. In other words, we reason from prior cases, hence the name of the subfield, case-based reasoning (CBR). It is felt that this model-based approach will prove more flexible than the brittle, rigid rule structures that have dominated AI efforts. While rule-based system performance tends to degrade as more rules and operators are added, CBR systems should perform better with increased experiential knowledge [McDougal 93].

In the discussion on classical planning, we explained that many planners generate a successful plan, execute the action and throw the plan away. Case-based planners, on the other hand, store a plan, any failures that it encountered during planning, and the alterations that it needed to make in order to repair these failures. When the planner is confronted with a new problem, it first searches its memory to see if it can find a similar scenario and its solution. If possible, the system can simply use the old plan, but often, adaptation must be made due to slightly different constraints on the new problem. A planner like CHEF [Hammond 89] can be reminded of past failures and their repair strategies, thus making it much more efficient than a traditional system. A simple augmentation can also allow it to index opportunities that led to success.

CHEF and its descendents interest us for various reasons. There is strong belief that musical memory is based on strategies much like this [Smoliar 90, Sloboda 85]. Through years of experience of listening to music, explicit memories are created. It seems that we have highly sophisticated mechanisms for storage and retrieval of musical information. As well, it appears that music is not necessarily indexed in terms of itself: it also has relations with non-musical events [Smoliar 90, Davies 78]. The questions to pursue are how and to what extent do composers draw upon their previous knowledge while creating a musical piece? As well, in a computational model, it is important to consider the nature of the structures that would elicit a musical reminding.

There are indications that composers are making use of prior musical knowledge in the protocol. In many cases, this seems to be actual thought on music theory, *e.g.*, discussions of form, tonality, *etc.* In fact, the Younker & Smith protocol turns out to be a poor indicator of the reminding behavior discussed above. However, in Sloboda's discussion of his self-generated protocol (collected as he composed a setting of Psalm 92), he speaks of a realization that features of material previously composed by him had entered the new work almost unconsciously, perhaps modified to fit the constraints of the new harmonic structure [Sloboda 85]. The nature of the tasks in the two bodies of data, however, are slightly different. In Younker and Smith's study, there is a slightly more rigid goal framework for the subject to work with — recall that the rhythmic shell and the tonal changes were given. Sloboda has more flexibility with his piece since it is more of a free task, constrained primarily by the lyrical content.

In theory, it all sounds quite plausible, and yet there is one issue that remains unsolved: the *indexing problem* [Riesbeck & Schank 89]. In order to be reminded of something, one must (a) have actually experienced that something and **stored** it in memory, and (b) be able to **retrieve** it from memory. The job of *indices* is to provide a means for accomplishing these tasks. Indices must be chosen to decide where new events will be inserted and where to search during retrieval. Obviously, we want our indices to be able to discriminate an event from all other similar ones to insure the "best" reminding. Considering the amount of detail that is contained in the average scene, the indexing problem becomes one of deciding how much information is necessary to store a case such that it can be successfully retrieved. For a computer model, this suggests the formulation of a (complex) vocabulary expressing the types of details that might be present in the domain under study.

What might the indices look like for a musical reminding? Let's think about this from the standpoint of the protocol once again. Again, we have a constrained task in that the rhythm and tonal framework have been specified. In the case of the adult expert composer, say, we see him add additional constraints in terms of form ("... so I wonder how many, whether I should make this some sort of classical phrase like antecedent-consequent ...") and tonality ("And I'll end on middle C, just because it's lower, and it'll sound more final." [Younker & Smith 92, p. A1]), constraints that are also related to stablization. It has been shown that a piece of music can be described by an increasing set of constraints [Levitt 93, Marsden & Pople 89], that such information could be used as a representation for composition and improvisation tasks. We have started investigating an indexing scheme which uses such constraints as differentiating conditions. Specifically, we are considering the use of affect as a high-level semantic primitive, characterizing pieces by their emotive connotations. The constraints will restrict these affective categories in ways which are perceptually plausible as well as providing discrimination measures. We are unsure of the psychological validity behind such a division, but a plan for further research is an empirical study of musical indices.

5 The hypermedia browser

Because of the complexity, nonlinearity, and linkability of the various dataforms, a popular hypermedia platform (see [Nielson 90]) was chosen as a vehicle for the display and analysis of the expert's data from the [Younker & Smith 92] study for the first phase of this cooperative project. The HyperCard environment for the Macintosh personal computer, a popular choice for use in schools and universities, provides for ease in the managing and viewing of data. This interface allows researchers, teachers, and students the ability to make connections between (a) the general, graphic modalities model and the expert's specific production system model; (b) the text protocol and its implementation in the production system model; (c) the text and digitized speech of the protocol; and (d) the music productions *en route* and the final product. An "automate" function will allow users to "experience" the composition task continuously. In addition, the users will have the option to parse the datastream as they see fit, in effect suggesting their own structure of the composer's thinking instead of endeavoring to understand the researchers' "imposed" structure through the real-time or step-wise display.

Figure 1 consists of a screen shot from the first version of the adult expert "stack" (the term for "file" or "program" in HyperCard language). The parts of this opening screen of the stack are outlined below, based on recent hypertext mapping principles [Horn 89]:

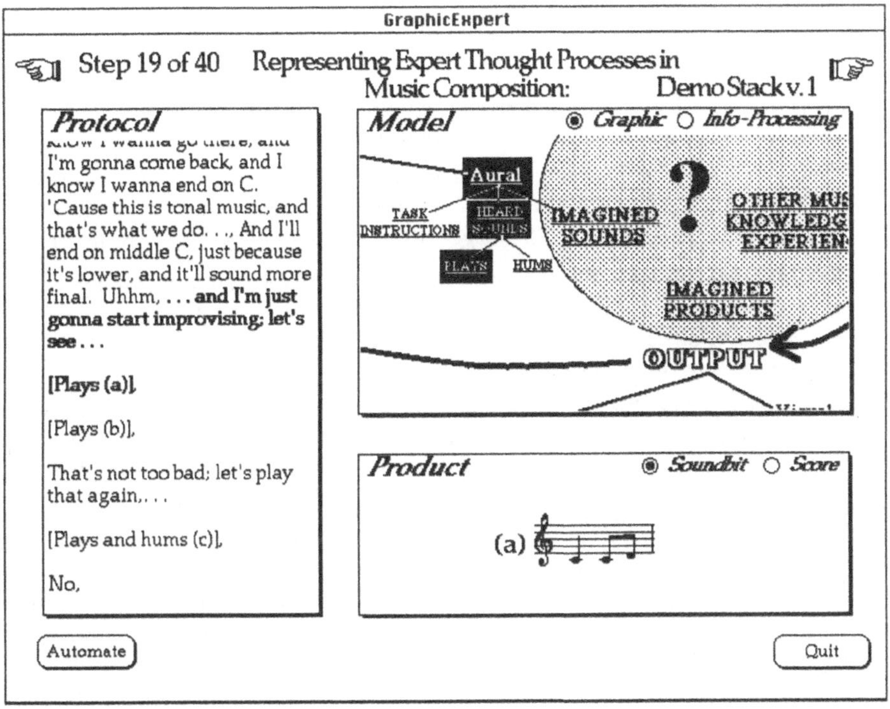

Figure 1: Illustration of card nineteen of the hypermedia simulation.

Step Number: *"Step 19 of 40"* indicates where in the process the composer's thoughts currently exist. If the "unstructured" toggle is highlighted, the user decides which cards make up a "step".

Text Window: This left-hand window contains the transcription of the verbal protocol; boldface text indicates which step is highlighted by this card when the "structured" toggle is selected. By clicking in this window, the user may hear the digitized speech of the composer. If the *"See Keywords"* toggle is selected, clicking on the text will show its implementation in the production system model.

Model Window: The user may toggle between a zoomed-in view of that part of the graphic, general model which is highlighted by this card, or a zoomed-in view of part of the production system ("Info-Processing") model. By clicking in this window, the user is zoomed-out to cards representing the entire model(s).

Product Window: Here, the user may see the transcribed "soundbits" — played, sung, or hummed musical productions. Or the currently written line of the score may be viewed. By clicking in this window, digitized or MIDI'ed versions of the music may be heard. The user also has the option, through the "sound-symbol" toggle in the help menu, to zoom out to a screen showing all soundbits or the entire score.

Left- and Right-Point Buttons: Clicking on these buttons takes the user to the previous or next step in the composer's process when the "structured" toggle is selected. These buttons become "grayed" (inactive) when the "automate" option is selected or when the "unstructured" toggle is chosen.

See/Hide Keywords Toggle: This button allows grouped text from the protocol, which are keyed to text used in the production system model, to be underlined and relationships shown. This toggle disables the digitized speech option.

Show/Hide Notes Toggle: This button brings up a "Researcher's Notes" field where users may type in their own qualitative analysis as to what may be happening at each step along the way, either as prescribed by the researcher ("structured") or decided by the users ("unstructured").

Automate/Step Thru Toggle: When selected, this option allows the user to watch, listen, and experience the composer's process automatically from beginning to end of the task. The task can be paused or stopped altogether at any point.

Data, in the form of notes made by users on the composer's process, and critiques of the stack's effectiveness and usefulness will be used to further refine the design of the stack. Although we found it valuable to construct the stack from an educational perspective (see [Webster 92]), future forms of this germinal stack must be designed and programmed more elegantly in order to collect, analyze, and guide users in learning how to compose. As principles of AI are incorporated in these and other model-tools, it is hoped that flexible, individualistic composition tutoring programs may be created for use with developing student-composers.

6 Reflections on the Models

Because of the influence of the Younker & Smith paper in this work, we feel it necessary to reflect on their ideas and the subsequent research agenda we will pursue. Our analysis of the protocol data has led us to consider different directions for reasons explained in this section.

The first comment deals with the AI approach that we have set forth in this paper. The situated view of composition described in this paper conflicts with Younker & Smith's production system model, and yet this may simply be a question of granularity and scope. Much like the productions in Anderson's ACT* [Anderson 83], their rules seem to reflect a domain-dependent sequence of operations. Anderson claims that his theory describes cognition at an algorithmic level [Anderson 87], the abstract principles that underlie some mental behavior. Younker & Smith present much the same in their paper, a difference being that their productions would probably be described by Anderson as declarative, pre-compiled knowledge. It is important to remember that Anderson's work is centered around well-defined domains, simplifying the efforts needed to express productions at a more generalized level. For composition, we currently lack sufficient data to begin making general statements.

The response to this was the formulation of the situated planner described here. We consider this abstraction comparable to Anderson's architectural level [Anderson 87]. That is, we have tried to define the components which contribute to the algorithmic level, the components which would need to be constructed by a lower, implementational level. The leap to this level was prompted by a desire to construct a computer model to simulate the algorithmic principles of composition. In order to do this, it is necessary to speculate about the nature of the algorithms themselves. Currently we are investigating higher level components in greater detail as well as developing a preliminary implementation.

Our interaction with the HyperCard stack should be noted. We found it advantageous to have such a tool for viewing the large amounts of data collected by Younker & Smith. Since it presents the protocol along with the sound fragments played by each composer, it allows a unique way for traversing information of different modalities. The added benefit of having their models at hand for perusal and comparison heightens the benefit of working with the tool. We found that we were able to reflect on our ideas in conjunction with theirs, keeping close to the algorithmic level that was established and allowing it to guide our architectural decomposition.

In order to further develop our ideas about composition, we will need several components. Firstly, just as Younker & Smith derived a taxonomy of modalities, we believe it will be necessary to do the same for the space of opportunities and stabilization constraints. This will require some effort, but it will be interesting to see, as we continue an analysis of the data, what sort of commonalities, if any, run through the subjects. Some of this information can be captured in the form of formal musical principles, but others may prove to be much more individualistic, and our presumption is that the more experienced composers will present control decisions that will have to be uniquely accounted for. Secondly, as pointed out, studies of musical memory are called for to begin refining our current thoughts about the structure of indices. Finally, decisions about architectures have been considered in terms of implementing a computational model, but as we proceed, more alternatives will present themselves, influencing the eventual implementation.

7 Conclusions

We have dealt with many issues in this paper, but there is a strong interest in educational implications within this work. As stated earlier, when viewing music composition as problem solving, we must recognize that it is an ill-defined task. In both the hypermedia browser and this planning formulation, we have assumed "correctness" on the basis of the actions of *one* composer. In domains like physics, mathematics, *etc.*, this might be an acceptable thing to do, since the metacognitive skills of experts in these domains might be reasonably similar, but creativity seems to manifest itself differently in artistic realms. The very fact that unique, individual styles manifest themselves in creative tasks presents difficulties when trying to generalize the cognitive workings of musicians.

One of our goals is to address the problems involved with understanding ill-defined cognitive tasks. We recognize that studying one composer will provide with us with minimal information and are in the progress of performing more detailed comparisons with the remaining Younker & Smith data. Just as intelligent tutoring systems have had well-formed psychological models as a foundation for their pedagogical implementations, we hope to better understand how to construct musical composition environments congruent with cognitive and metacognitive skills viewed in composers. This effort represents a first step in this approach to musical understanding.

It is recognized that the majority of the literature on intelligent tutoring systems (ITS) revolves around scientific domains because their structures make them appropriate for student modeling and feedback delivery. If our interest is in teaching music theory, methods embodied in a typical ITS would certainly be applicable: theory provides a well-developed set of rules. However, our wish is to consider seriously the possibility of systems that assist students in maximizing their creative potentials. The HyperCard simulation represents a first step towards making compositional processes explicit and comprehendable for the learner. If properly deployed in a learning environment, we feel that it could be an effective tool. The fact that it does **not** provide tutorial support is interesting in itself; we hope that the tool could empower learners to begin the active construction of their own compositions. Future work in this direction would include greater scaffolding to facilitate such engagement.

This project brings together a set of ideas borne out of a concern for understanding the structure of musical thought. We believe that discoveries about the nature of compositional processes and how those processes develop deserve attention in music education in light of recent advancements in computer music technologies. These developments are giving rise to new music technology labs and composition-related courses in the schools [Reimer 89a]. The development of research and instructional tools which help teachers understand and guide the music composition process with their students is vitally important, especially when the majority of school music educators come to the profession from a performance background and lack composition experience. By understanding more about the ways in which composers think, we hope to strengthen our understanding of the musical mind in order to build and support learning environments.

8 Acknowledgements

Our thanks to the participants of the workshop on music education and AI during AI-ED 93 for suggestions and comments on this research. We also thank Betty Anne Younker for her assistance during this collaboration and the anonymous reviewers for their informative feedback.

References

[Agre & Chapman 90] PE Agre and D Chapman. What are plans for? *Robotics and Autonomous Systems*, 6:17–34, 1990.

[Anderson 83] JR Anderson. *The Architecture of Cognition*. Harvard University Press, Cambridge, MA, 1983.

[Anderson 87] JR Anderson. Methodologies for studying human knowledge. *Behavioral and Brain Sciences*, 10:467–505, 1987.

[Blythe & Reilly 93] J Blythe and WS Reilly. Integrating reactive and deliberate planning for agents. Technical Report CMU-CS-93-155, School of Computer Science, Carnegie Mellon University, Pittsburgh, PA, 1993.

[Brooks 91] RA Brooks. Intelligence without reason. In *Proceedings of the International Joint Conference on Artificial Intelligence*, pages 569–595, 1991.

[Copland 57] A Copland. *What to Listen for in Music*. Penguin Books, New York, 1957.

[Davidson & Welsh 88] L Davidson and P Welsh. From collections to structure: The developmental path of tonal thinking. In J Sloboda, editor, *Generative Processes in Music: The Psychology of Performance, Improvisation, and Composition*. Oxford University Press, New York, 1988.

[Davies 78] JB Davies. *The Psychology of Music*. Stanford University Press, Stanford, CA, 1978.

[Dowling & Harwood 86] WJ Dowling and DL Harwood. *Music Cognition*. Academic Press, Inc., San Diego, CA, 1986.

[Englemore *et al* 88] RS Englemore, AJ Morgan, and HP Nii. Introduction. In RS Englemore and AJ Morgan, editors, *Blackboard Systems*. Addison-Wesley, Wokingham, England, 1988.

[Hammond 89] KJ Hammond. *Case-based Planning: Viewing Planning as a Memory Task*. Academic Press, Boston, MA, 1989.

[Hammond *et al* 90] K Hammond, T Converse, and C Martin. Integrating planning and acting in a case-based framework. In *Proceedings of the Eighth National Conference on Artificial Intelligence*, pages 292–297, 1990.

[Hammond *et al* 92] KJ Hammond, TM Converse, and JW Grass. The stabilization of environments. Available from the Department of Computer Science, University of Chicago, Chicago, IL, 1992.

[Hammond *et al* 93] K Hammond, T Converse, M Marks, and CM Seifert. Opportunism and learning. *Machine Learning*, 10:279–209, 1993.

[Hayes-Roth & Hayes-Roth 79] B Hayes-Roth and F Hayes-Roth. A cognitive model of planning. *Cognitive Science*, 3:275–310, 1979.

[Horn 89] R Horn. *Mapping Hypertext: Analysis, Linkage, and Display of Knowledge for the Next Generation of On-Line Text and Graphics.* The Lexington Institute, Lexington, MA, 1989.

[Johnson-Laird 88] PN Johnson-Laird. *The Computer and the Mind: An Introduction to Cognitive Science.* Fontana, London, 1988.

[Laske 89] O Laske. Composition theory: An enrichment of music theory. *Interface*, 18:45–59, 1989.

[Levitt 93] DA Levitt. A representation for musical dialects. In SM Schwanauer and DA Levitt, editors, *Machine Models of Music.* The MIT Press, Cambridge, MA, 1993.

[Marsden & Pople 89] A Marsden and A Pople. Modelling musical cognition as a community of experts. *Contemporary Music Review*, 3:29–42, 1989.

[McDougal 93] TF McDougal. Using case-based reasoning and situated activity to write geometry proofs. In *Proceedings of the Fifteenth Annual Conference of the Cognitive Science Society*, pages 711–716, 1993.

[Merrill *et al* 92] DC Merrill, BJ Reiser, R Beekelaar, and A Hamid. Making processes visible: Scaffolding learning with reasoning-congruent representations. In C Frasson, G Gauthier, and I McCalla, editors, *Proceedings of the International Tutoring Systems Conference.* Springer-Verlag, New York, 1992.

[Meyer 56] LB Meyer. *Emotion and Meaning in Music.* University of Chicago Press, Chicago, 1956.

[Meyer 89] LB Meyer. *Style and Music: Theory, History, and Ideology.* University of Pennsylvania Press, Philadelphia, 1989.

[Narmour 90] E Narmour. *The Analysis and Cognition of Basic Melodic Structures: The Implication-Realization Model.* The University of Chicago Press, Chicago, 1990.

[Nielson 90] J Nielson. *Hypertext and Hypermedia.* Academic Press, New York, 1990.

[Palatano *et al* 93] AL Palatano, CM Seifert, and KJ Hammond. Predictive encoding: Planning for opportunities. In *Proceedings of the Fifteenth Annual Conference of the Cognitive Science Society*, pages 800–805, 1993.

[Reimer 89a] B Reimer. Music education as aesthetic education: Toward the future. *Music Educators Journal*, 75(7):26–32, 1989.

[Reimer 89b] B Reimer. *A Philosophy of Music Education.* Prentice Hall, Inc., Englewood Cliffs, NJ, 1989.

[Riesbeck & Schank 89] CK Riesbeck and RC Schank. *Inside Case-Based Reasoning.* Lawrence Erlbaum Associates, Hillsdale, NJ, 1989.

[Schank 82] RC Schank. *Dynamic Memory: A Theory of Learning in Computers and People.* Cambridge University Press, New York, 1982.

[Sloboda 85] JA Sloboda. *The Musical Mind: The Cognitive Psychology of Music.* Clarendon Press, Oxford, 1985.

[Smoliar 90] SW Smoliar. The mental processes of musical composition. In *Proceedings of Colloque International "Musique et Assistance Informatique"*, pages 171–178, Marseille, France, 1990.

[Solomon 93] G Solomon, editor. *Distributed Cognitions.* Cambridge University Press, New York, 1993.

[Webster 92] P Webster. Custom-designed software in the arts: The educator as expert. *Design for Arts in Education*, 93(6):37–44, 1992.

[Younker & Smith 92] BA Younker and WH Smith. *Modeling the thought processing structure of high school and adult expert and novice composers.* Presented at the Music Educators National Conference, New Orleans, LA, 1992.

Section II: Representation of Musical Knowledge

Representations of the MONK harmonisation systems

Daran Coates*
Department of Computing
Faculty of Mathematics and Computing
Open University
Milton Keynes MK7 6AA, England
d.coates@open.ac.uk

Abstract

This paper describes the music representation approaches used in MONK, an implemented group of software modules from which harmonisation systems can be built. The basic design issues are outlined in relation to two preparatory studies, namely an examination of three recent harmonisation systems and an informal protocol analysis of practitioners performing harmonisations. The development of a symbolic model of the Longuet-Higgins map of harmony, LHSpace, is described and the manipulation of LHSpace by the MONK systems outlined. The representation of melody is outlined and compared with Conventional Music Notation. Approaches to representing other musical knowledge using traditional Artificial Intelligence techniques are discussed. The educational implications of the MONK representations are considered.

1 Introduction

MONK (Modules Of iNterconnectable Knowledge) is an implemented group of modules, of which a subset can be built into a harmonisation system. The input to a MONK harmonisation system is a symbolic representation of a melody and the output is a bass line and set of chords which accompany that melody. The system is explicitly modular, and the modules can by used by more than one system. The representations for such a system have to be general and flexible. MONK has been designed so that only a general adherence to a hierarchical framework is needed, allowing maximum expandability. This report details some of the open representations used by the systems which facilitate this modularity. Educational uses of MONK are examined.

2 Design of MONK

The design of MONK was influenced by two preparatory studies. The first examined three recent harmonisation systems identifying approaches, motivation

*The author carried out the research reported here at the Department of Computing Science, King's College, University of Aberdeen, Aberdeen AB9 2UB, Scotland.

and techniques. Shortcomings and limitations were also identified. The second study was an examination into how human practitioners perform the task of harmonisation.

The three systems examined in the preparatory study were CHORAL [Ebcioglu 86], Vivace [Thomas 85] and CHORALEARN [Sirkin 87]. Although the work achieved their respective project aims, there were some areas left to explore in the domain of computer harmonisation.

- The building of systems which can harmonise in more than one style. Sirkin [Sirkin 87] claims CHORALEARN can perform harmonisations in more than one style due to the open architecture, but he presents no examples to support his claim.

- Ebcioglu's CHORAL system (described in [Ebcioglu 86]) is the only one of the three examined which can handle modulating material. Thomas [Thomas 85] outlines a plan to include modulation software into a future version of Vivace. It is not clear from [Sirkin 87] how CHORALEARN could be updated to handle modulations. This is a very common musical activity and should be addressed in any substantial harmonisation system.

- Each system is capable of harmonising a melody in only one way. These systems model just one approach to the problem. However, comparing the strategies of harmonisation between Vivace and CHORAL [*op. cit.*] it can be seen that there is more than one way to perform the task adequately.

- It is not clear whether the systems, in whole or in part, could be reused or recycled for a different purpose. Basic representation issues are of a similar nature for all music systems. If suitably general representations are found, there is no reason why they cannot be used in a variety of music applications.

To try and address general design issues which would help tackle these areas, the constraints of modularity and expandability were formed. If a system is explicitly modular, and the modules are of a small enough size to allow skill or knowledge based sizes (for example, knowledge about building triads residing in one module), these modules are more recyclable. Choosing the most comprehensive representations available allows expandability. Future versions of MONK could use software written on the first day of the project. To harmonise in a variety of styles using a variety of methods indicates the need to build a number of systems with, in many cases, duplicate knowledge and skills. Expandable and modular software allow a recycling of modules between systems, creating a flexible and open system of constructing a variety of harmonisation systems.

[Sloboda 85] makes the interesting point that:

> "most of [the literature concerning composition] deals with the production of the composition, not the process."

This can be seen to be true for the CHORALEARN system, for example, which has learned from Bach's examples and not his composition process. To try and address this issue, five people who could perform basic four part harmonisations were asked to harmonise a phrase of a hymn tune. The subjects were asked to talk aloud, whilst performing the task, to explain what rules, constraints and knowledge were being used. This informal study was performed to identify what knowledge, constraints and knowledge were being used. The answers of the subjects were not examined for their quality. The main aim was to find an indication of the interrelation of rules, domain knowledge and constraints. A layered model was observed in all the subjects and became the basis for the outline MONK systems design.

- A top level strategy, which controls how the task was performed, makes decisions about how the material should be developed, and manipulates subtasks.
- A subtask layer, where sequences of fundamental skills are combined to form recognisable harmonisation skills.
- A fundamental skills layer, where essential skills and knowledge are singly stored.
- A basic knowledge layer, where factual knowledge about music are stored, including note and key relations.

This was developed into the overview layered MONK design which forms Figure 1.

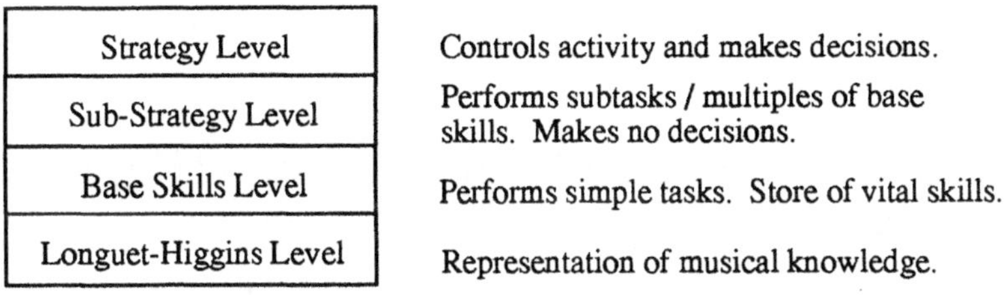

Figure 1: The MONK layered design, with brief level descriptions.

All harmonisation systems built with MONK modules follow this outline design. An illustration of a possible MONK system forms Figure 2. The following points may help the reader understand the workings of a MONK system.

- The flow of control is from the Strategy layer down. The Strategy module for any MONK system initiates any request for information throughout the system directly (by calling the relevant routine) or indirectly (by calling an intermediate program to retrieve on its behalf).
- The flow of information is from the Longuet-Higgins layer up. The LH-Space model is the fundamental repository for harmonic information. This model is discussed later in the chapter.

- The level of granularity is finer in the lower layers of the design. The Base Skills modules are very small programs performing single tasks. The Strategy modules are larger, more complex software modules.
- Creative decisions about the harmonisation are taken only by the Strategy module. It is the function of the other layers of the design to provide the information to allow the creative decisions to be made.

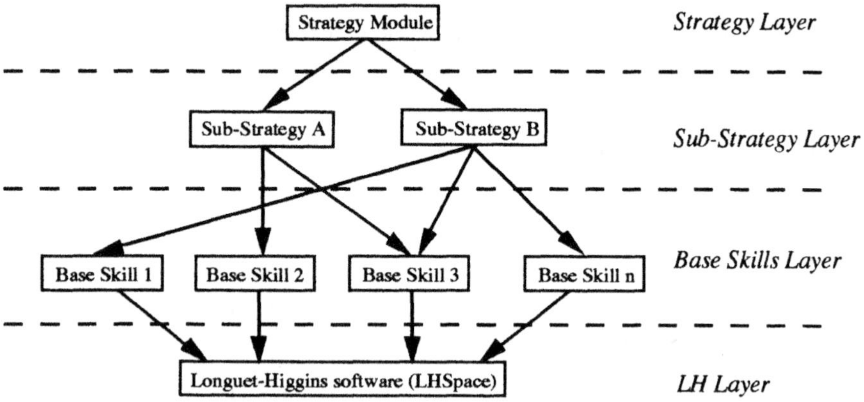

Figure 2: Flow of control within a simplified MONK system.

A detailed description of the Design issues and details can be found in [Coates ?].

3 Implementation of the Longuet-Higgins Map of Harmony

[Longuet-Higgins 62a] describes a map of harmony, built from major third and perfect fifth relationships. It has been used in a variety of musical applications, for instance as a method of visually describing musical concepts [Longuet-Higgins 62a] and [Longuet-Higgins 62b], as part of a melody analysis system [Steedman 72] and adapted and implemented as a direct manipulation tool for learning harmony [Holland 89]. The map can be viewed as an implicit repository of musical knowledge ([Holland 89], explores the educational aspects of this). Distinct musical concepts can take a unique and consistent shape in the map. Using a symbolic version of the map (LHSpace) and coordinate manipulation definitions (which are essentially representations of the concept shapes) MONK models essential harmonic knowledge in a succinct but comprehensive way.

LHSpace is essentially a codification into Prolog of the map from [Longuet-Higgins 62a]. Each element of the map has been represented by a two element entry in a Prolog database. The entries are of the following form.

```
lhspace( [row,column] , [pitch,accidental] ).
```

The row and column coordinates[1] for each database entry were derived from the version diagram seen in Figure 3. The natural symbol is denoted by '*', the flat by '−' and the sharp by '+'. Double sharps and flats are represented by '++' and '−−' respectively. Example Prolog representations of notes in the Longuet-Higgins map can be found in Figure 3. The map is the version that appears in [Longuet-Higgins 62a].

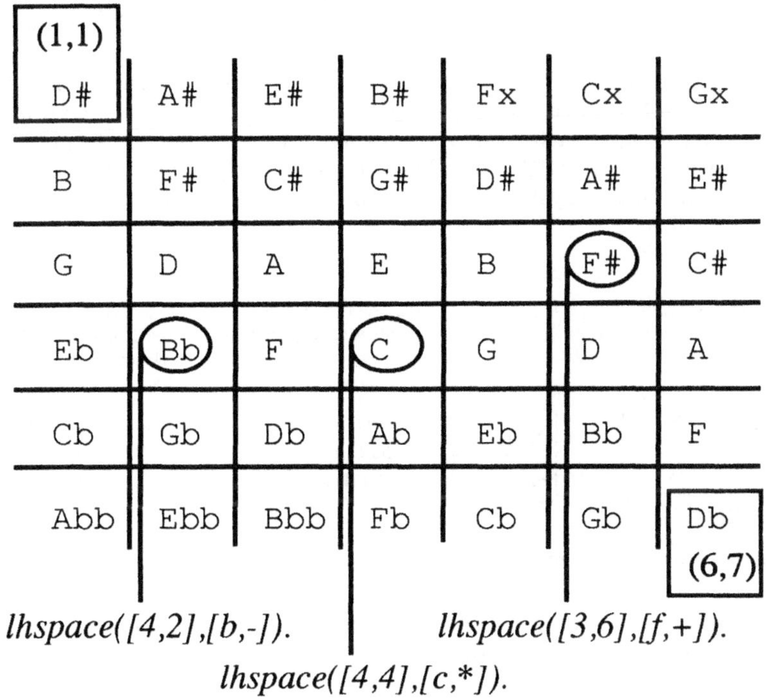

Figure 3: Example LHSpace definitions in relation to the original map.

Manipulations of LHSpace are conducted with reference to coordinate manipulation definitions. These definitions, referred to in MONK as concept recipes, each represent a distinct musical concept. To illustrate the use of these coordinate manipulations, the relatively simple example of the major triad will be taken. The major triad in the Longuet-Higgins map takes a quite distinct 'L' shape. The root is found at corner of the 'L'. The third and fifth are above and to the right of the root respectively. As has been previously stated, this shape/concept is consistent throughout the map. If the major triad whose root is F♯ is desired, the concept of the 'L' can be used, using the following instructions.

[1]Position [1,1] is the top left of the grid. The coordinate references take the form [row,column].

- Find the chord root. Its map coordinate will be [row,col].
- The chord's third will be found at coordinate [row-1,col].
- The chord's fifth will be found at coordinate [row,col+1].

F♯ can be found at [2,2]; therefore the third can be found at [1,2] and the fifth at [2,3]. The hidden constraint in this instruction set is the need to find the root in the map so that the rest of the notes can be retrieved. This constraint can be represented simply as [col $<$ 7] and [row $>$ 1]. The process of converting Longuet-Higgins map concepts to LHSpace manipulation definitions can be seen in Figure 4.

The combination of the symbolic model of the Longuet-Higgins map (LH-Space) and the LHSpace concept recipes allow for a succinct but comprehensive and expandable approach to music knowledge representation. Implicit musical knowledge is held in LHSpace. The LHSpace recipes provide a general and flexible manipulation system, forming the interface between LHSpace and the MONK systems.

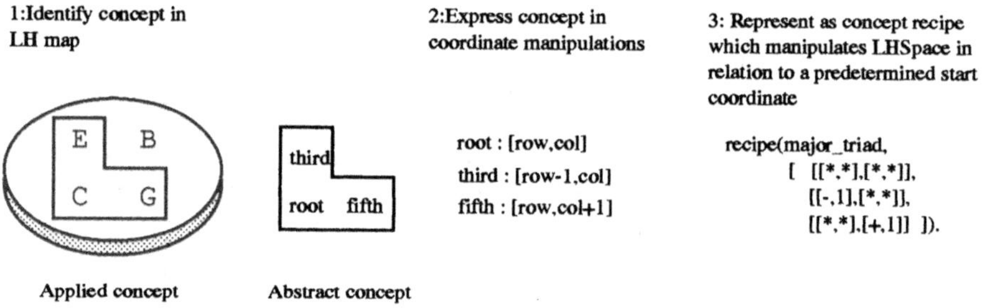

Figure 4: The conversion of concepts in the Longuet-Higgins map to LHSpace coordinate manipulation definitions.

4 Melody Representation

The MONK systems use a symbolic version of Conventional Music Notation (CMN) to represent the input melody. This system, the Melodic Data Structure (MDS), is able to represent almost any single line melody written in CMN. This was seen to be advantageous for several reasons.

- Musicians use CMN as a standard method of communication.
- Students and many practitioners of harmony use CMN to express their solutions.
- CMN is capable of representing music from various genres and styles.

- Harmonisation is commonly treated as a paper and pencil exercise. The faults of CMN as a performance specification language are not relevant to this application.
- A future development for a graphical CMN interface would be helped enormously as MDS could be used without redevelopment or conversion.

As CMN can represent music from many different styles and cultures it was seen as the most open and the most general of current music representation systems. The MDS satisfies the design constraint of expandability, as it can be expanded to deal with more complex material as the need arises. No rewrite of the melody representation project standard would be needed if the systems were expanded to deal with more complex material, for instance.

The basis of the MDS design is the view that a melody can be seen as a series of events, namely notes and rests. Much of the extra markings, for example, slurs, ties and bars can be viewed as extra events that affect the basic notes and rests. The definition of the note and rest events are based on noting their onset in relation to the rest of the events in the melody and their duration in relation to the initial or current time signature. The notation of the peripheral markings depend on their function. A bar of material, for example needs only to be defined when it begins in MDS. Its end is marked by the beginning of the next bar. The only end of bar marking in MDS is the double bar line. With more subtle markings such as the slur and tie, there needs to be a begin/end pair of statements defining which inclusive events are to be slurred or tied. The basic concepts are best described by a comparative example, representing the same musical information in CMN and MDS. Figure 5[2] compares the representation of a simple bar of material.

CMN Version :

MDS Version :

(1) keysig([c,*],major).
(2) timesig([2,4]).
(3) event([bb,1,_,1,_]).
(4) event([n,1,[c,*],4,[2,1]]).

Figure 5: Note representation in CMN and MDS.

Each statement of the MDS description in Figure 5 is fully explained below :

(1) `keysig([c,*],major).`

This statement defines the key signature of the piece. The element [c,*] defines the tonal centre of the key, in this case C natural. The second element, 'major', denotes the scale type, in this case the major scale.

(2) `timesig([2,4]).`

[2]The numbers (1) through (4) in the MDS description are included for legibility only. They are not part of MDS.

This statement defines the time signature of the subsequent material. This statement is a simple translation of the numerical representation of the time signature in CMN.

(3) `event([bb,1,_,1,_]).`

This event refers to the beginning of the bar, in this case bar 1. The first field denotes the activity type; 'bb' refers to the bar begin activity. The second field is the event number, in this case '1', denoting the beginning of bar one is the first event of the melody. The fourth field, also filled with '1' is a reference to the bar number. This event structure defines the first bar as beginning at event number one.

(4) `event([n,1,[c,*],4,[2,1]]).`

This melody event is a note event; the first field of the event list is 'n'. The second field is the event number, which is '1'. Notice that both the start of the bar and the first note happen at the same time, as in the CMN representation. The third and fourth fields define what note is being described. The third field, [c,*], describes the note in abstract, in this case C natural. The fourth field defines exactly which note is to be sounded; the '4' indicates the note is the octave above middle C. The fifth field describes the duration of the note in relation to the time signature. The two numbers can be thought of as a fraction, so [2,1] converts to 2/1. As the key signature is noted in crotchets, the note duration is two crotchets (a minim).

In the above example, a minim C was represented using a single note description. It is interesting to contrast this case with others where the same aural effect can be gained from writing two or more tied notes for an equivalent duration. These equivalent sounds look different in CMN and therefore are represented differently in MDS. In the case of two tied crotchets, each crotchet would be defined as well as the tie. This contrasting example can be seen in Figure 6.

CMN Version :

MDS Version :

```
keysig([c,*],major).
timesig([2,4]).
event([bb,1,_,1,_]).
event([tb,1,_,_,_]).
event([n,1,[c,*],4,[1,1]]).
event([n,2,[c,*],4,[1,1]]).
event([te,2,_,_,_]).
```

Figure 6: Notes and ties in CMN and MDS.

In this example the key and time signatures are defined as in Figure 5. Instead of a minim definition there are now two crotchet definitions as note events one and two (note events are the events which begin *event([n,...*). The tie is defined as an event pair. The events have the following format:

```
event([tb,m,\_,\_,\_]).
event([te,n,\_,\_,\_]).
```

where *tb* is tie begin and *m* is the first tied note event number, and *te* is tie end and *n* is the last tied note event number.

MDS has proved flexible enough to be able to represent more complex melodies. Several jazz compositions have been implemented in MDS (Thelonius Monk's 'Gallop's Gallop' is one), as well as classical melodies. These representations and a comprehensive description of MDS can be found in [Coates ?].

5 The Melody Analysis Tool (MAT)

The melody provides not just the raw notes which are harmonised, but other surface information which is used by human practitioners to guide the task not only at a note level but also at a higher conceptual level.

A surface feature such as the melody contour can shape the contours of other voices in traditional four part harmony exercises, if the rules of voice leading are to be observed. Unusual accidentals could signify the modulation of the melody. The form of the piece is important if recurring themes are to be treated in a similar way harmonically. If the melody was written to the plan AABA, there would only have to be a harmonisation of the A and B themes, with suitable adjustments for the cadential links between themes, and the coda. It was observed during the interviews with the practitioners that they examined the melody before starting and re-examined at regular intervals during the harmonisation task.

To model this top level plan building activity, the Melody Analysis Tool was designed. This tool examines the melody before the harmonisation process begins to build a high level picture of the melody, describing such recognisable features as form, possible modulations and melody contour. The Strategy module then can operate in a more intelligent manner. It has not only a conception of the notes at the low, note processing level but also a higher level conceptual model giving the Strategy module different views of the same material.

The current implementation can handle modulating material and can deduce melodic contour for voice leading. The form finding aspect is currently in a rather elementary stage of development. A full description of the MAT can be found in [Coates ?].

6 Other Knowledge Representation in the MONK systems

Harmonisation is a creative task which has had built up around it a formidable corpus of rules, constraints and heuristics. This section outlines how a few of the more common tasks, rules and constraints in harmonisation have been represented in MONK. Using Artificial Intelligence in this domain gives the developer access to a tried and tested range of tools and techniques which allows the codification, or approximate codification of parts of the formal harmonisation corpus. It should be noted here that strict adherence to rules is not a method for producing excellent solutions to harmonisation problems; rather it allows the production of solutions which avoid the obvious pitfalls of the task and make for a reasonable harmonisation.

The most important task modules currently developed concern the controlling of the harmonisation process. The modules are referred to as the strategy modules and they occupy the Strategy Layer of the outline MONK design, discussed in the section 'Design of MONK'. The strategy modules currently implemented are concerned with two different methods of harmonisation.

- The first is a model of the Thomas approach, used in Vivace and documented in Thomas [Thomas 85]. Harmonisations are built by harmonising phrase by phrase. A phrase is split into three, namely the first note, the phrase body and the cadence notes. The first note and the cadence are fitted with appropriate material. The phrase body is harmonised from the cadence to the first note.

- The second strategy is similar, harmonising phrase by phrase and splitting the phrase into three, but harmonising the phrase body forwards from the first note to the cadence point.

The selection of chords is an ideal problem to represent using constraints The constraint of the note or notes to be harmonised reduces the search space enormously. Avoiding an adjacent chord repetition may exclude another chord. In MONK, a codification of the root chord preferred progression table found in Piston [Piston 89, p. 23] is used to weight the remaining chords, according to their suitability. The most suitable chord is chosen, although it should not violate the consecutives rule, discussed below.

The only current hard coded rule in MONK concerns the occurrence of consecutive fifths and octaves. The previous note harmonised and the current note with a proposed chord are considered. The check performed, with reference to the LHSpace model, returns true for a violation and false for no violation. At the Strategy Level, the rule is enforced as part of the strategy module. This is one of the rare examples where the Sub-Strategy layer is bypassed. It was implemented this way to keep all decision making exclusively in the Strategy Layer.

There is a comprehensive overview of knowledge represented in MONK and the techniques used to represent that knowledge in [Coates ?].

7 Educational Issues

Whilst the MONK project did not directly address topics in education, there are several issues which have educational implications. Holland [Holland 89] states:

> "the first requirement for an Intelligent Tutoring system is that it has to have some ability to perform, or at least to discuss articulately, the task in hand."

MONK can perform the task. Because the system has been implemented in such a modular way, the scope for extending and even changing its functionality is wide. Thus, it is not impossible to see the use of some MONK code in an ITS or other educational software. Although the previously discussed Protocol Analysis was conducted as an informal fact-finding exercise, it did unearth the various skills and knowledge present in all harmonisation systems. What is interesting is the way these agents interact. The linear flow of information between Vivace's modules was not mirrored in the subject's attempts at the task[3]. It should be stressed here that the subjects were not experts, and a wider group of subjects with a wider range of ability may have resulted in a different set of findings. The MONK design reflects the emphasis on the architecture, particularly extendibility, which is a feature of the human model rather than the emphasis on the quality of the output, which was the motivation behind the traditional systems. Wenger [Wenger 87] states:

> "for the design of useful instructional systems, the shift to building explicit computational models of domain and pedagogical expertise introduces a cognitive orientation that broadens the scope of the enterprise."

As has been described earlier, the MONK systems are a conscious attempt to model the ways in which human practitioners (practitioners can be experts, capable performers of the task and learners) tackle the task. Although Thomas does model her own thought processes in Vivace, it is likely there is more than one way to perform a creative task, even one so constrained as harmonisation. It seems more reasonable to be able to model multiple approaches to the same task, as is possible within the MONK architecture.

A plausible application of a MONK harmonisation system in education is to use it as a 'machine expert' which could be consulted by an Intelligent Tutoring System. Figure 7 depicts a possible design, whereby the MONK system would be manipulated by the ITS at various layers to provide different levels of detailed domain knowledge. Interaction between the tutor and the student would be in both natural language and CMN. The student would be able to hear as well as write the material. Tutorial material could be generated by MONK during the student session, using the melodies under examination. Various solutions to a single problem could be generated to show the concepts in action.

Figure 8 contains an illustration of a a dialogue between a student and a tutoring system built around MONK. In the dialogue, MONK is being used by the tutoring system to spot the change of key in a melody. The melody starts in C major but modulates in the phrase discussed in the dialogue. The student is envisaged to be capable of basic, non-modulating harmonisations and just beginning to study modulatory material.

---

[3]It should be noted that a MONK system could be built to mirror the Vivace architecture; each linear module would conforms to the four layer MONK design.

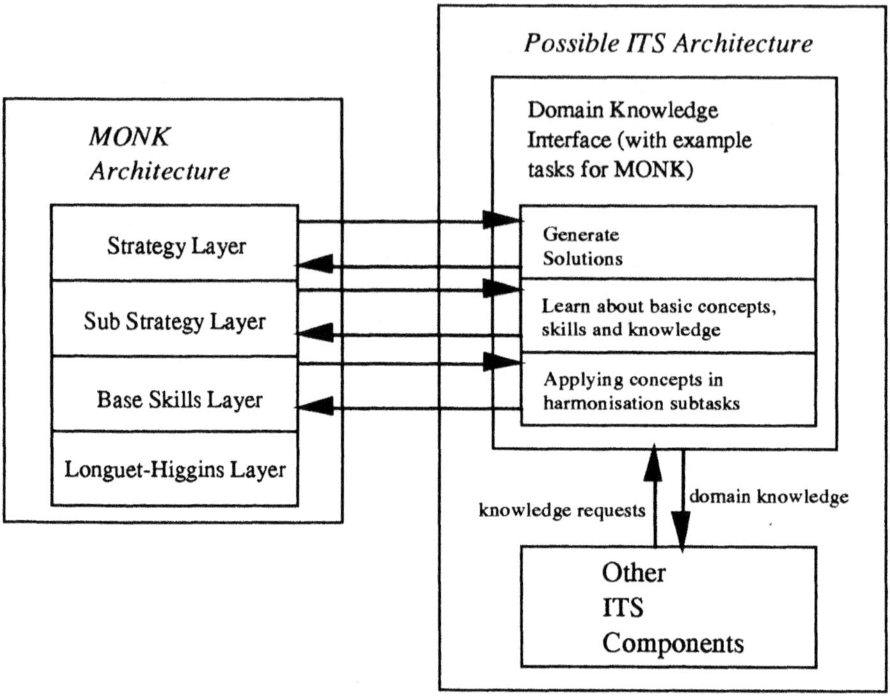

Figure 7: MONK as part of an Intelligent Tutoring System for harmony.

8 Further Work

The future of the MONK project lays in extending the current functionality within the existing design framework. The implementation of new harmonisation activities is one of the major tasks. This would entail the development of new Strategy modules to perform new tasks, such as three and four part harmonisations (the reader will recall that the system currently performs 'bassline and chords' harmonisations). The Melody Analysis Tool (MAT) needs to be further developed to allow more subtle melodic information to be understood and so produce more convincing harmonisations. The chord vocabulary needs to be expanded to allow MONK systems to produce texturally richer solutions. These issues have, in the main, been dealt with at the Design phase of the project, and thus need only to be implemented. The interviewing of a larger number of harmony practitioners would be beneficial. It would allow a different perspective to be taken on the problem. The small number of interviews carried out at the Design stage of the project proved to be a very useful part of the project as a whole. The integration of one or several MONK systems into a larger ITS structure is an interesting and challenging longer term development. It is felt that this would prove the versatility of the design and the modularity of the systems built to that design.

TUTOR : What can you tell me about this phrase of the melody?

(student is shown this phrase)

STUDENT : There are accidentals in the phrase.

TUTOR : Does that lead you to any conclusions?

STUDENT : Play the phrase.

(the phrase is played)

STUDENT : I think the material may modulate.

TUTOR : How can that modulation be made harmonically? What device could be used?

The tutor would then lead the student to the concept of the pivot chord. In conjunction with the LHSpace model and the Melody Analysis Tool the material would be examined.

TUTOR : What keys might the material be moving to?

STUDENT : D major or D minor.

The tutor uses the routines in the Melody Analysis Tool to find out which keys the material is really moving to. LHSpace is manipulated to find the Closely Related Keys and the list is constrained by the phrase. For instance if the Closely Related Keys for C major are generated, and the material contains an F#, F major and D minor could be discounted.

TUTOR : Why did you suggest D minor?

The tutor is now trying to determine why the student suggested D minor as MONK has thought it less likely than D major. The evidence of the F# will be used by the tutor to justify the more plausible interpretation of D major.

Figure 8: An example tutorial dialogue between a student and possible tutoring system built around MONK

9 Conclusions

The MONK systems use a combination of techniques to model a non-trivial task. The use of the LHSpace and the manipulation definitions has proved to be a succinct and thorough method of representing musical knowledge. The Melodic Data Structure (MDS) is capable of representing CMN material, capturing not only notes and rests, but other information used by the practitioner such as bar lines, ties and slurs. The process of harmonisation has been modelled in relation to the human processes found by observing and questioning real practitioners. The final MONK modules allow for the construction of explicitly modular harmonisation systems.

10 Acknowledgements

The author would like to thank Matt Smith and Simon Holland for help with the paper, the Department of Computing Science at the University of Aberdeen for the extended use of computing facilities, the Department of Computing, Faculty of Mathematics and Computing at the Open University for computing facilities and the comments and suggestions of the anonymous reviewers. This work was undertaken with the funding of a SERC studentship.

References

[Coates ?] D. Coates. Description of the monk harmonisation systems. Technical report, Aberdeen University, ?.

[Ebcioglu 86] K. Ebcioglu. *An Expert System for Harmonization of Chorales in the Style of J.S. Bach.* Unpublished PhD thesis, State University of New York at Buffalo, 1986.

[Holland 89] S. Holland. *Artificial Intelligence, Education and Music.* Unpublished PhD thesis, published internally as OU IET CITE Report No. 88, July 1989, 1989.

[Longuet-Higgins 62a] H.C. Longuet-Higgins. Letter to a musical friend. *Music Review*, pages 244–48, 1962.

[Longuet-Higgins 62b] H.C. Longuet-Higgins. Second letter to a musical friend. *Music Review*, pages 271–80, 1962.

[Piston 89] W. Piston. *Harmony (4th impression).* Gollancz Ltd, London, 1989.

[Sirkin 87] D.W. Sirkin. Choralearn : A system that learns from examples to write simplified figured bass harmonizations of chorales using the pls1 clusterer. Unpublished M.Sc. thesis, University of Illinois at Urbana-Champaign, 1987.

[Sloboda 85] J. Sloboda. *The Musical Mind : The Cognitive Psychology of Music.* Clarendon Press, Oxford, 1985.

[Steedman 72] M. Steedman. *The Formal Description of Musical Perception.* Unpublished PhD thesis, University of Edinburgh, 1972.

[Thomas 85] M.T. Thomas. Vivace : A rule based AI system for composition. In *Proceedings of the International Computer Music Conference*, 1985.

[Wenger 87] E. Wenger. *Artificial Intelligence and Tutoring Systems.* Morgan Kaufman, Los Altos, California, 1987.

Slappability: A New Metaphor for Human Computer Interaction

Daniel V. Oppenheim*
Computer Music Center
IBM T. J. Watson Research Center
P.O. Box 218, Yorktown Heights, NY 10598
Music@watson.ibm.com

Abstract

I present *Slappability*, a new metaphor for Human-Computer Interaction. I suggest that the common unidimensional approach taken by user-environments is undesirable, and that various views and techniques need to be unified, in order to yield more comprehensive and comprehensible software systems. The approach is demonstrated by reference to a system for manipulating music and sound on a computer.

1 Introduction

Under current computer technology, as applications evolve into more complex systems, they also become harder to use. Multiple views and representations, direct graphic manipulation, user-configured graphic interfaces, and extensibility via user programming are techniques widely recognised as improving the human computer interaction (HCI). However, there is no uniform methodology for using multiple views or, more important, for being able to use different underlying representations and move between them within a single application[Honing 92][1]. Moreover, user-environments often take a unidimensional approach that enables either direct-graphic-manipulation or user programming – the former is typically chosen for non-technical users and the latter for "computer experts".

The thesis put forward in this paper is that a blending and unification of the above techniques within a single user-environment is highly desirable. This should enable the design of more comprehensive and complex software systems that are yet more natural to use, quick to learn, easy to extend, and accessible to a more diverse community of users.

Slappability is an object-oriented mechanism that helps bring out many of these capabilities. I developed it at the Center for Computer Research in Music and Acoustics (CCRMA), Stanford University, between 1992 and 1993. This paper explains Slappability, provides specific examples from its implementation within the DMIX environment, and discusses its potential applicability to human computer interaction. The reader should bear in mind that the ideal

*This work was carried out at the Center For Computer Research in Music and Acoustics (CCRMA), Stanford University.

[1] For a general discussion of music representations see [Dannenberg 93] and [Wiggins *et al* 93].

place to implement Slappability would be within the framework of an operating system rather than within specific applications.

2 Motivation: Harnessing the Complexity

My recent work at CCRMA has focused on the design and implementation of software to support composing and performing music – namely, the DMIX environment [Oppenheim 93], written in ParcPlace Smalltalk-80. A major concern has been to support the user's creativity, or at least to minimise the system's interference with his/her natural flow of ideas. As a result, DMIX has evolved into a large and complex environment. It includes many different components which are not grouped together in any other system: a programmable algorithmic input language (Quill [Oppenheim 90]), MAX-like real-time interactive modules, high-level graphic and real-time editors, numerous high-level tools such as Modifiers, Extractors, and Enumerators, score tracking capabilities, and more. The rationale for this diversity in tools, and hence overall complexity, is that each such tool has a different appeal to different people and that its usefulness changes as musical conditions evolve. The overall goal is to enable composers to move easily between such diverse tools and representations, thus aiding them in expressing their creativity.

Unfortunately, the ever-evolving environment eventually became overwhelmingly complex. In an effort to make it more natural to use, yet without sacrificing functionality, system complexity, or extendibility, I finally came up with the idea of Slappability. Slappability has been fully incorporated into the DMIX environment. My evaluation of Slappability is based on my observations of composers using the system and on my experiences in teaching composition using the DMIX system at CCRMA, Laboratorio de Investgacin y Procuccin Musical (LIPM) in Argentina, Bar Ilan University in Israel, and the National Chaio Tung University in Taiwan. Users background was varied and included non-musicians and seasoned instrumental composers with little prior experience in computer music, as well as experienced computer musicians. The ease with which they performed complex tasks that otherwise require expert programming skills, and the short time in which novices could harness the system towards their creative goals, illustrates the merits of Slappability.

3 Slappability

In desktop environments with mice, *drag and drop* allows the user to select a source object by clicking. A target is selected by dragging the source and releasing the mouse button. This mechanism merely initiates a transfer of data between the source and target objects. Typically, the source pastes data into a global clipboard so that the target may retrieve it. This mechanism is a convenient shortcut that, in its very essence, is limited to simple operations involving data transfer, such as Copy and Paste.

Slappability takes this mechanism a crucial step further. Once the source and target have been selected, a direct communication between the two objects is initiated. The target object receives a single message with the source object as an argument:

```
target getSlappedWith:  source
```

It is now entirely up to the source and target objects to negotiate a response. Different objects respond in different ways and since the two objects themselves are now interacting directly, a world of endlessly rich possibilities becomes available. In DMIX, for example, Slapping text onto Graphics enables non-technical users to extend graphic manipulation in ways that would otherwise require skilled programming (see the example in section 5.2); carefully worked out compositions can be Slapped onto interactive MAX-like objects that allow the user to 'perform' them and add expressive nuances, and much more (extensive examples follow).

The method `getSlappedWith:` is implemented in Class Object, ensuring some default action that will always take place. Every subclass may override this method in order to implement more appropriate behaviours. There are several additional bells and whistles, such as using menus when several Slap-behaviours make sense, passing the screen points at which the user clicked as an argument, or using a double-dispatch message passing technique – but these additions do not change the basic concept.

Three basic responses might take place: the source or target objects might be modified, they could both participate in modifying a third object, or a new object might be created. There are often several plausible responses, in which case a pop-up menu would offer different alternatives.

Slappability seems to have a magical effect on users: they quickly take advantage of the system's complexity and frequently jump between different tools and representations, or find ways of transforming their musical materials into tools, and vice versa. In fact, it apparently takes users less time to become comfortable in using DMIX than is the case with other high-end environments that implement only a single facet (*i.e.*, either programming, or graphic editors, or real-time interaction, *etc.*).

4 Examples in DMIX

The first two examples will demonstrate the basic concepts of Slappability in some detail. The examples that follow illustrate less obvious possibilities.

4.1 Modifying music objects via Slappability

Figure 1 is a DMIX piano roll view of the Bach Prelude no. 1 in C major. Time is represented on the X axis and pitch on the Y axis. The length of a note is proportionate to the length of its rectangle.

Figure 2 is a standard DMIX sine Function. Note the default window settings of the Function (second line in the label above the view): the X axis is interpreted as time and is set from 0 to 1 second, the Y axis is set to accommodate MIDI values of 0 to 127.

The Slapping mechanism is initiated by keying COMMAND-S within the Function's view. In Figure 3 the Function is dragged and Slapped onto the Bach Prelude.

Unlike a drag and drop, a dialog now takes place between the Function and the music-object representing the Bach Prelude. The Function finds out

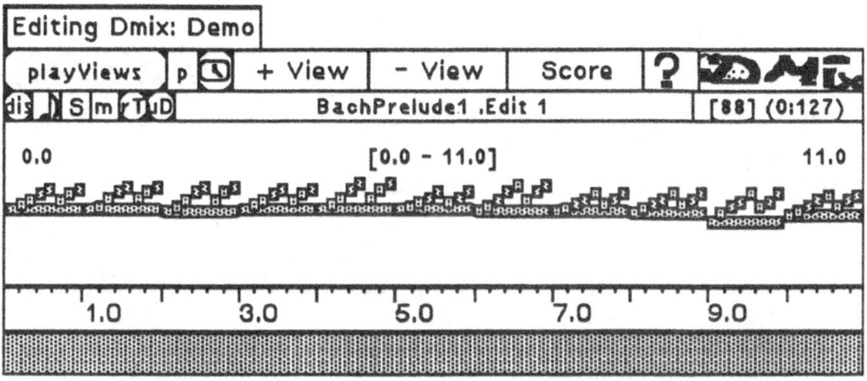

Figure 1: A graphic view of the Bach Prelude no. 1

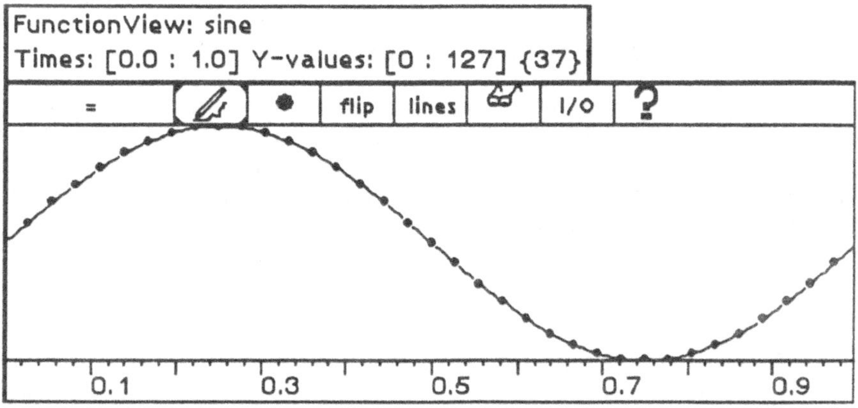

Figure 2: Standard DMIX sine function

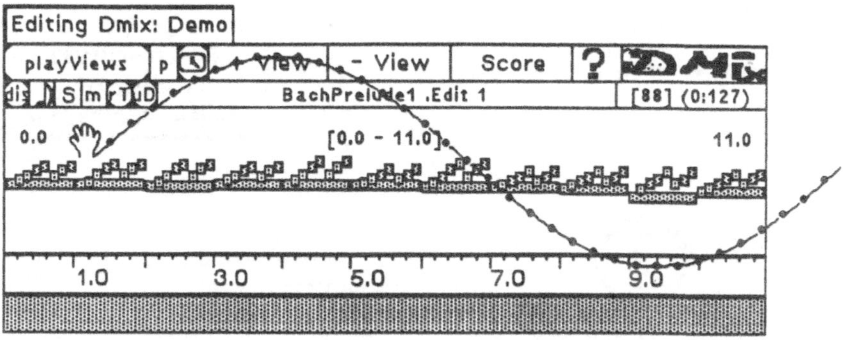

Figure 3: Slapping the sine Function onto the Bach Prelude

the duration of the Prelude and adjust its X axis accordingly (note the new window setting in Figure 6). Then, the music-object requests the Function to apply itself on its pitch-parameter (a default). Figure 4 shows the result.

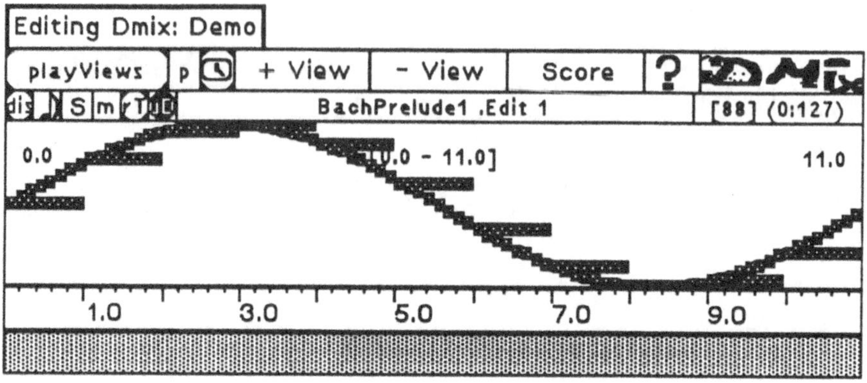

Figure 4: The result (by default, pitch is affected)

4.2 Additional Slap options: modifying tempo

Note that there are many different ways in which a function might affect the Prelude. For example, it might be used to set any other parameter, such as velocity, duration, or MIDI channel number. It might also be used to scale a parameter, to modify time, or to modify tempo. A completely different intent might be to first transform the function into a music object and then merge or insert it into the Prelude. In the current implementation, a SHIFT-Slap pops-up a hierarchical menu that offers the non default alternatives:

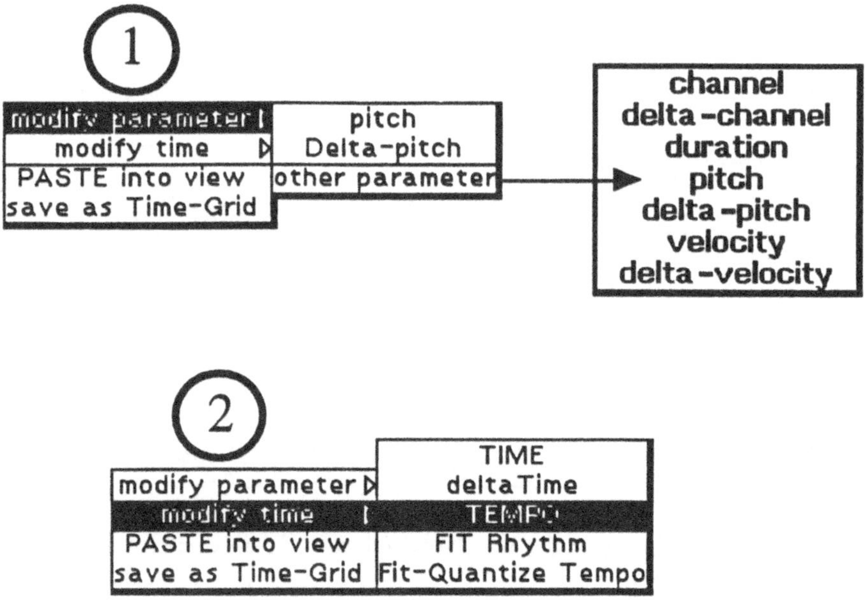

Figure 5: Other Slap options become available by SHIFT-Slapping

Figure 6 demonstrates how the same Function can now be used to further modify the tempo of the already modified Prelude. Modifying tempo requires a scaling of the delta-times between notes. To facilitate this, the Function's mode is set from '=' to '/' (division). The Function's Y axis is also changed and set to the range of 0.5 to 2 so changes in tempo are set between half and double that of the original. Note that the Function's X axis is already set between 0 and 11 seconds – this was changed by the music object during the dialog that took place in the previous Slap.

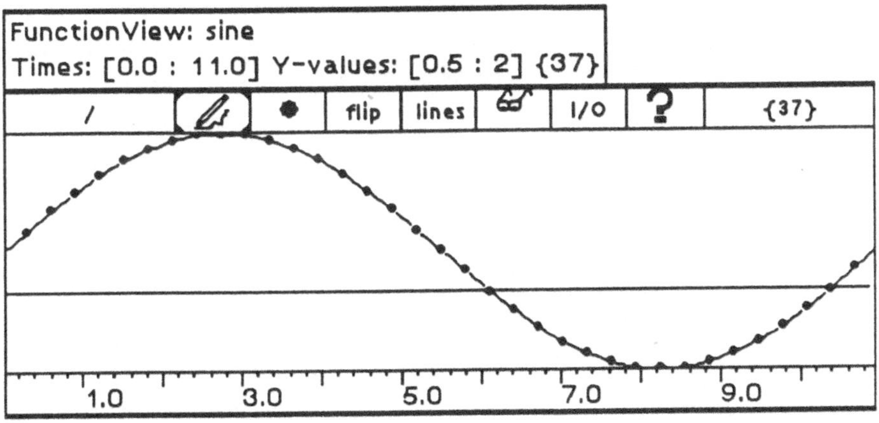

Figure 6: Setting the function to enable tempo modification

The Function is SHIFT-Slapped onto the graphic view, and the option: 'modify time: TEMPO' is selected from the hierarchical menu shown in Figure 5. The result is seen in Figure 7.

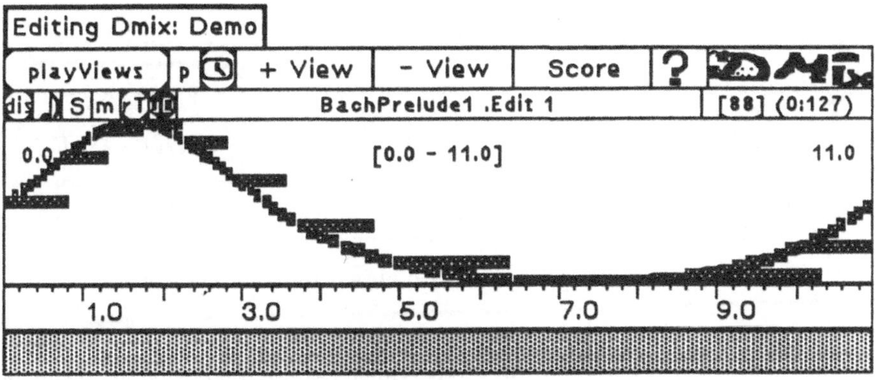

Figure 7: Result of modifying tempo

4.3 Transmogrification

In the previous examples a Function was Slapped onto the Bach Prelude and modified the music. Slapping a music object onto a Function has a completely different effect. Now, the music object is modifying the Function. The Function's data (collection of x-y points) are replaced with new points that are collected from the Slapping music object. In Figure 8, a 4.6 second phrase from of the Bach Prelude (a) is Slapped onto an arbitrary Function (b). As a result, each x-y point in the Function's data now corresponds to a begin-time and pitch of a note in the corresponding phrase (c). The pitches are represented in the Y axis, and the onset times, or rhythms, on the X axis:

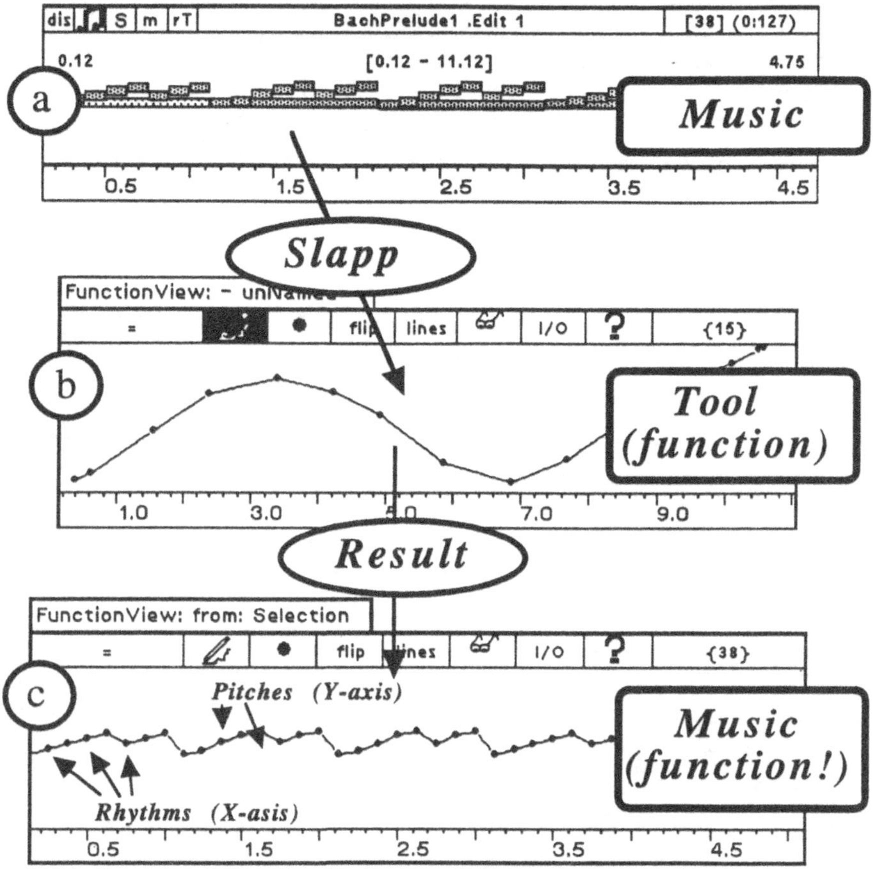

Figure 8: Slapping a music object onto a Function

Two subtle, yet extremely important, points should be noted. Firstly, the Function is now a representation of the music, though some information was lost (*i.e.*, velocity and MIDI channel). In fact, the technique demonstrated above could be used to represent the music as a collection of functions, one for each parameter (pitch, velocity, *etc.*). In other words, the user is thus able to actually modify the underlying music representation he/she is using. Secondly, whereas a user would naturally think of the piano roll notation as a representation of music, and of the Function as representing an abstract, high-level, mathematical tool, Slappability helps blur these conceptual differences. Now the user may think of the Function in musical terms, such as a phrase from the Prelude, or as a collection of the rhythms, or as gestural or dynamic information.

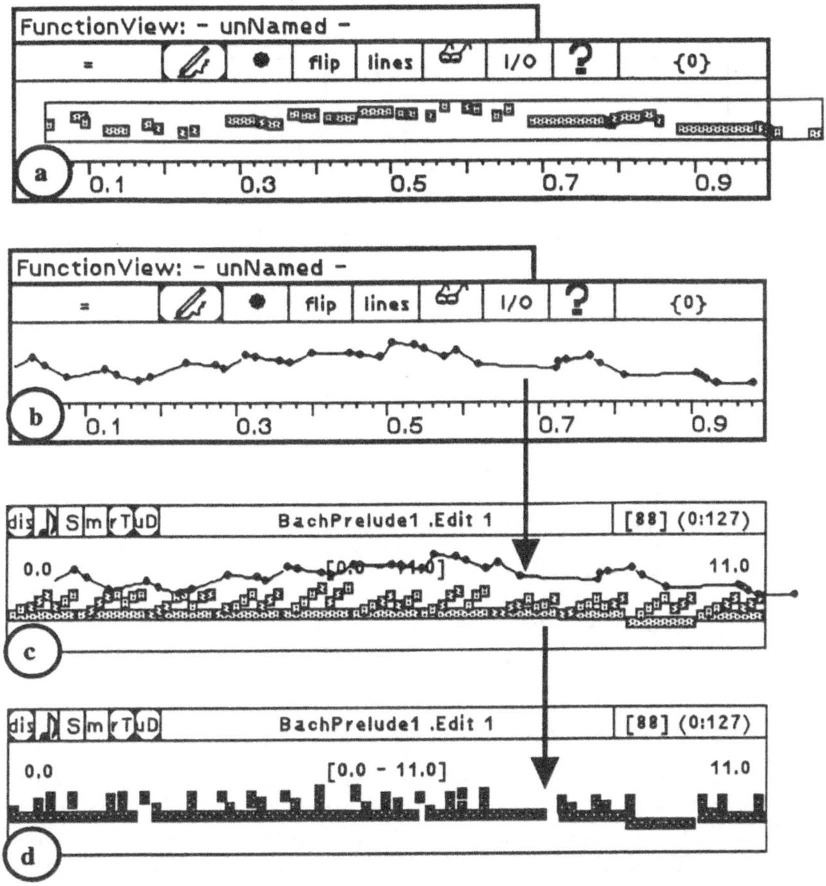

Figure 9: Transformations between music and tools

This property of Slappability that enables the transformation of one object, or representation, into another, seems particularly useful and I call it *Transmogrification.* In Figure 9, a Jazzy improvisation is Slapped onto a Function (a), the resulting rhythms are extracted and become the Function's data (b). The new Function, or rather the Jazzy rhythm, is then Slapped onto Bach's Prelude in C major (c) with the result being a rhythmically Jazzed-up Prelude (d). The onset time of each note in the Prelude is shifted to the closest onset time in the Jazzy improvisation, often forming interesting chords.

4.4 Creating new objects

Slapping can also produce new objects. Slapping one Function onto another can create a new Function that is the resultant of some mathematical operation between them. In Figure 10 a sine-wave Function is Slapped onto an up-ramp

Function (a). In (b) the Functions are multiplied by each other and in (c) they are added. Tools can thus easily be personalised either by transmogrifying some other object into a tool, or by creating new tools based on existing tools.

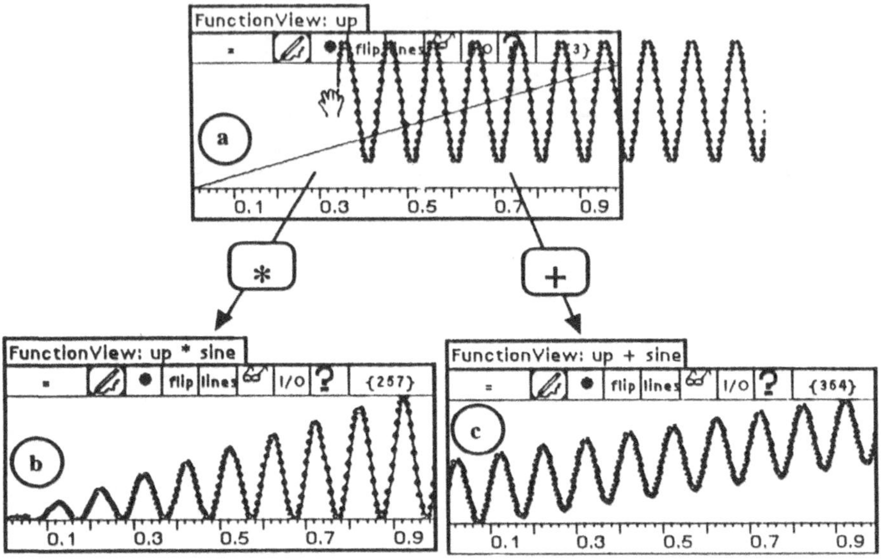

Figure 10: Slapping one Function onto another

4.5 Graphics and Algorithms

In the example of Figure 11, music was selected in a graphic view and then Slapped onto an empty edit window of a QUILL algorithmic music generator [Oppenheim 90]. The music-event, which is 13 notes long, is transformed into an ASCII algorithmic description using the QUILL syntax. Compiling this text will regenerate the same music. However, the algorithm can now be changed to produce a musical result that cannot be obtained via graphic manipulation.

The `voiceLoop` syntax in the figure is closely modeled after the VOICE construct in PLA [Schosttstaedt 83] and the PART construct in Common Music [Taube 91]. A loop creates a voice named `fromSelection`. The loop will iterate 13 times (`notes: 13`), once for each note in the original phrase. Two variables are declared: pitches and durations. In an initialise block (`init::`) each variable is assigned a Pattern – a list accessing object. The list provided to each Pattern is the collection of a parameter field from each of the 13 notes. The loop (`loop::`) simply assigns the next parameter in the list each time it iterates.

The `voiceLoop` syntax used above is almost pure Smalltalk, and a composer who is also an experienced Smalltalk programmer could add conditionals, use Functions to modify parameters, and many other objects made available by Smalltalk and DMIX. However, a novice user will need a considerable investment in time in order to acquire the programming skills needed to work on this level. In order to make Quill accessible to non programmers, a much simpler

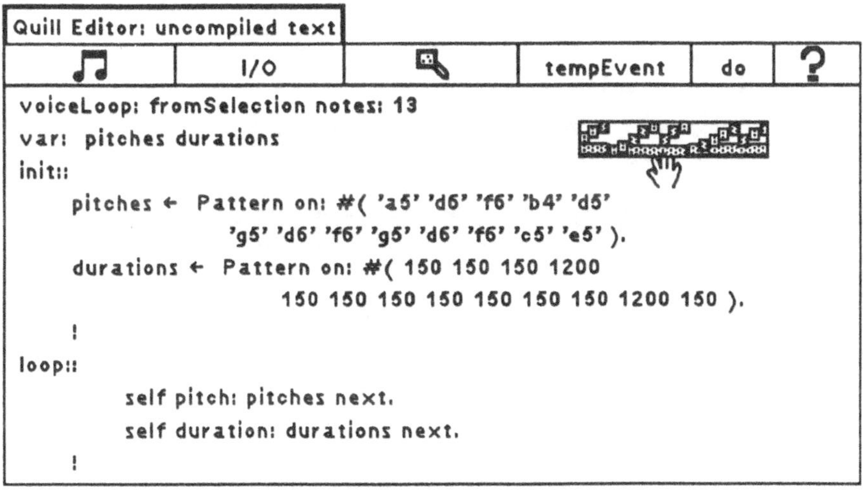

Figure 11: Converting music-events into algorithms

input format was implemented. The first five notes could be entered in this manner (comments are surround by double quotes):

```
p:  a5   d6   f6   b4    d5   ''list of pitches"
d:  150  150  150  1200  150  ''list of durations"
```

An interesting discovery I made was that Slappability enabled me to significantly extend the power and flexibility of this simple syntax. The key to this improvement was the ability to Slap any object into Quill, where it would become available to the user. For example, the Bach Prelude in Figure 9c could be Slapped into Quill as a motive. Similarly, the Function used to 'Jazz up' its rhythm in Figure 9b could be Slapped and saved in Quill. Assuming this has been done, the entire syntax needed to obtain the exact same result that was obtained graphically in Figure 9 would be the following:

```
t:  [beginFunction:  'Jazzy Rhythm']  "mark begin time (t:)"
insertMotive:  'Bach Prelude'
t:  [endFunction:  'Jazzy Rhythm']    "mark end time"
```

4.6 Composition and Performance

Figure 12 shows a graphical view of already composed music being Slapped onto an ECHO – a MAX-like real-time algorithmic music processor. The ECHO accepts the music as if it were being input by a performer in real-time. The composer can now interact with the music and add expressive nuances as it is being processed.

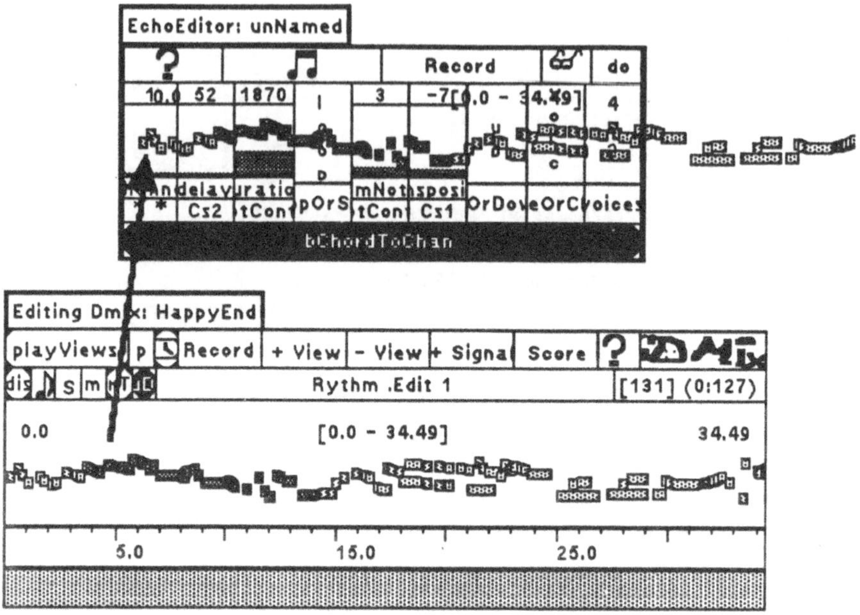

Figure 12: Performing Compositions

5 Complexity versus Usability

As programs become more complex, they also become harder to use. Examining this problem from several perspectives will demonstrate how Slappability should prove useful.

5.1 Menus, Buttons, and Libraries

In the evolution of commercial applications, it seems that as newer versions become more sophisticated they also become more complicated to use. For example, Microsoft Word used only about 20 menu-items in the 1984 release, but by 1992 there were over 50 [Microsoft 92]. Similarly, the first version of Aldus SuperPaint required about 350K of disk space. Two versions later it occupied about 3.2 Megabytes, and the number of menu-items and tools increased proportionally. Unfortunately, so did the difficulties in using it (based on my experiences and those of my colleagues). The direct relation between complexity and difficulty of use may be an inevitable result of what I term a Linear Design Paradigm. The issue of interface is taken quite literally: for each operation that the program can support there is one menu item (or button) for the user to click on. As applications get more sophisticated their user-interface invertibly becomes more cluttered and therefore harder to use.

My premise is that no matter how many menu-options are available, a creative user will always want to do something NEW for which there is no menu button. Simply increasing the number of menu-items in new releases to accommodate for users' "wish lists" is counterproductive since the added complexity in the user interface hampers the efficient use of the application.

With Slappability I have discovered two things. Firstly, for many operations menus can be bypassed altogether, making the system much more manageable and natural to use. Secondly, I discovered unexpectedly that users who were working via Slappability rather than menus started doing things that I, as a designer, never thought of and for which no menu-item was available. In other words, not only was the user's creativity less impaired by the system's design, but also the system's design was enhanced by the user's actions, and that is no small matter!

5.2 Graphic Manipulation vs. Programming

There seems to be a dichotomy between two fundamental approaches to user-interface design: namely direct-graphic-manipulation and programming. Compare Microsoft Word, which is menu driven and simple to use, with EMACS or TEX, which are more flexible due to their programmable interface but require a large investment in time to take full advantage of their flexibility. Similarly, compare commercial MIDI sequencers (with graphical interfaces) to high-end, programmable, ASCII-based environments such as Common Music [Taube 91]. Regrettably, the application designer must compromise and choose between one approach or the other.

Through Slappability, however, I found ways that avoid such a compromise and bridge between the two. By typing text (source code) into any text-window and Slapping it onto a graphic editor DMIX users can achieve results that otherwise require expert programming skills. Moreover, by a careful factoring of the design I eliminated the need to know about the underlying data-structures or implementation. Thus even novices can enjoy many of the benefits of programming while working with a familiar, and reassuring, graphical interface. For example, Slapping the following line of text onto a graphic view will cause the MIDI pitches (key numbers) to equal that of the same notes' velocity + a random value between 0 and 5:

```
event pitch :  event velocity + (random next * 5)
```

and the following text will access the currently selected notes in the graphic editor, extract their `#pitch` parameter, transform that into a Function , then open a graphic editor on that Function:

```
(activeSelection asEvent asFunction:  #pitch) edit
```

5.3 Formalism and the Creativity Flowchart

Software design has traditionally consisted of two stages. First the domain, and then the task (the way a user works), are formalised and modeled in software. The domain is modeled as a set of data structures and primitives. The task is modeled and implicitly formalised in the overall application design and user-interface. In many domains this works well – NASA can fly astronauts to the moon in auto-pilot mode. But in domains where the user's creativity plays a vital role, such as music composition, or graphic design and animation, pre-determining how a user must work can have a profoundly negative effect on the end result. Below is an example and discussion of this potential problem, but due to the limited scope of this paper it must be kept somewhat simple.

Let us go back in time and consider a computer system that might have aided Classical musicians to compose. The user might have gone through three stages:

stage 1.	define a key
stage 2.	write (an 8 bar) melody
stage 3.	harmonise

This is obviously oversimplified, but plausible: many Classical works could have been composed using such a system since most works of this period conform, more or less, to this sequence. But now comes an intriguing question: could Beethoven's Fifth Symphony have been conceived and/or implemented with such a system? I claim unequivocally that the answer is no: in the Symphony's first introductory measures the key is ambiguous, no melody is presented, and the motive is not harmonised – even though things become clear soon after. If Beethoven would have limited his creative thinking to the above three-stage process this profound creation would never have come to be. Whereas this hypothetical system would indeed support creativity, it would be restricted to a superficial level that shares a broad common denominator with many compositions. However, it is precisely the individuality of each composer, his or her unique way of thinking, of putting ideas together, personal techniques for working out materials, and so forth, that give birth to new creations (this is not to claim that every work of art must be innovative). I suspect that no system having a formalised preconception of how a human should use it will ever fully support creativity in the sense that it will encourage a "Beethoven" to create a unique work such as the Fifth Symphony or the late Quartets; rather, such a feat would probably be accomplished in spite of the system's limitations. Current formal approaches seem oriented less towards encouraging the discovery of the new and the unique, and more towards a rehashing of the mundane and mediocre. This problem stems from the implicit need to formalise the task, and I refer to to this problem as a creativity flowchart syndrome: computers are formal systems; but humans that use computers are not, and should not be expected to behave as such. Object-Oriented technology offers interesting alternatives.

5.4 Non-formal Alternatives

Object-oriented methodologies provide a powerful paradigm that might help avoid the rigidity implied by the creativity flowchart syndrome and better support the unexpected ways people might decide to use systems creatively. In such applications, objects seemingly 'float' in the system with no preconception of what other objects they will interact with or when. Thus, a careful design could leave all notions of 'where to begin' and 'what to do next' to the user's discretion (for a more detailed discussion see [Oppenheim 91]).

Regrettably, such a design still requires an equally flexible user-interface to take full advantage of its potential, and to enable unpredictable interaction with the system. Direct-graphic-manipulation using Slappability implements this interface in a unique and powerful way. It not only allows the user to jump quickly between presentations, but also extends the idea of multiple presentations by enabling one object-type to transform itself into another. For example, in DMIX music can be transformed into Functions (tools) as seen in Figure 9, but also into Quill algorithms (Figure 11), Filters, Patterns, and more. Slappability also offers a natural way to jump between different modes of creation: improvisation, programming and algorithms, scoring, and graphics, among others. Moreover, the user can continuously switch between a top-down, bottom-up, side-in, or side-out approach. In short, the system can provide an extremely rich, unconstrained compositional environment. The user is able to express himself or herself uniquely, and in ways that seem more natural. Moreover, by and large the structure of the underlying applications gets configured by the user as he or she works, rather than be determined by the programmer.

5.5 Tools, individuality and transmogrification

Tools used by composers tend to be highly personalised. Every artist uses different tools which play an important role in developing a unique style that expresses his or her individuality. Software tools enable users to perform high-level operations of a more general nature than those obtainable through buttons or menu-items. There is a trade-off between high-level ease of use, generality, and individuality. High-level tools are easy to use but perform a more generic action; low-level tools require configuration and hence can be made more personal, but are harder to use. Paradoxically, the tools intended to "free" one's creativity often end up limiting it via the narrowness of the channel of common choices. For example, if books were written by hand I expect we would find much more variety in layouts or ways of attracting attention to important points. High-level formatting tools tend to produce documents that appear similar to each other (this is not necessarily a drawback) but they also tend to discourage individual expression. Slappability enables the creation of tools from musical materials, or from combinations of other tools, and thus encourages the building of unique tools.

6 Conclusions

The strength of Slappability lies in the ways in which it allows users to control complex systems with ease. With the availability of Slappability, DMIX users now welcome the complexity of the system, whereas before they were often overwhelmed by it. The fact that non technical users can achieve results that otherwise require expert users suggests that it might be ideal in fields such as music education, where programs could be devised for children to use without sacrificing the more complex musical issues.

Like copy-and-paste or drag-and-drop, Slappability is a but a mechanism. It becomes especially useful as a metaphor for users if the underlying application is flexible, modular, extensible, and supports object-transformations. It should ideally be located in an operating system, where it could enable the sharing of applications in novel ways. For example, editing a sound file in a music program, defining a digital filter in an unrelated application such as Mathematica, and then Slapping the sound file onto Mathematica to have it processed (see Figure 13). I believe this would have a beneficial impact both in the way applications

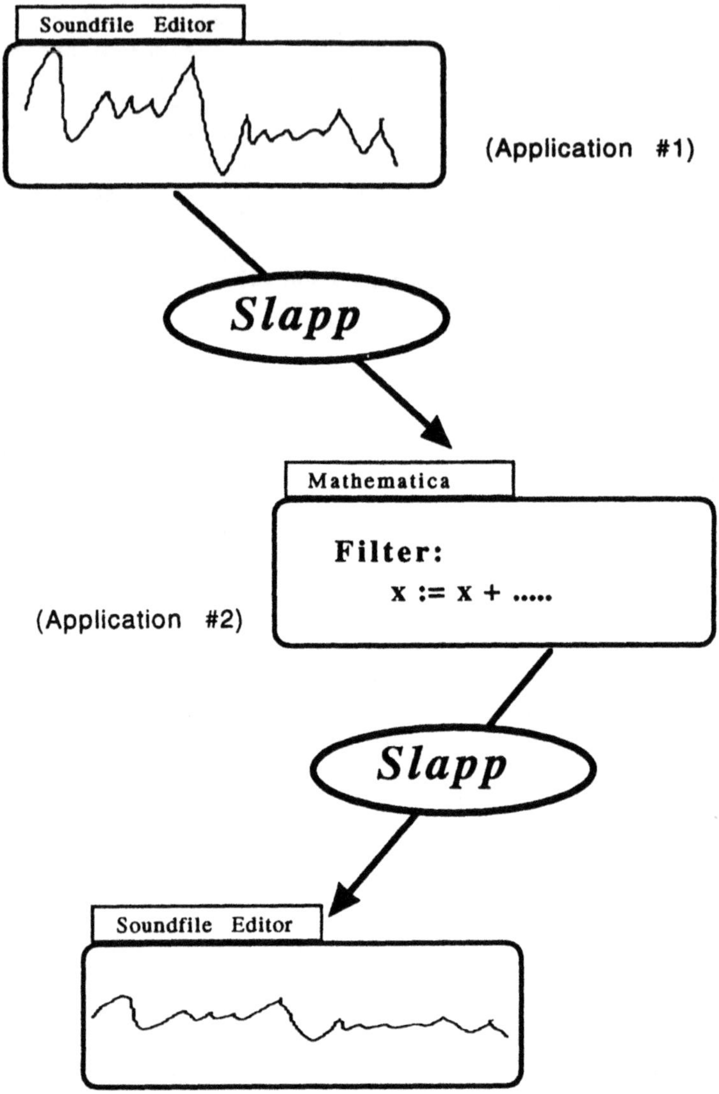

Figure 13: Using Slappability between applications

would be designed as well as on the overall user environment, user interface, and general human computer interaction.

Creativity is a fundamental component of human thinking and behaviour, and this is by no means limited in its domain to the arts. Hence the problem of supporting creativity is general and relevant to all domains of human computer interaction. Slappability is one way to improve the support of users in their creative work.

7 Acknowledgements

This work could not have been done without the continuous support and encouragement from everyone at CCRMA. It was Bill Schottstaedt that pointed out that an easy way to move between the numerous representations in DMIX would be useful – an innocent remark without which Slappability would not have come to be. I am especially grateful to the numerous composers and students who used DMIX and gave precious feedback and much encouragement, including Joanne Carey, Eitan Avitsur, Kui Dong, Jan Vandenheede, Celso Aguiar, Peter Bramble, and many many others.

References

[Dannenberg 93] R. Dannenberg. Music representation issues, techniques, and systems. *Computer Music Journal*, 17(3):20–30, 1993.

[Honing 92] H. Honing. Issues in the representation of time and structure in music. In *Music, Mind and Machine: Studies in Computer Music, Music Cognition and Artificial Intelligence.*, Amsterdam, The Netherlands, 1992. Thesis Publishers. Also in Proceedings of the ICMC 1990, Glasgow, England.

[Microsoft 92] *Microsoft Word manual*, 1992.

[Oppenheim 90] D. Oppenheim. Quill: An interpreter for creating music-objects within the dmix environment. In *Proceedings of the International Computer Music Conference*, Glasgow, Scotland, 1990.

[Oppenheim 91] D. Oppenheim. Towards a better software design for supporting creative musical activity (cma). In *Proceedings of the International Computer Music Conference*, Montreal, Canada, 1991.

[Oppenheim 93] D. Oppenheim. Dmix: A multi faceted environment for composing and performing computer music: its design, philosophy, and implementation. In *Proceedings of the SEAMUS Conference*, Austin, Texas, 1993. Also in proceedings of the Arts and Technology Symposium, Connecticut College, Connecticut.

[Schosttstaedt 83] W. Schosttstaedt. Pla: A composer's idea of a language. *Computer Music Journal*, 13(3):49–55, 1983.

[Taube 91] M. Taube. Common music: A music composition language in common lisp and clos. *Computer Music Journal*, 15(2):21–32, 1991.

[Wiggins *et al* 93] G. A. Wiggins, E. Miranda, A. Smaill, and M. Harris. A framework for the evaluation of music representation systems. *Computer Music Journal*, 17(3):31–42, 1993.

Music Representation – between the Musician and the Computer

Alan Smaill
Department of Artificial Intelligence
University of Edinburgh
80 South Bridge, Edinburgh EH1 1HN, Scotland
smaill@ai.ed.ac.uk

Geraint A. Wiggins & Eduardo Miranda
Departments of Artificial Intelligence* and Music†
*80 South Bridge, Edinburgh EH1 1HN, Scotland
†Alison House, 12 Nicholson Square, Edinburgh EH8 9DF, Scotland
geraint@ed.ac.uk; miranda@music.ed.ac.uk

Abstract

In any automated tool designed for use in a musical context, the choice of representation language is crucial. The *Charm* system, as presented in [Wiggins *et al* 93], was designed as a general purpose musical representation system. In this paper we consider how a system intended to foster the creative exploration of a musical soundworld could make use of such a representation. The ability to support multiple perspectives upon musical material is thought to be important, and we explain how this is supported. We also indicate how to incorporate automated support for the process of generalising from musical examples to a higher-level description.

1 Introduction

There is a growing interest in the use of Artificial Intelligence techniques in musical domains, from musical cognition to composition tools (see [Laske *et al* 92]). In constructing AI systems, the problem of designing a suitable representation is always important. In this paper we describe an approach to music representation that we believe is appropriate for a wide range of musical systems.

In previous papers [Wiggins *et al* 89, Harris *et al* 91, Smaill *et al* 90, Wiggins *et al* 93], we have attempted to build a framework for the representation of music that would be useful for a wide range of musical tasks, from composition to analysis. Our aim has been to provide a description of a system that the user can configure to the purpose at hand; user configurability is crucial given the disparate range of activities we want to support. The system should also support the automated manipulation of music objects and structures in a way that is intuitive to the musician. Finally, we aim to remain neutral between the description of musical phenomena as processes in the physical world, and music as perceived by the musician and listener.

should also support the automated manipulation of music objects and structures in a way that is intuitive to the musician. Finally, we aim to remain neutral between the description of musical phenomena as processes in the physical world, and music as perceived by the musician and listener.

In this paper, we first describe properties that we believe are needed in a system to allow non-expert users to explore the process of combining musical elements, going beyond simple juxtaposition. We then review our proposal for an *abstract musical representation*, and its configurability by an appropriate hierarchical organisation of the musical material. We indicate how these ideas can be used in constructing such exploratory musical systems. A partial implementation of the system exists, and could easily be linked up to a sound generation device, yielding a basic musical exploratorium. Systems such as Xenakis's graphical UPIC system (based on ideas in [Xenakis 92]) suggest that with appropriate technological support, musical creativity outwith conventional styles can be encouraged without needing a deep musical background. We believe that the capability to move between different underlying pitch and rhythmic perspectives would encourage such openness, and that the proposed representation provides the basis for such a system.

Such systems aim to allow the user to communicate with the system in terms as close to a natural musical vocabulary as possible – that is to say allowing the user to use something close to the vocabulary that she would use to communicate her musical ideas to fellow musicians.

To support this argument, we also indicate how Machine Learning techniques may be used to allow the system to infer abstract musical concepts from a set of examples.

2 A tool for musical invention

We now outline briefly what capabilities we believe should be present in a tool for musical exploration.

The user should be able to:

- enter simple musical objects (notes, motifs, ...),
- transform the objects, using some system-provided routines,
- group together objects by fiat,
- build new ways of grouping and characterising objects, and
- build new ways of transforming objects.

Of these, the last is probably the hardest to come to terms with, both for the user and for the provision of automated support. But we believe it is an important feature for a system aimed at encouraging exploration.

What sort of representation language is appropriate for such a tool?

3 Languages for music

A good knowledge representation language lets the user express knowledge of a given domain naturally and concisely, and supports an efficient reasoning regime to retrieve and manipulate the knowledge encoded. The expression should be *natural* in that the formalism used to express the knowledge should correspond closely to a description that the user might employ spontaneously in the course of communicating with others information about the domain.

Much work has gone into the development of such formalisms, which allow a declarative reading of the encoded knowledge [Brachman & Levesque 85, Brachman & Levesque 92].

General purpose Knowledge Representation systems can be used for musical applications: for example, KL-ONE [Brachman & Schmolze 85] has been used as the basis for the system described in [Camurri *et al* 92]. We have chosen to develop a representation system specifically for musical applications, where certain musical parameters receive special treatment.

It is notoriously hard to find a vocabulary to describe musical experience. Supposing we want to start by paying attention to some note-like events (rather than, say, looking primarily into the timbre of individual sounds). We propose to take such notes as the building blocks of our representation – yet we do not want to be committed to any particular organisation of pitches or rhythms. Our primary interest is in the music itself, either considered as a physical phenomenon, or as experienced by the listener; our interest is not (for example) the scores of the Western music tradition (which form one particular way of notating some aspects of a piece of music).

The *Charm* system (Common Hierarchical Abstract Representation for Music) is an attempt to free the representation of music from application- or domain-specific influence. The proposal (based on the notion of *abstract data types* from computer science) is that we need to know only some underlying properties of the pitch and time organisation for the representation to function. In different instances, we might work with a classical even-tempered semitone scale, or with a quarter-tone scale, or with some non-regular scale, or indeed with a notion of pitch where intermediate pitches are always available. Each one of these is a realisation of the *abstract* data type of pitch that we have adopted for the *Charm* system.

In *Charm*, what we require of the pitch organisation is

- a pitch value corresponding to each note, and
- a notion of *interval* between notes,

together with ideas of how these fit together. We suppose that temporal information is organised in a similar way, with points in time, and time intervals corresponding to pitches and pitch intervals respectively; there is provision too for description of timbre and dynamics.

A piece of music is then represented as a set of *events*, each of which is characterised according to pitch, time and timbre characteristics. Note that this is done without any commitment to some particular organisation of pitch (say), so that manipulation of pitches can be arranged as appropriate for the case in hand.

This provides us with a representation of the musical "surface", in the sense of Jackendoff ([Jackendoff 87]). Music as experienced and constructed involves of course a lot more than a set of isolated and independent events. The next representational problem is how to deal with the enormous range of ways of thinking about music that are possible, in such a way that the power of the computer can be harnessed to musical description and invention.

4 Hierarchical structures

So far, we have described music in terms of individual notes arranged in a space of pitch and time. The performer and listener have a richer idea of music than this, and we describe a very general mechanism for the grouping of musical events that can be used both for representing salient features in some given musical experience, and as the basis for the creation of new experiences. It is widely agreed that the use of hierarchical descriptions is especially important for music representation ([Balaban 92, Buxton & *et al* 78], so as to allow expression of local stylistic features as well as global structuring properties.

Organisation at this level is something that systems like the UPIC do not support well. Yet the organisation of music around notions of similarity and contrast is basic to musical understanding.

Charm events can be grouped by the construction of "constituents". These are arbitrary collections of "particles", that is of events (which do not have to be contiguous), or of other constituents. Each constituent has a unique name, and may be labelled with a set of first order logical formulae describing the properties of its particles or of the constituent as a whole.

The idea is that formal logic gives us a language to describe the particles of a constituent, and to state properties of the particles that justify grouping them together. For example, two groups of notes can be said to *overlap* if some notes from one group and some from the other sound at the same time; this relation can be captured by a logical formula, in terms of the abstract time representation.

It is also possible to label a constituent "definitionally" — to state that a particular collection of particles should be considered as a unit (*e.g.*, a piece or motif). Thus, properties without a basis in deductive logic can be represented by associating a label with a particular set of musical structures.

We thus have two ways of building up our higher-level descriptions, corresponding to the two ways in which sets of objects are commonly defined in mathematics. Suppose we have already some notes $n_1, n_2, \ldots$ and some constituents based on these notes $C_1, C_2, \ldots$ We could then form a new constituent based on logical properties of the n_i and C_i; for example:

$$D_1 = \{\ x : P(x)\ \},$$

where P is a logical formula, gives a constituent that picks out those n_i and C_i that make P true. We can also pick out some combination explicitly:

$$D_2 = \{\ n_1, n_5, C_2, C_3\ \}$$

Because of the use of logical formulae in the constituent specification, *Charm* allows the expression of complex relationships between different musical objects. It is also important that these relationships can not only be expressed, but that automated techniques are available to manipulate such representations, and to construct objects with the required properties. (This is, of course, the basis of Logic Programming (see [Kowalski 79]).)

To take a simple example, the following fragment of Webern can be analysed in several ways.

The figures 1 and 2, respectively, show a conventional score representation, and an instantiation of *Charm*'s basic event representation for the same frag-

Figure 1: Webern, Op 27, bars 1-4

ε(e00, ⟨f,♮, 4⟩, 1/4, 1/2, 10/1, ...)
ε(e01, ⟨e,♮, 5⟩, 1/4, 1/2, 10/1, ...)
ε(e02, ⟨b,♮, 3⟩, 1/2, 1/4, 10/1, ...)
ε(e03, ⟨f,♯,3⟩, 3/4, 1/4, 10/1, ...)
ε(e04, ⟨g,♮, 4⟩, 3/4, 1/4, 10/1, ...)
ε(e05, ⟨c,♯,5⟩, 1/1, 1/4, 10/1, ...)
ε(e06, ⟨a,♮, 2⟩, 3/2, 1/2, 10/1, ...)
ε(e07, ⟨b,♭, 3⟩, 3/2, 1/2, 10/1, ...)
ε(e08, ⟨e,♭, 4⟩, 7/4, 1/4, 10/1, ...)
ε(e09, ⟨c,♮, 4⟩, 4/2, 1/4, 10/1, ...)
ε(e10, ⟨d,♮, 5⟩, 4/2, 1/4, 10/1, ...)
ε(e11, ⟨g,♯,4⟩, 9/4, 1/4, 10/1, ...)

Figure 2: Webern, Op 27, bars 1-3

ment. This takes the form a set of note descriptions, where the arguments shown are successively identifier, pitch, start time, duration, and dynamic.

The passage can be thought of (and heard) in several ways – in terms of texture, or pitch symmetry, or temporal symmetry, or as a series. Our contention is that the ambiguity that allows this passage to be heard in many ways is central to this musical experience, and that our representation language should support such multiple viewpoints upon a single musical surface (to use the term of [Jackendoff 87]).

Many people have stressed the importance of multiple viewpoints in computational descriptions of music (for example, [Minsky 81, Lerdahl & Jackendoff 83, Ebcioglu 88, Holland & Elsom-Cook 90, Conklin & Witten 91]). We would like not just to be able to translate easily between different representations, but even more – to have a single representation in which the multiple viewpoints can be expressed and compared.

The constituent mechanism allows precisely this. For example, various constituents are shown in figure 3.

Constituent *c*00 is an enumerated constituent that we have chosen to call *subject*. Constituent *c*01 contains the same notes, but satisfies the logical specification of a *series*. *c*03-*c*06 satisfy the logical specification for *chord*, and so on.

κ(c00, _ , subject, { e00 e01 e02 e03 e04 e05 e06 e07 e08 e09 e10 e11 }, _)
κ(c01, ⟨series,{}⟩, _ , { e00 e01 e02 e03 e04 e05 e06 e07 e08 e09 e10 e11 }, _)
κ(c03, ⟨chord,{}⟩, _ , { e00, e01 } , _)
κ(c04, ⟨chord,{}⟩, _ , { e03, e04 } , _)
κ(c05, ⟨chord,{}⟩, _ , { e06, e07 } , _)
κ(c06, ⟨chord,{}⟩, _ , { e09, e11 } , _)
κ(c07, ⟨alternation,{}⟩, _ , { c03, e02, c04, e05, c05, e08, c06, e11 } , _)
κ(c08, ⟨triple,{}⟩, _ , { e00, e01, e02 } , _)
κ(c09, ⟨triple,{}⟩, _ , { e03, e04, e05 } , _)
κ(c10, ⟨triple,{}⟩, _ , { e06, e07, e08 } , _)
κ(c11, ⟨triple,{}⟩, _ , { e09, e10, e11 } , _)

Figure 3: Constituents for Webern Op 27

This brief description is intended to show that this approach allows the flexibility of multiple representations of the musical material. Such flexibility should subsequently allow high-level manipulation of the musical material in ways that make sense to the musician, who will have tailored the system to her way of thinking in the course of collecting together salient groupings, and indicating which logical descriptions are relevant.

5 Using the representation

We now show how the capabilities set out in section 2 can be built on top of this representation system.

- Simple musical objects can be built up from a repertoire of provided ingredients, preferably using a visual interface like the system UPIC, as developed by Xenakis. At this point, the higher level structuring properties are not in play, and UPIC has shown the effectiveness of this approach at this level.

- Simple transformations (repetition, augmentation, transposition, inversions, *etc.*) are easily written in terms of the underlying abstract representation and provided to the user.

- Collecting objects together is a matter of simply indicating which among the full set of objects under consideration are to be taken. Again, mouse clicking on a graphical representation is an obvious approach.

- Building descriptions of new groupings, and new ways of transforming objects, are two faces of the same problem in this approach. However, we do not necessarily expect the user to write logical specifications directly. A more intuitive approach would allow a mixture of two sorts of user input, as follows.

- On the one hand, the user can ask the system to generalise from a set of examples – "here are three motifs – give me a description of a class of motifs that they come from." This is a problem in Machine Learning, and there are several well-known techniques available. We discuss this further in section 6.
- On the other hand, the user should be able to require that parts of a full logical specification hold – for example, Boolean combinations of previously defined relations should be made available to the user.

These facilities together allow in principle the construction of musical objects with great flexibility, as is possible in systems that incorporate the computational power of a full programming language (*e.g.*, [Vercoe 91, Pope & *et al* 92]). We believe it could also provide a good intermediary between the manipulative power of the computer and the intuition of the musician.

6 Assistance in concept formation

6.1 Introduction

In this section we discuss a possible role for inductive machine learning in systems intended to aid musical invention. We will focus here on the modelling of a particular aspect of human cognition which is believed to play an important role in musical creativity: the generalisation of perceptual attributes. By this we mean the process by which the listener, when confronted with a series of sounds, instead of hearing each sound as unique, tries to find common features, perhaps of timbre, or pitch, or rhythm.

For the particular example we will describe, the object of attention is the *timbre* or tonal quality of particular sounds. This has not so far been integrated into the *Charm* representation. However, the example has been implemented in the context of a system we have built for musical exploration (of timbre), and the general approach applies equally to a system based on *Charm*.

We introduce below the fundamentals of inductive machine learning followed by the presentation of a example inductive learning engine.

6.2 Inductive learning fundamentals

Inductive learning is to do with making generalisations, or classificatory rules, out of a collection of examples given in a training set. In our case the training set is constituted of sounds described by means of their perceptual attributes.

Broadly speaking, the problem of learning concepts from examples can be formalised as follows: let U be the universal set of objects, – that is, all of the objects that the learner may encounter. There is in principle no limitation on the size of U. A concept C is formalised from a subset of objects in U. That is to say that the elements of a certain subset of objects in U share certain features (or properties) that can be formalised by a concept C. We say that the formalisation of a concept C defines a class C of objects in U. To learn a concept C means to learn to recognise objects in the class C. In other words, once C is learned, the system is able, for any object O in U, to recognise whether O belongs to class C or not.

Let U be the set of all sound events able to be produced by a certain digital instrument. Suppose C corresponds to a certain class of sounds in U. Once C is learned, the system can decide whether any sound event SE from U is in C.

The task of generalising a class C from a training set can now be stated as follows: given a training set S of examples, find a description F expressed in an appropriate language, such that for all objects X, if X is a positive example in training set S then X satisfies F, otherwise X does not satisfy F. As a result of learning, F is the "system's understanding" of the class C.

Inductive learning in our case is aimed at learning how to recognise novel sounds with respect to C – that is, sounds contained in U but not contained in the training set S. Consequently, the learned concept description F should be more general than the training elements themselves.

6.3 The example inductive machine learning engine

We have implemented a machine learning engine which uses two inductive learning algorithms: the ISCD (for Induction of the Shortest Concept Description) and the IDT (for Induction of Decision Trees). Detailed algorithm specifications are not within the scope of this paper, and can be found in [Bratko 90, Miranda 92]. In this paper, we describe how the first method functions.

We have implemented a timbre generation program which builds up sounds according to a user specification, which involves specifying values for attributes in a relatively high-level language, for example *vibrato, openness, attack, smoothness* ... (see [Miranda 92, Miranda *et al* 93, Miranda 94] for a discussion of the meaning of these attributes). Each of these is implemented in the lower-level terms of the sound synthesis algorithm. The user may, however, be interested in describing sounds with a different vocabulary. Having designed a number of sounds (by experimenting with the values of the attributes available), the user can then specify that some number of these sounds have the quality the user is looking for. For example, the user might be searching for a sound described as an "open vowel". The learning system will attempt to discover what combinations from the given attributes are important in differentiating between the sounds in this set that are and are not "open vowels" according to the user's classification.

The result of learning here is a set of rules which characterises the sounds of the training set that are positive examples of the concept in question. The main requirement of ISCD is that the rule set exactly matches the positive examples. Such a rule set is said to be complete and correct: complete because it includes all the positive examples and correct because it includes no negative examples.

Learning in ISCD is viewed as a search among possible rules with the objective of minimising the number of attributes in it. In other words it searches for the shortest concept description. Because of the high combinatorial complexity of this search, the ISCD resorts to a heuristic of scoring functions.

An example ISCD rule, when looking for a description for "open vowel" on the basis of some examples, is as follows (Recall that "normal vibrato" and "high openness" are terms from our given sound description language.):

A sound event is "open vowel" if
it has "normal vibrato",
and "high openness".

No matter how many attributes an "open vowel" has in the training set, according to the above ISCD rule the most relevant attributes for this sound class are "vibrato = normal" and "openness = high". "Most relevant" here means what is most important to distinguish an "open vowel" from other sound classes.

This algorithm has been used to construct a number of similar generalisations, as described in [Miranda 94]. Once the concept has been learned, the user may use the description directly in specifying new sounds, different from those that were originally picked out as typical of the new sound description.

6.4 Concluding remark

Our main reason for inducing rules about sounds is that the computer now can aid the user to explore among possible alternatives to accomplish a goal, namely in this case to design a certain sound. The user can ask the computer to "play something that sounds similar to a bell sound" or even "play a kind of dull sound", for example. In these cases the engine will find out rules for deducing which attributes are relevant for synthesising a bell-like sound or a sound with a dull colour attribute and which values they should take.

As for knowledge representation, we believe that supporting multiple perspectives upon learned musical material is important in the case of timbre, just as it is for the notions discussed earlier. This explains why we use more than one inductive learning algorithm in our machine learning engine.

The Machine Learning approach thus allows us to include logical descriptions of more abstract musical concepts, without requiring the user to formulate such descriptions explicitly, by generalising from examples.

7 Summary

We have indicated how a suitable representation language can play a central role in automated systems aimed at the encouragement of musical creativity and the exploration of the possibilities inherent in musical material, here considered at the level of notes and above. Similar considerations apply to organisation of timbre and "non-musical" sounds, though our underlying basic representation is not aimed at that sort of exploration. We have shown how the automated construction of musical descriptions from examples can be carried out.

At this stage, our conclusions can only be speculative. While we have implemented some of the representational background required, the worth of this approach can only be properly evaluated after a system along these lines has been built and used in a controlled way. We hope to be able to do just this in the future.

References

[Balaban 92] M. Balaban. Music structures: Interleaving the temporal and hierarchical aspects in music. In O. Laske, M. Balaban, and K. Ebcioglu, editors, *Understanding Music with AI – Perspectives on Music Cognition*, pages 110–39. MIT Press, Cambridge, MA, 1992.

[Brachman & Levesque 85] R.J. Brachman and H.J. Levesque, editors. *Readings in Knowledge Representation.* Morgan Kaufmann, California, 1985.

[Brachman & Levesque 92] R.J. Brachman and H. Levesque. *Knowledge Representation.* MIT Press, London, 1992.

[Brachman & Schmolze 85] R.J. Brachman and J.G. Schmolze. An overview of the KL-ONE knowledge representation system. *Cognitive Science*, 9:171–216, 1985.

[Bratko 90] I. Bratko. *Prolog Programming for Artificial Intelligence.* Addison Wesley, 1990.

[Buxton & *et al* 78] W. Buxton *et al.* The use of hierarchy and instance in a data structure for computer music. *Computer Music Journal*, 2:10–20, 1978.

[Camurri *et al* 92] A. Camurri, M. Frixione, C. Innocenti, and R. Zaccaria. A model of representation and communication of music and multimedia knowledge. In B. Neumann, editor, *Tenth European Conference on Artificial Intelligence*, pages 164–8, Vienna, 1992. John Wiley and Sons, Chichester, England.

[Conklin & Witten 91] D. Conklin and I. H. Witten. Prediction and entropy of music. Technical Report 91/457/41, Department of Computer Science, University of Calgary, Alberta, Canada, December 1991.

[Ebcioglu 88] K. Ebcioglu. An expert system for harmonizing four-part chorales. *Computer Music Journal*, 12, 1988.

[Harris *et al* 91] M. Harris, A. Smaill, and G. Wiggins. Representing music symbolically. In *IX Colloquio di Informatica Musicale*, Genoa, Italy, 1991.

[Holland & Elsom-Cook 90] S. Holland and M. Elsom-Cook. Architecture of a knowledge-based music tutor. In M. Elsom-Cook, editor, *Guided Discovery Tutoring*, London, 1990. Paul Chapman Publishing Ltd.

[Jackendoff 87] R. Jackendoff. *Consciousness and the computational mind.* MIT Press, Cambridge, MA., 1987.

[Kowalski 79] R. Kowalski. *Logic for Problem Solving.* Artificial Intelligence Series. North Holland, 1979.

[Laske *et al* 92] O. Laske, M. Balaban, and K. Ebcioglu. *Understanding Music with AI - Perspectives on Music Cognition.* MIT Press, Cambridge, MA., 1992.

[Lerdahl & Jackendoff 83] F. Lerdahl and R.S. Jackendoff. *A Generative Theory of Tonal Music.* The MIT Press, Cambridge, MA., 1983.

[Minsky 81] M. Minsky. Music, mind and meaning. *Computer Music Journal,* 5(3):28–44, 1981.

[Miranda 92] E.R. Miranda. From symbols to sound: Artificial intelligence investigation of sound synthesis. Research Paper 640, Dept. of Artificial Intelligence, Edinburgh, 1992.

[Miranda 94] E.R. Miranda. ARTIST - an AI-aided working environment for the design of intelligent sound synthesis device. *Languages of Design,* 1994. To appear.

[Miranda *et al* 93] E.R. Miranda, A. Smaill, and P. Nelson. A knowledge-based approach for the design of intelligent synthesisers. In *Proceedings of the X Reunion Nacional de Intelligencia Artificial,* Mexico City, 1993.

[Pope & *et al* 92] S. T. Pope *et al.* The Smallmusic Object Kernel: A music representation, description language, and interchange format. Anonymous ftp from ccrma-ftp.stanford.edu:/pub/st80, 1992. N.B. draft only.

[Smaill *et al* 90] A. Smaill, G. Wiggins, and M. Harris. Hierarchical music representation for analysis and composition. In *Proceedings of the Second International Conference on Music and Information Technology,* Marseilles, France, 1990. Also in *Computers and the Humanities,* vol. 27.

[Vercoe 91] B. Vercoe. *The Csound Reference Manual.* Addison-Wesley Publishing Company, Cambridge, MA, 1991.

[Wiggins *et al* 89] G. Wiggins, M. Harris, and A. Smaill. Representing music for analysis and composition. In M. Balaban, K. Ebcioglu, O. Laske, C. Lischka, and L. Sorisio, editors, *Proceedings of the 2nd IJCAI AI/Music Workshop,* pages 63–71, Detroit, Michigan, 1989.

[Wiggins *et al* 93] G. Wiggins, E. Miranda, A. Smaill, and M. Harris. A framework for the evaluation of music representation systems. *Computer Music Journal*, 17(3):31–42, 1993. Machine Tongues series, number XVII.

[Xenakis 92] I. Xenakis. *Formalized Music: Thought and Mathematics in Composition.* Pendragon Press, Stuyvesant, New York, 1992.

Section III: Music Theory and Computational Models

Pragmatics in Language and Music

Kenny R. Coventry & Tim Blackwell
Department of Psychology
University of Plymouth
Drake Circus, Plymouth PL4 8AA, England
p02218@uk.ac.plymouth.prime-a

Abstract

This paper argues for the importance of the application of pragmatics to music, and in particular to spontaneous composition. Indeed pragmatics, it is proposed, provides a more fruitful link between natural language and music than syntax or semantics. Furthermore, it is demonstrated that the semantic problems associated with music can be solved by viewing meaning as arriving through shared experience and cooperation. Specifically, Gricean pragmatics is applied, by way of example, to spontaneous composition. It is demonstrated that Gricean pragmatics can provide a framework to improve understanding of not only choice and analysis of musical ideas within each genre, but also of the emotional reactions of the listeners. Finally, the ramifications of these principles are outlined for direct application in educational settings, and issues of representation are considered.

1 Introduction

The aim of this paper is to examine how musicians communicate with each other from a psychological point of view as a precursor to the consideration of how to get a machine to interact musically with a human improviser. Much of the first half of the paper deals with these issues, and argues that one cannot address issues of representation without a careful consideration of the nature of the interactions between musicians. It is only when we know what the problems are that we can then go on to consider the nature of the representation of the problems. In order to do this, one can begin with an examination of communication in general, and specifically to the study of how communication takes place in the more familiar domain of natural language understanding.

There have been many attempts to forge a relationship between natural language and music (for a review see [Sloboda 85, ch. 2] and [Clarke 89]). To this aim, a tripartite theory of language understanding is assumed, with the separate study of syntax, semantics and pragmatics. Research into the relationship between natural language structure and musical structure has almost exclusively focused on the first two enterprises, namely using syntax from natural language to aid the analysis of musical structure (for example, [Lerdahl & Jackendoff 83], and trying to somehow work out semantic equivalents in music (for example, [Cooke 59]). The purpose of this paper is to explore the third enterprise, that of pragmatics, and its relation to musical structure. In particular, we examine what we call spontaneous composition (improvised music), and will demonstrate that Gricean maxims can be applied successfully to the description of different 'conversational' musical styles in the history of jazz. Finally, it is argued that pragmatic analysis offers a more realistic bond between musical structure and natural language structure from the point of view of structural analysis.

As [Clarke 89] has commented, there have been many attempts where

> "Music theorists and psychologists have used the abundant superficial resemblances between [music and language] as a pretext for a somewhat ill-considered extension of linguistic theory into the study of the structure, aesthetics, meaning, mental representation and affective content of music." [Clarke 89, p. 20]

It is therefore important to provide a clear foundation and justification for the analogy in order to demonstrate utility beyond the level of superficial resemblance. The rest of the introduction will deal with this issue.

Much of linguistic and psycholinguistic theory deals with written language as opposed to spoken language. Often there is the assumption that written and spoken language are one and the the same. Recently there has been much evidence to suggest differences between forms. For example, [Miller 85] points to differences in syntax between spoken and written language, and [Watt 93] provides evidence for differences in the processing of spoken and written language. The parallel we wish to explore is between that of spoken dialogue and improvised music, initially where musicians are improvising freely. The position adopted throughout this paper is that spoken language is the primary form of language, and that written language is a secondary form. Evidence for this comes from numerous sources. In many countries written and spoken languages are different. For example, an ability to speak Mandarin Chinese is separate from an ability to write Mandarin Chinese (they are in fact different languages). Across languages, some speech sounds map more closely onto written forms. An acceptable spoken sentence is not necessarily an acceptable written sentence. Developmentally spoken language is also primary in terms of stage of acquisition. The child develops an ability to communicate using the spoken word before the child acquires the ability to read and write. Children appear to have a natural ability to learn the rules of language through exposure to examples, and spontaneous speech is first apparent early on (between one to two years of age). It is only later that the child learns to read language. [Sloboda 85] discusses the close parallels between the acquisition of language and music, and argues that the pattern of development of the acquisition of language and music are very similar. Spontaneous singing occurs during the first and second years of life, and the natural medium for both language and music is auditory-vocal.

With music, a similar focus on written music is apparent. Most musicologists deal with composition to the neglect of improvised music. However, as [Bailey 92] has pointed out, improvised music is a key feature of music across all cultures, and historically has a strong tradition. Indeed, music at the end of the Renaissance period was affected by the advent of the printing press, which was to have a major influence in determining the destiny of Western music. The development of music from the Renaissance period can be characterised as movement away from the improvisatory elements apparent in early music, to an increasing emphasis on reading and writing music. Composers became more and more specific in the written instructions given to musicians. This lead to the need for musicians to spend more and more time acquiring reading skills, and therefore to the neglect of skills involving improvisation. The paradox is that, with language, we speak and communicate before we learn how to read and write, but in music, we learn to read and write without being able to improvise and interact musically in spontaneous ways. Of course, this becomes more ironic based on the knowledge that spontaneous singing, for instance, occurs before the ability to read and write music.

As an aside, it can be noted that the spoken language situation seems much more common than the analogous freely improvised musical situation. This is natural based on the move towards written forms in the history of Western music. Spoken language remains primary as it has a fundamental function not shared with music. Language is fundamental for communication/planning activities. Music is not.

There is therefore considerable justification with the starting point of spoken language and improvised music, and it is to the outline of these problems that we now turn.

2 Spoken and Musical Dialogue Situations

Before proceeding further, we can can outline two parallel situations one wishes to understand in the domains of music and language, and suggest that the mode of explanation required for a set of questions of interest in both situations is the same. The situations are depicted in figure 1 below. In the figure, a, b, c, and d represent four conversants; 1, 2, 3, and 4 represent four musicians[1]. No conversational or musical materials are prepared in advance. The situation on the left represents a spoken dialogue situation, and the situation on the right represents a musical dialogue situation. The questions we can ask are similar in each situation. For example, if person b speaks, how do people a, c and d understand what person b means, and therefore contribute to the conversation. How does person b know when to speak? Similarly, when person 2 plays a musical idea, how do people 1, 3 and 4 know how to respond and contribute to the situation? How does person 2 know when to play? How does the dialogue in each situation proceed? What do the observers, who are listening to the dialogue, musical or spoken, understand and make of it all? These, then, are the questions and issues the rest of the paper will address.

Now that it has been established that we are interested in dialogue situations, and particularly (as a starting point), the situations in figure 1, we can now introduce pragmatics.

3 Pragmatics in Natural Language: Co-operative Principles

Pragmatics is concerned with language use, and the background conditions and specific contextual conditions which enable understanding of an utterance to take place. Thus, with the focus on spoken language, pragmatics is of central importance. Here we wish to focus on one particular theory in pragmatics,

[1] The group size of four has been chosen because it is a common number for a group in improvised music. The figure is otherwise arbitrary.

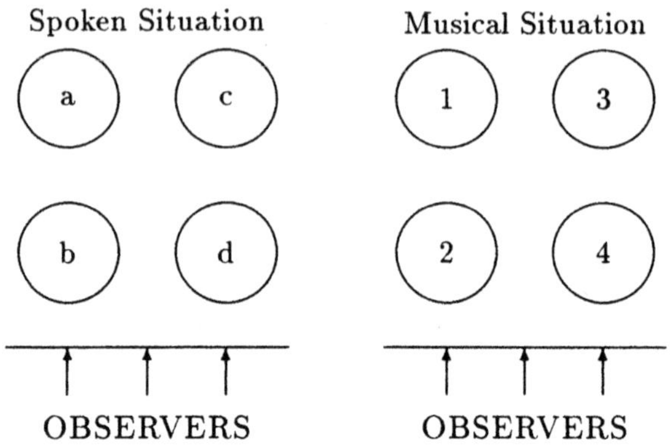

Figure 1: Two dialogue situations

that of H. Paul Grice, and specifically on the Gricean maxims outlined in [Grice 75]. Grice's theory is concerned with language use, and the assumptions that speakers make during the act of communication. For Grice, there is a set of over-arching assumptions speakers use which guide the conduct of conversation.

Grice introduces the notion of conversational implicature, which is one of the most important ideas in pragmatics. Implicature can be viewed as central for four main reasons. Firstly, and most importantly with respect to the analysis of music below, implicature is a type of pragmatic inference which lies outside the organisation of language, in some general principles for cooperative interaction. They may then be applied to other domains as they are not specific to language. Secondly, implicature provides an account of how it is possible to mean more than what is 'said'. Thus pragmatic inference can help resolve problems of specification in the semantics by enabling one to go beyond the semantics without explicit representation. This, it will be argued, allows us to bypass many of the problems associated with meaning in music. Related to this point, implicature allows a simplification of the semantics by limiting the problems of meaning that semantics has to deal with. Finally, the principles underlying the generation of implicature have a general explanatory power.

The set of assumptions guiding conversation involve the notion of cooperation, and are indeed realised as a cooperative principle which has four subprinciples or maxims. These principles can be expressed as follows:

The cooperative principle

Make your contribution such as is required, at the stage at which it occurs, by the accepted purpose or direction of the talk exchange in which you are engaged.

The maxim of Quality

Make your contribution one that is true, specifically;

1. Do not say what you believe to be false
2. Do not say that for which you lack adequate evidence

The maxim of Quantity

1. Make your contribution as informative as is required for the current purposes of the exchange
2. Do not make your contribution more informative than is required

The maxim of Relation

Make your contribution relevant

The maxim of Manner

Be perspicuous, and specifically:

1. Avoid obscurity
2. Avoid ambiguity
3. Be brief
4. Be orderly

These maxims specify what participants have to do in order to converse in a maximally efficient, rational, cooperative way: they should speak sincerely, relevantly and clearly, while providing sufficient information. Rather than being arbitrary conventions, Grice argues that these maxims describe rational means for conducting cooperative exchanges. If this is the case, then one would expect them to govern aspects of non-linguistic behaviour too. Indeed, within the realms of spontaneous composition we have such a vehicle.

Conversational maxims enable inferences to appear beyond the semantic content of the sentence, thus enabling speakers to go beyond what is said, and listeners to work out what is meant based on what is said. An example should make this clear:

A: "Have you seen Miles?"
B: "There's a red Ferrari outside Gil's house."

In this example B's contribution, taken literally, fails to answer A's question, and thus appears to violate at least the maxims of Quantity and Relevance. We might therefore expect B's response to be interpreted as a non-cooperative response, a brushing aside of A's concerns with a change of topic. Semantically the best we could do here would be to assume that Miles is a red Ferrari, and that red Ferrari indeed refers to Miles, mentioned in the original question posed by speaker A. Yet despite this apparent failure of cooperation, we try to interpret B's utterance as nevertheless cooperative at some deeper (non-superficial) level. We do this by assuming that it is in fact cooperative, and then asking ourselves what possible connection there could be between the location of Miles and the location of a red Ferrari, and thus arrive at the suggestion (which B successfully conveys) that, if Miles has a red Ferrari, he may be in Gil's house.

We can give examples of the operation of the maxims for both linguistic and nonlinguistic exchanges. With the maxim of quantity, if one says, "I have three trumpets", then the assumption is that one has only three trumpets. If one owns six trumpets, then one is speaking the truth when one says one has three, but one is flouting the maxim of quality. Similarly, at a particular stage if you are helping me to fix my car, and at a particular stage I need three screws, then I expect you to hand me three rather than two or ten.

With the maxim of quality, one expects a genuine contribution from those involved in an exchange. For example, if one says that one is feeling ill and needs a doctor, then the assumption is that one is actually ill and needs a doctor. If that is not the case, then the maxim of quality is not being adhered to. Similarly, if I need sugar as an ingredient in a cake I am baking (with your assistance) and you pass me salt (knowingly) then you are flouting the maxim of quality.

The maxim of relation specifies that one should act or say something relevant to the purposes of the current exchange. For example, singing "Rule Britannia" in a discussion about a political crisis is not appropriate, thus flouting the maxim of relation. Similarly, dancing the tango during a waltz when your partner is dancing a waltz is not appropriate.

Finally, if one needs three screws to fix one's car, then the request, "Pass me the screws" assumes an immediate response. If I am tinkering with my car engine, and you (in your role as helper) walk off, then you need to make it clear that the purpose of this is to fetch some screws which you know I need at that moment in time. If you do not do this, then you are flouting the maxim of manner. Similarly, in a fire, walking in slow motion to a fire exit knowing one must head to the nearest exit is not appropriate, and flouts the maxim of manner.

In relation to figure 1, it is clear that Gricean principles can be applied to either the spoken dialogue situation, or the musical dialogue situation. Indeed, Grice argues that the cooperative principle applies not only to conversational exchanges, but to all cooperative activities, and we have given examples above.

Thus Grice stresses the point that a rational conversation must have a purpose or goal, such as the exchanging of information about a topic of mutual interest. These maxims enable different types of implicature to occur, and one can distinguish between standard implicatures, which arise from observation of the maxims, and floutings of the maxims (which are deliberate exploitations of the maxims). We have already given an example of a standard implicature, so we will restrict ourselves here to an example of a flouting of maxims. An example of the flouting of the maxim of relation is the following:

A: I think Mrs. Bloggs is a lousy cook.
B: Lovely weather we're having for July, isn't it?

The response of B is irrelevant to the topic of conversation at hand. B's utterance may implicate that Mrs. Bloggs is standing close by.

Grice provides the start of a theory of conversational implicature, by which it is possible to go beyond what is said, in terms of the semantics of a sentence, to what is meant. The key to this, as should be clear by now, lies in the assumptions of cooperation as outlined in the cooperative principle and the maxims. Before proceeding to music, some points should be raised as to the validity of this approach.

Grice comments that the maxims are not separate and are incomplete. For example, Grice recognises that there are other conventions influencing the nature of talk exchanges, such as 'Be polite'. The focus on four maxims lies in the belief that these are

> "specially connected with the particular purposes that talk is adapted to serve and is primarily employed to serve."[Grice 75, p. 47]

One important modification that is needed for our purposes is to contextualise the realisation of the maxims. Grice's work is based on a set of principles required to get at what is meant through what is said. The importance of the principles, in other words, are about going beyond what is actually said. However, Grice is stuck in truth conditional semantics with the assumption that conversation should proceed is a maximally efficient manner. A more realistic account is to emphasise the second part of the cooperative principle, which is;

> "by the accepted purpose or direction of the talk exchange in which you are engaged."

By this, one can imagine that the contributions required in the contexts of an academic board meeting and a conversation with a neighbour may be very different. The maxim of quantity, one can argue, would be realised differently in each case. In the first case, efficiency is a requirement, but in the second case, redundancy of language content is not a problem. Often it is the fact that one is involved in a conversation that is important, emphasising the social function of conversation.

Davidson [Davidson 84, Davidson 86] offers a semantic theory compatible with the views adopted here. He reacts against the definition of meaning as relating to generalisations in a speakers community. For Davidson, communication is much like a game. Before the start of a conversation, the hearer has a semantic theory which he believes will be adequate for the interpretation of a specific hearer's utterances. This is what is termed the speaker's prior theory. However, the prior theories vary greatly depending on who the hearer is about to communicate with. Once the communication is underway the prior theory originally adopted by the hearer may not be working sufficiently well, so adjustments have to be made. A new theory is then adopted by the hearer (a new semantic theory) which Davidson terms a passing theory. If the passing theory is successful, it may become a new prior theory (for further communication with that person). If not, the hearer can resort back to the previous prior theory. Thus successful communication occurs when speaker and hearer have the same (or equivalent) passing theories. Thus Davidson offers a view of linguistic competence which relates to the flexibility in the adjustment of passing theories. This view is in contrast with the Chomskyan view of competence, but is more directly applicable to musical dialogue.

Evidence supporting the Davidsonian position comes from spoken language in the form of the work of [Clark & Wilkes-Gibbs 86, Garrod & Anderson 87, Garrod & Doherty 93]. Garrod and colleagues have extensively studied spoken communication during performance on a maze game task (*cf.* [Garrod & Anderson 87]). Each player was seated in a different room confronted with a VDU on which a maze game was displayed (of the types displayed in figure 2). The task was for each one of the pair to describe the location of a point on the maze to the other, thus directing the other player to that point on the maze.

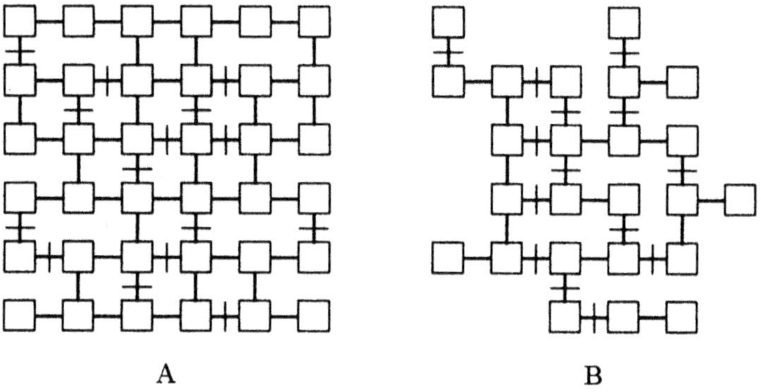

Figure 2: Mazes

The results are explained with recourse to mental models. Each description scene exhibited in the spatial dialogue pairs, Garrod and Anderson claim, is based on a particular mental model of the maze configuration, which in the case of effective communication would become "agreed upon" by the participants. Thus subjects were observed to adopt distinct but consistent description schemas which they readily classified into four basic types : path descriptions, line descriptions, co-ordinate descriptions and figural descriptions. Each of these descriptions treats the maze in a different way, illustrated by the following (taken from [Sanford & Garrod 81, pp. 48-49]);

Path description – "See the bottom left, go along one and up one, that's where I am"

Line description – "I'm on the second level, second from the left"

Co-ordinate description – "I'm at E two"

Figural description – "See the rectangle at the bottom left, well I'm in the middle box of the bottom of it"

When a pair of conversants adopt some particular model of the maze configuration this was observed to have the effect of constraining their locative descriptions to the extent that the 'local' meaning of any expression can only be derived through the model itself. Such an example would be the sometimes long-winded and bizarre descriptions resulting from the use of a particular model. With the maze in figure 2, for example, speakers that adopted the path model produced a dialogue to describe point X thus:

A: Right, see the bottom left-hand corner.
B: The bottom left.
A: There's a box and then there's a gap.
B: Uh-huh.
A: And there's a box and there's another box.
B: Uh-huh.
A: I'm right here.

Furthermore, it was found that dialogue pairs developed quite specialised description subschemes based on a single type of model. For example, Garrod and Anderson found evidence for at least three variants of the basic horizontal line type of model.

Garrod and Anderson therefore find evidence to support the idea that, through experience with a communicator, a way of talking about the world is established, and thus a solution to what [Lewis 68] has called the semantic co-ordination problem is found. Competence on this task can be measured in terms of how easily an individual is able to develop and co-ordinate a new schema to deal with the task at hand. This is akin to Davidson's notion of a passing theory. Lewis has argued that language is inherently ambiguous and vague, yet we manage to communicate with it. The ability of subjects on the maze task to agree, through shared goals, on a mutual schema to talk about the maze provides a solution to this problem. We will return to a further consideration of this work after a discussion of pragmatics (and semantic co-ordination) in music.

4 Pragmatics in Music

4.1 Free Music and Cooperation

We are now in a position to examine the application of pragmatics to spontaneous composition. From figure 1, it is clear that the place to start, as already indicated, is free improvisation, where no material is prepared in advance. Free music may be more rigorously defined as

> "improvisation not based on a predetermined, underlying harmonic structure, and without a fixed number of bar-lines." [Carr *et al* 88]

This is the direct parallel with spoken dialogue, again, as should be clear. Given four individuals, meeting for the first time, how do they establish a communication, when does each individual know when to communicate, and how does each individual know what the others mean by their utterances, *etc.*?

In the spoken dialogue situation, it is clear that there is a common set of assumptions all four individuals will bring to the situation. Assuming that they all speak the same language, they will all have a similar competence (in Chomskyan terms) for the language. They will therefore all be able to produce syntactically well-formed sentences, and so understand syntactically well-formed utterances. In Davidsonian terms, they will all have knowledge of standardisations in a speaker's community, and will have the ability to adjust passing theories appropriately for the situation required.

With respects to free music, there are problems which are apparent at this early stage. Musicians, in Davidsonian terms, will have different prior theories, and therefore may find it difficult to establish common ground in order for the musical dialogue to proceed. Additionally, and crucially, music does not have a semantics in the way that language does. One cannot say that musical idea X means Y in the same way that one can argue that 'the cat is on the mat' means Y. Furthermore, it is unlikely that all musicians will agree as to the meaning of musical idea X. In contrast, all competent speakers of English would agree on the meaning of 'the cat is on the mat'. The need for conversational implicature has obvious relevance in domains where arriving at a palpable semantics is extremely difficult. Indeed, the quest to find meaning in music has not been very fruitful. This is largely because of the problem of reference, in that one cannot point to a category, real world entity or even abstract idea to which a musical idea (chord, phrase, piece) can meaningfully be said to refer to.

Putting this another way, musicians are unlikely to come to a free improvisational situation with the same prior theories, and therefore are unlikely to be able to communicate with each other. Furthermore, as experiences differ, it is unlikely that musicians can be said to have the same competence. This means that musicians must be very sensitive to cooperation during improvisation, and perhaps meaning in such music can be understood in terms of cooperation, and how successful the cooperative activity is. From a Davidsonian perspective, a prerequisite for good free improvisation in a good setting would be familiarisation with the other participants in the situation in advance. In other words, one needs to have a prior theory as to how the other participants produce musical utterances. Alternatively, all musicians involved would need to have had similar (or perhaps identical) past musical experiences (that is, interactive musical experiences) in order to have a meaningful dialogue. As has already been indicated, this second possibility is a remote one.

The reliance on cooperative activity moves us to a consideration of Gricean maxims in this domain. From a Gricean perspective, the maxims within free improvisation can be very widely interpreted. The assumption of cooperation has to hold, but how one identifies how contributions are made is much more difficult than in the spoken dialogue situation, where prior theories on first meeting will have some relation to generalisations in the speakers' community. Firstly, we can consider the maxim of quality. In music, it is difficult to talk meaningfully in terms of truth of an utterance. A better definition here would be 'say what you believe to be of relevance to the current dialogue in which you are engaged'. Therefore, quality is subsumed under the maxim of relation. Quantity is flexibly defined in terms of 'play for the amount of time that is appropriate in the context in which you are improvising'. The problem here, as should be apparent, is that there is no way to evaluate whether a dialogue will make sense or not *a priori*. Evaluation of free improvisations has to be *post hoc*, and will be in terms of how successfully the musicians are interacting with one another. This is the only barometer of evaluation one can use, unless one assesses the similarity of the dialogue to familiar dialogue. Indeed, this is where the observers come in. The success of an improvisation on stage can only be judged by two sets of criteria. In this respect, the beliefs of an audience about the success of what has happened on stage is as much a reflection of the prior theories of the audience, or the ability of the audience to generate sufficient passing theories. In this respect, Jackson Pollock is right when he argues that the process is more important than the finished product. Familiarisation with a particular style of composition, and the development of the composer's work, lead to better theories as to how the finished product was conceived, and therefore *vis-a-vis* the nature of the finished product.

The success of free improvisation, therefore, lies in the ability of performers to interact with each other in ways that are predictable. That is, it is necessary for each musician to have knowledge as to where the other musicians in the dialogue are likely to go musically. This is unlikely unless the musicians have developed joint plans, or mutual schemas which work in future contexts. Indeed, [Garrod & Doherty 93] have compared, again using the maze task, language co-ordination between speakers who always interact with the same partner (isolated pairs) versus speakers who interact with different partners drawn from the same group (group pairs). The isolated pairs show higher degrees of inter-speaker convergence than the group pairs at the start of the experiment, but the situation was found to be reversed by the time all subjects had played six games. This suggests that, for free improvisations to be maximally effective, it is necessary for musicians to interact in an improvisational community, with each musician in the community interacting with every other member. This way, a common set of principles in the community will appear which provide some form, or principles of interaction, which guide the dialogue. The Company is such an outfit, and is considered to comprise the most gifted improvisers in Europe. Nevertheless, the suggestion from this discussion is that, for musical interaction to be most successful in improvisational setting, some structure or rules guiding the interaction should be present prior to the interaction.

The problems that should now be apparent for free improvisation suggest that predetermined structures or rules for improvisation are necessary to guide musicians in the cooperative activity of music making. It is to this approach that we now turn.

4.2 Gricean Maxims and Stylistic Movements in the History of Jazz

The history of jazz can be characterised as a development through a series of distinct stylistic forms, often in conflict with each other. These can be summarised for present purposes as a development from New Orleans through swing to bebop, cool and then onto free jazz and fusion of various sorts. However, the consensus of opinion as to the classification of stylistic forms in the history of jazz does not mean that an understanding of each form is forthcoming. For example, how would a cool school performance, such as a Miles Davis performance of a standard differ from a performance of the same piece by a bebop musician, such as Dizzy Gillespie? The problem here is that there is currently no appropriate vocabulary to use to describe the differences in performance. Simply saying that Dizzy Gillespie plays more notes is uninformative. It does not get at the intentionality of the performer, and does not give insight into the choice of notes that are played.

For the present purposes, we will take two successive periods in the history of jazz, and will provide an analysis of each style from the point of view of pragmatics. The periods which will be our focus of attention are bebop and cool school jazz styles. The reason for this choice is that there are many available recordings of both styles, unlike periods before. This enables us to take what are considered paradigmatic examples of each genre and provide an explanatory framework which can be applied to all spontaneous compositional genres.

Bebop is the

> "classic style which came to fruition in New York in the early 1940's, masterminded by Dizzy Gillespie and Kenny Clarke and brought to life by Charlie Parker." [Carr *et al* 88]

Cool is more difficult to define as it refers more to a way of playing than a particular period in jazz history. However, the early works of Miles Davis provide what are considered to be classic examples of this style. In particular, the work with Gil Evans, released as a recording under the title "The Birth of the Cool" provide paradigmatic examples of this type of playing.

Again, the questions we wish to address relate to the diagram in figure 1. The crucial difference between cool, bebop and free jazz is that (as has been already stated above) free jazz does not have predetermined material, whereas cool and bebop do. However, we wish to argue that cool and bebop differ in terms of the types of musical contributions each style licenses, which is based on a different emphasis on and realisation of Gricean type cooperative maxims.

We can begin with the cooperative principle itself:

The cooperative principle

> Make your contribution such that is required, at the stage at which it occurs, by the accepted purpose or direction of the talk exchange in which you are engaged.

Both musical contexts involve a melody written over a series of chord changes. Therefore, it is not simply the predetermined material in terms of chord changes that determines what is played. Here the distinction made earlier between an academic conversation and a conversation with a neighbour is relevant. How the cooperative principle is realised constrains the types of musical expressions allowed by each style, which relates to the differing purposes of cool and bebop. This becomes clearer when we examine the individual maxims.

The style of bebop can be understood in its historical context. Bebop is the first kind of jazz where the musicians involved could be regarded as artistic elitists. As [Carr *et al* 88, p. 33] comment,

> "this has to be seen in context with the short-lived social gains of black Americans during World War II, as a musical attempt to build a bridgehead for greater respect of black contributions to US society."

Thus bebop is characterised by a need to be as musically and technically sophisticated as possible. Cool, on the other hand, can be regarded as the opposite of this. Indeed [Carr *et al* 88, p. 110] comment that

> "cool described the ability of certain jazz improvisers to sound more detached and less 'hot' than their colleagues."

Turning to the maxims, the differences in style become clearly articulated. To begin with, we can dispense with the maxim of quality as it does not apply:

The maxim of Quality

Try to make your contribution one that is true, specifically:

1. Do not say what you believe to be false
2. Do not say that for which you lack adequate evidence

This is because truth conditional semantics is not a viable enterprise with respect to music. Gricean theory can be criticised for still taking on board the objectivist semantic thesis. The most relevant avenue related to the level of commitment by performer. A performer reproducing somebody else's ideas is not remaining faithful to his own intentions, which means that there is not an adequate basis for truth to be established. This is particularly true of cool, as will be apparent below. At another level, it is assumed that the contributions made to a musical dialogue are genuine, and that the performers are trying and contributing in a way that should be the musician's goal to be clear to the others in the dialogue.

The maxim of quantity can be readily applied to differentiate between styles.

The maxim of Quantity

1. make your contribution as informative as is required for the current purposes of the exchange;
2. do not make your contribution more informative than is required.

In bebop, the amount of information required in a solo is immense compared with that of cool school. Bebop was a musical form, which can be (in terms of quantity) defined as follows;

> "Say as much as you can in as short a space of time as you can without pausing."

The bebop musician wishes to dazzle the audience with the show of knowledge he has and his ability to reveal new connections within the form (for example, playing a riff and playing it across different chord changes). The bebop musician has to be able to perform. In this respect, bebop can be viewed a similar to horse racing commentary in an off-course betting office, in which the goal is to give out as much information as possible in a short space of time to keep the punters' attention. The commentator must keep up with the changing positions of horses in a race while still informing the punters of how their horse is doing. This means that the race commentator speaks extremely quickly, with escalating pitch. Asking punters what position their horse was in several furlongs ago is not really a relevant question to ask in this context. As with bebop, horse racing is about the moment, the instant excitement that a communication can have. Indeed, this excitement is transferred to the audience. This is clear when we compare the experience of punters during horse-racing commentary with those of the bebop musician listening to a solo:

> "One long, intense solo like Tranes can bring about any or all of the following conditions, sometimes after the end of a solo:
>
> 1. heavy breathing,
> 2. drenching perspiration,
> 3. trembling,
> 4. Nausea,
> 5. uncontrollable exhilaration,
> 6. fatigue,
> 7. depression, and
> 8. muscular tension (residual) and soreness...
>
> If we could measure the energy level for a given duration, say, for one thirty-two measure chorus by each artist, and then measure and compare Trane's energy output to that of Lester Young, for example, Trane's level would probably be somewhere between five and ten times greater." Jerry Coker (cited in [Priestley 87])

[Dickerson & Adcock 87] report a list of symptoms exhibited by off-course betters during gambling. These include heart rate increases during a race (up to 50 beats per minute change during a four minute race), sweating, tension, digestive system difficulties (constipation and/or diarrhoea), and depression. Their characterisation of the excitement of horse racing for the punter bears a striking resemblance to Coker's characterisation of the bebop audience.

Cool, on the other hand, specifies that one should only say something if one has something worthwhile to say. Miles Davis has commented that, when improvising there is careful selection of musical ideas, such that improvisation is 'a process of saying no, no, no, no, yes, until one settles on a good idea' (Miles Davis, cited in [Carr 92]). For Davis, the judge of a good musician was 'does the man project, and does he have ideas' (Davis, cited in [Carr 92]).

When we turn to the maxim of relation, the bebop musician does not have to observe the maxim to any great degree. As bebop is about the thrill and excitement of ideas from moment to moment, relevance is hard to distinguish from the maxim of quantity. Each individual note does not matter for the bebop musician. It is foolish to think of a particular note in bebop as being right or wrong during a performance. The musician can play any sequence of notes, as long as there are still references to the underlying chord structure in some way, although this itself is difficult to define. Musicians can quote from other contexts, such as well known tunes from popular standards. This hooks on the the listeners' prior theories in terms of quoting ideas which are perhaps already familiar to the audience.

For the cool school musician relevance is more important. It is important not to play any material for immediate impact, such as quoting from other tunes. This would be viewed as crude and stylistically inappropriate. It is necessary to improvise in the style of the material given, without spurious replication of ideas and use of irrelevant and irreverent material.

Finally, the maxim of manner has relevance for cool, but little for bebop. In cool musicians have to play no more than is required, thus obeying the manner of being brief. The musician must also be orderly - each successive phrase must relate to the last, and the overall context and form of the solo.

Thus, we have seen that bebop and cool involve a different emphasis and realisation of the cooperative maxims specified by Grice. This type of analysis allows us to avoid the necessity of being able to state specifically which sequences of notes are correct in a style, and which sequences are incorrect (which is necessary within a standard framework). From a Davidsonian point of view, the notion of acceptable utterance is itself defined by the nature of the users of that language. Therefore, what may be 'correct' in one context within a style may not be correct in another context. What is key is that each context provides a different emphasis on the way that musicians can contribute to the musical dialogue and therefore interact in each musical situation.

5 The Origins of Language and Music

One alternative to the failed quest of trying to define a semantics for music is to argue that meaning in music arrives through structure. Hence, one should study the syntax of music in order to approach anything resembling a semantics. Indeed, the structure of language provides a framework which can be applied directly to the structure of music. For example, [Lerdahl & Jackendoff 83] have attempted to analyse the structure of music within the framework of generative grammar.

It is beyond question that syntax is an important field of study in the domain of music. However, this study is very much geared towards analysis *post hoc*, and looks less attractive when one turns to the art of composition, and of performance. The *raison d'être* of language is communication and therefore it must be in the interests of an individual involved in the enterprise of communication to have knowledge about other communicators, and how they communicate. One such principle would be that other communicators will act in the same way as ourselves. The Gricean maxims can be seen to fall out of such motivation. With respect to music, and in particular to spontaneous composition, it is entirely plausible that there exist similar motivations.

As we have seen, in developmental terms spoken language is primary in terms of stage of acquisition. The child develops an ability to communicate using the spoken word before the child acquires the ability to read and write. Furthermore, [Trevarthen 83, p. 145] has argued that the acquisition of spoken communication is preceded by

> "a set of interpersonal abilities [that] regulate and drive forward the growth of cooperative awareness and that first steps in language acquisition rest on mutual confidence."

The infant is born with an ability to know another human [Trevarthen 80], and the first few months of life are governed by emotional exchanges between mother and infant, exchanges which importantly result in better communication when the partner shows positive empathy. Thus, the origin of pragmatics can perhaps be seen in early development, where the child makes the assumption that the partner will be cooperating in the exchange. If the partner does not do so, the infant communication is inhibited. The infant, according to Trevarthen, is born with an innate mechanism for 'emotional' communication, which lies at the root of communication, we have argued, in spontaneous improvisation. It is impossible to separate the music from the listeners and performers, just as it is impossible to separate language from the users of that language, and the overall goals that language serves.

6 The Representation of Musical Knowledge

We are now in a position to consider issues of musical representation and the ramifications of our approach for educational practice. We will consider the former issue first.

[Marr 82] distinguishes between three different levels of explanation which relate to any information-processing device. The first level is that of the level of computational theory, which is concerned with the specification of the goal of the computation, and the logic of the strategy by which it can be carried out. Levels two and three deal with the issues of how this computational theory can be carried out and implemented. We will deal exclusively with the level of computational theory.

We can examine existing systems for the representation of musical knowledge. These in general are governed by syntax and by the idea that musical knowledge can be captured using a set of rules, such as a generative grammar. The problem then is the one of how to finitely enumerate the rules and specify the conditions under which specific rules are applied. In other words, musical knowledge is symbolic manipulation where the symbols stand for musical sounds.

We can take the example of learning how to improvise, together with the task of designing a computer system which can improvise in a variety of contexts. One approach is to jump in at the level of algorithm, and work out, for each style, a finite set of rules which can generate all the possible (and admissible) strings in the style. Together with this, we would have to incorporate a nondeterministic element or an algorithm based on incoming information. This is the algorithmic interface. Let us see how we can take a generative grammar and interface this to the environment. Indeed, David Baker's approach to teaching bebop [Baker 87] provides us with a model grammar.

In Baker's approach melodic lines are drawn from a nine-note scale (normal major scale plus minor seventh), designed so that chordal tones inevitably appear on down beats or strong beats. Using a repertoire of standard endings and chord arpeggios, one generates bebop phrases/lines. These ideas can be extended by *enclosure* which chromatically encloses a chord tone. *Syncopation* is achieved by beginning the phrase on a weak beat and then using chromaticism to return to the original scale. Melodic variety and some degree of dissonance is achieved by starting on a note outwith this scale and returning to the original scale and rhythm by enclosure or a chromatic link. The rhythm can be doubled for semiquaver runs and these scales can be smoothly linked to one another using these rules, thus enabling the performer to negotiate the fast-moving chord sequences.

The types of rules specified by [Baker 87] can easily be written as a set of rewrite rules and put in a machine, and then the claim can be made perhaps that the machine represents musical knowledge. We can then ask the question as to how well this hypothetical machine improvises within an interactive context. We can ask, for instance, whether the machine could pass a version of the Turing test within the setting of a jazz quartet. This situation is depicted in figure 3 below.

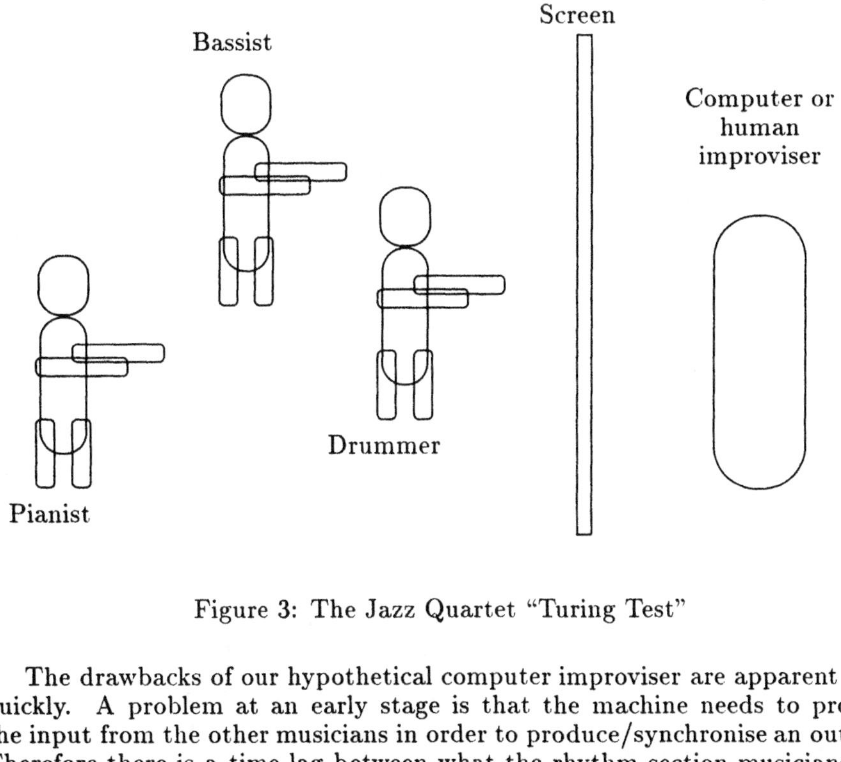

Figure 3: The Jazz Quartet "Turing Test"

The drawbacks of our hypothetical computer improviser are apparent very quickly. A problem at an early stage is that the machine needs to process the input from the other musicians in order to produce/synchronise an output. Therefore there is a time lag between what the rhythm section musicians are doing and what the improviser is doing. In reality, improvisers such as Charlie Parker are ahead of the beat. It is perhaps possible to programme the improviser to tacit for a few bars in order to work out the beat, and again it is possible for the chord sequences in a standard to be preprogrammed, which is the case with many sequencers. However, this does not mean that the machine would pass the Turing test. This is because the pulse is defined interactively within the group, and the pulse is constantly changing. Even if the machine had a processing capacity infinitely quicker that that of the rhythm section musicians, it is still left to explain how musicians can interact within a group setting in a cohesive way (and in an ever-changing pulse), given that humans presumably process information at similar rates to each other.

The above model assumes a static view of music making, and lacks psychological plausibility. What is missing is a characterisation of the problem space at the level of computational theory. We prefer a dynamic viewpoint, whereby heuristics can be viewed as continually changing and developing within the realms of communicative exchange. In Davidsonian terms, what is important is to characterise how one is able to develop passing theories, as opposed to the mainstream view of language as a static set of rules which specify correct and incorrect strings in the language. The function of language is to provide a framework to aid interactive activities and joint planning, and therefore the nature of representations should be such as to cope with the overall goals.

We can now turn to the issue of music education. Specifically, how does one learn to improvise in a variety of contexts? Just giving people the rules, such as Baker's principles for playing bebop, does not mean that they can instantly play bebop. It is the experience of interacting with other similar entities which leads to one's ability to improvise in real contexts. This in essence is a distinction between learning through experience and learning in terms of building up a declarative knowledge base. It is being able to apply knowledge flexibly in an ever-changing context which is primary. Thus the ability to interact, as embodied in an understanding of pragmatics, is a necessity when it comes to producing successful improvisations. What we need is an interface between the musical situation, and the information we bring to that situation; a model which is dynamic in nature and is constructed through interactive processes and a knowledge of principles governing interaction.

References

[Bailey 92] D. Bailey. Improvisation. its nature and practice in music. British Library National Sound Archive, 1992.

[Baker 87] D. Baker. *How to Play Bebop.* Alfred Publishing Company, Van Neys, California, 1987.

[Carr 92] I. Carr. *Miles Davis, A Critical Biography.* Quartet Books, London, England, 1992.

[Carr *et al* 88] I. Carr, D. Fairweather, and B. Priestley. *Jazz: the Essential Companion.* Paladin, 1988.

[Clark & Wilkes-Gibbs 86] H. H. Clark and D. Wilkes-Gibbs. Referring as a collaborative process. *Cognition*, 22:1–39, 1986.

[Clarke 89] E. F. Clarke. Issues in language and music. *Contemporary Music Review*, 4:9–22, 1989. Proceedings of the Symposium on Music and the Cognitive Sciences 14-18 March 1988, Centre National d'Art et de Culture 'Georges Pompidou', Paris, France.

[Cooke 59] D. Cooke. *The Language of Music.* Oxford University Press, London, England, 1959.

[Davidson 84] D. Davidson. *Inquiries into Truth and Interpretation.* Clarendon Press, Oxford, 1984.

[Davidson 86] D. Davidson. A nice derangement of epitaphs. In R. Grandy and R. Warner, editors, *Philosophical Grounds of Rationality: Intentions, Categories, Ends.* Clarendon Press, Oxford, 1986.

[Dickerson & Adcock 87] M. Dickerson and S. Adcock. Mood, arousal and cognitions in persistent gambling: Preliminary investigation of a theoretical model. *Journal of Gambling Behavior*, 3:3–15, 1987.

[Garrod & Anderson 87] S. C. Garrod and A. Anderson. Saying what you mean in dialogue: A study in conceptual and semantic coordination. *Cognition*, 27:181–218, 1987.

[Garrod & Doherty 93] S. C. Garrod and G. Doherty. Conversation, coordination and convention: An empirical investigation of how groups establish linguistic conventions. Manuscript, 1993.

[Grice 75] H. P. Grice. Logic and conversation. In P. Cole and J. L. Morgan, editors, *Speech Acts.*, volume 3 of *Syntax and Semantics.* Seminar Press, New York, 1975.

[Lerdahl & Jackendoff 83] F. Lerdahl and R. Jackendoff. *A Generative Theory of Tonal Music.* MIT Press, Cambridge, MA, 1983.

[Lewis 68] D. Lewis. *Convention: A philosophical study.* Cambridge University Press, 1968.

[Marr 82] D. Marr. *Vision: A Computational Investigation in the Human Representation of Visual Information.* Freeman, San Francisco, 1982.

[Miller 85] J. Miller. *Semantics and Syntax : Parallels and connections.* Cambridge University Press, 1985.

[Priestley 87] B. Priestley. *John Coltrane.* Apollo, 1987.

[Sanford & Garrod 81] A. J. Sanford and S. C. Garrod. *Understanding written language : explorations of comprehension beyond the sentence.* Wiley, Chichester and New York, 1981.

[Sloboda 85] J. A. Sloboda. *The Musical Mind.* The Clarendon Press, Oxford, 1985.

[Trevarthen 80] C. Trevarthen. The foundations of inersubjectivity: development of interpersonal and cooperative understanding. In D. R. Olson, editor, *The Social foundations of thought and language.* Norton Press, 1980.

[Trevarthen 83] C. Trevarthen. Interpersonal abilities of infants as generators for transmission of language and culture. In A. Oliviera and M. Zapella, editors, *The Behaviour of Human Infants.*, pages 145–176. Plenum, London and New York, 1983.

[Watt 93] S. Watt. *The Auditory Parsing of Complements.* Unpublished PhD thesis, University of Dundee, Scotland, 1993.

The Role of Musical Memory in Creativity and Learning: a Study of Jazz Performance

Geber Ramalho & Jean-Gabriel Ganascia
LAFORIA-IBP-CNRS
Université Paris VI
4 Place Jussieu, 75252 Paris Cedex 05, France
ramalho@laforia.ibp.fr; ganascia@laforia.ibp.fr

Abstract

As an alternative to most current approaches, we propose to model musical composition tasks by emphasizing the role of a "musical memory". We present how this model can deal with some features of creativity and learning in music. More specifically, the problem of simulating the behavior of a jazz trio that follows a live soloist is studied. We discuss the two main knowledge acquisition problems encountered in the implementation of this system. The first one is the problem of building the musical memory, *i.e.*, defining what kind of musical events the memory is composed of and finding good descriptors to index them. The second problem is to elicit from experts the knowledge necessary to use the musical memory content, *i.e.*, to define how to retrieve musical events from memory and how to modify them to fit the current musical context.

1 Introduction

A young musician and his friend, an older musician, on vacation on Tzac island[1] are invited to attend their first Tzac-music concert. During the concert, their host notices how puzzled they are. To help them having a better understanding of his native music, he suggests to them the challenge of composing a 27-bars Tzac-music melody which would be played in the concert the following night. The young musician asks for a theory book on Tzac-music and goes right away to his room to start studying. The old musician, on the other hand, prefers to spent the whole night listening to the native musicians. Which one will compose the melody that is the closest to Tzac-music? It is argued in this paper that rules are not sufficient to formalize musical activities. On one hand, rules are very adequate to represent some musical tasks that have a more formal status (*e.g.*, motive development in two-voice counterpoint). But, on the other hand, for the more intuitive musical tasks (*e.g.*, drums performance in a jam-session), experience plays the most important role. It seems that experience is closely related to the material heard/listened to everyday that is accumulated in one's long term memory, *i.e.*, what we call the "musical memory". In this perspective, there is an analogy between natural language and music learning. In fact, nobody learns a language only by studying its grammar, even if grammar rules

[1] Fictitious island.

play a very important role in the processes of producing and understanding language. In this paper we propose a computational model of composition tasks that is based on the above notion of musical memory. We discuss the two main knowledge acquisition problems encountered in the implementation of system. The first one is the problem of building the musical memory, *i.e.*, defining what kind of musical events the memory is composed of and finding good descriptors to index them in the musical memory. The second problem is to elicit the knowledge necessary to use the musical memory content, *i.e.*, to define how to retrieve musical events of the memory and how to adapt them to the current musical context. The word composition is used throughout this paper in a wide sense which includes tasks such as creating bass-lines, chord sequences, solos, voice leadings, arrangements, etc. Indeed, we consider that these activities share many problems with composition in its classical sense. The theoretical ideas presented in this article are attached to a concrete project whose long-term goal is to build a machine that is capable of giving an intelligent assistance to arrangers in the domain of jazz. Such a machine is meant to perform some limited composition tasks but also to progressively improve its musical knowledge from its errors, through listening to musical examples and through an interaction with a human supervisor.

Our project is divided into two stages. Firstly, a great amount of musical knowledge must be provided to the machine. Secondly, based on the knowledge accumulated in the machine during the previous stage, the interaction between human and machine will be studied. So, in the first stage, man-machine interaction is rather defined as "composer aided composition". In fact, the user's requirements for an intelligent tool in the domain of jazz are different from the requirements in the domain of contemporary classical music. Contrary to contemporary composers, jazz arrangers often do not want to use programming languages and mathematical models. Thus, in order to provide an effective exchange between the arranger and the machine, the latter must be capable of understanding the arrangers' requests which are stated by means of musical jargon. That's why we decided to start the project by modeling the musical knowledge used by jazz musicians. In this perspective, we have chosen the problem of simulating the behavior of a jazz trio composed of bass, piano and drums. This trio must follow a live soloist given some arrangement instructions and a score in the Real-Book format[2].

In Section 1 and 2, we discuss the problems of modeling composition tasks and the limitations of some current approaches. In Section 3, we introduce the notions of musical memory, musical strategies and progressive knowledge acquisition as the basis of our alternative approach. The problem of representing musical events in a musical memory is treated in Section 4. The knowledge necessary to retrieve and use the fragments of such a musical memory is discussed in Section 5. Finally, we conclude by describing our current work as well as discussing some still open problems in our approach and the directions for further development.

[2]The Real-Book contains the most popular songs and pieces played by jazz musicians in the format "melody plus chord grid".

2 The Problem of Modeling Composition Tasks

2.1 Musical rules

Even in a culturally constrained musical style like jazz, the modeling of composition tasks is a difficult problem. Indeed, musicians have a hard time to express the rules they supposedly use and the rules provided by them cannot be directly interpreted in a computational formalism. Here are three examples of typical rules given by bass players [Pachet 87]:

- In general, I play the tonic of the chord on the first beat;
- I know some academic methods to pass from one chord to the next chord (*e.g.*, a two-five chord sequence);
- Sometimes I introduce passing notes among the chords notes;
- I avoid to "play over" the soloist phrases;
- I know some transgressions to the rules I've told you that I apply when I want (*e.g.*, pull-up, pull-down).

2.2 Musical choices and decision taking

Among the numerous facets of musical activities, two of them are by nature very difficult to formalize. Firstly, musicians cannot justify all the choices they make, typically at the note-level. For example, a trumpet player will not find a local explanation for each note that composes his solo, even if he has consciously applied some high-level strategies in his performance like "play in dorian mode". The second facet is that musicians set and solve problems on a real-time basis. There is no backtracking, in the AI sense, because musicians cannot change what they have already played. Moreover, musicians may reconsider strategies and constraints in the on-going process. Indeed, musical actions depend strongly on contexts that evolves over time. For example, the dynamic conditions imposed by the soloist's use of musical scales can lead the other musicians to violate some initial harmonization constraints given in the chord grid. These two facets reflect the three features of creative tasks proposed by Johnson-Laird [Johnson-Laird 92]: non-determinism (for the same given composition problem it is possible to obtain different musical solutions which are all acceptable); lack of well-defined and fixed goals (goals are refined or changed during the process of composition); and lack of consensus for evaluating results (aesthetic judgment varies from style, person, country, epoch, etc.). As it is discussed in the next section, it is rather difficult to obtain a computational model of these features that is flexible and simultaneously has an explicit semantic.

3 The Current Approaches

We will discuss in this section two groups of approaches that try to deal with some of the above problems. The first one is based on statistical or random considerations. The second one is based on grammars and specialized rules.

3.1 Composition as a statistic-based or random-based activity

Taking advantage of the fact that it is possible to identify frequent patterns in culturally-constrained music, the problem of generating an accompaniment can be partially treated by enumerating these patterns, assigning weights to them and using them according to their weights. Some good examples of the application of this technique is Charles Ames' Cybernetic Composer [Ames & Domino 92] and Francesco Giomi's work [Giomi & Ligabue 92]. They represent some jazz styles by means of grammars rewrite-rules or derivational trees with associated statistical parameters. These approaches offer a good simulation of the non-deterministic facet of music generation because of the flexibility provided by random-oriented choices. Nevertheless, there is no semantic associated to such choices. Moreover, this approach does not treat the temporal and dynamic aspects of live performances. The point doesn't seem to be how many times a musical pattern is played but why it is played. Another example of this kind of approach is the Vincinanza's application of the universal sub-goaling problem solving method proposed in SOAR [Laird J. & P. 87] to melody generation [Vincinanza & Prietula 89]. This method states that a goal must be broken into sub-goals when an impasse occurs. So, the task of creating a melody can be broken down into creating phrases and creating a phrase into choosing a rhythmic pattern and assigning pitches to it. At the next level, the choice of notes themselves is randomly oriented. This work tries to reach a certain level of cognitive plausibility by modeling musicians reasoning by means of a problem solving method. Unfortunately, at the note level a *random* choice occurs. So, the same criticisms made to the above works remain applicable.

3.2 Specialized description: trying to formalize musical choices

To avoid the lack of semantics and control associated to random-oriented choices, introduced by the above approaches, another direction of research focus on the richness of descriptions so as to achieve a better explanation of musical choices. In general, this more detailed knowledge is expressed in terms of production rules or grammars. However, the complexity of the problem leads either to reductions in rules or introduction of "artificial rules" that solve some computational problems but that do not correspond to the actual musician's reasoning. As a consequence, this kind of system looses flexibility which is an essential feature of creativity. Some examples of systems in which this problem is encountered are Kemal Ebcioglu's work on chorales in the style of Bach [Ebicioglu 92] and some implementations of the "Generative Theory of Tonal Music" [Lerdahl & Jackendoff 83]. In fact, there is a trade-off in modeling creative activities expressed in terms of: *randomness* versus *control*, *flexibility* versus *semantic relevance* and so on [Rowe & Partridge 93]. If creativity is neither a random or statistical activity nor a fully explainable one, so what happens when musicians create?

4 The Basis of our Approach

4.1 Experience is related to musical memory

We claim that musical memory is the main source of knowledge in intuitive or non-formalized composition tasks. Up to now, there is no exact explanation of how fragments of one's auditory history are used to understand and generate music but its importance for musical activities is undeniable [McAdams & Deliege 88]). The great difference between a young and an old musician is not their quantity of known theory but their acquired musical experience. Rules taught in music theory give a very important and basic support to composition tasks. However, the full development of the musical skills is only accomplished within a cultural medium by practicing, *i.e.*, a very fastidious understanding process of listening and repeating music [Sloboda 85] In this sense, the concept of musical memory used in this paper goes beyond the notion of short term memory or routine memory. The proposed musical memory is rather defined as a long term memory that accumulates all musical material (songs, arrangements, solos, nursery rhymes, etc.) heard during one's life. This memory might retain as well some information about situations, context features, strategies success and failures attached to the musical events previously heard or listen to.

4.2 Jazz rules act like Advisers rather than Dictators

If our first claim was related to the notion of musical memory, our second claim is that the most important strategies used in jazz performance are not at the note-level but at more abstract levels. For example, when creating or analyzing an improvisation jazz musicians emphasize higher-level concepts like color, scale references, tension, complexity, space, rhythm practices, velocity, etc. [Baker 80], [Baudoin 90]. Musicians also use note-level concepts or strategies (for example, the rule cited by the bass player as *academic methods*). Nevertheless, we claim that most of the time the note-level choices do not critically influence the general jazz expression. In other words, the constraints do not generally lie on the notes themselves but on more abstract musical structures.

Figure 1 gives a simple illustration of how we visualize the association of our two first claims in a computational formalism. A key idea is that during performance the musicians use dynamically different kinds of knowledge. So, the modeling of musicians' actions might have a hybrid framework integrating rules and memories. Sometimes, according to the musical context, some rules that directly determine the notes are applied. But for other contexts, any attempt to express musicians' actions in terms of rules can be seen as artificial, because these rules are actually not available. In these later contexts, a search for musical fragments in the musical memory is performed. The retrieval and adaptation of these memory fragments to the current musical context is guided by abstract musical concepts (such as the ones cited in the previous paragraph). The adapted material is played and stored in the musical memory, closing a learning cycle.

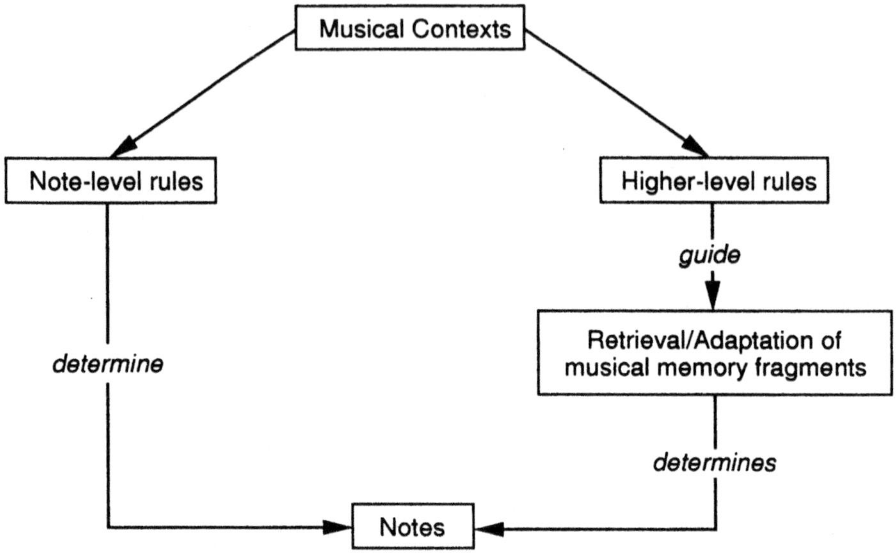

Figure 1: Schema rule-memories.

4.3 It takes a long time to make a musician

Our last claim is related to the way we in which we will proceed to implement our system. We state that in order to get a deeper insight into learning and creativity, it is useful to undertake a progressive approach for knowledge acquisition. In other words, instead of global formalization, an emphasis must be given to the knowledge evolution as an incremental process. Thus, the initial goal is not to model directly the knowledge of a highly expert musician but a medium musician and study the different modifications required in the machine knowledge so as to track and develop its musical behavior. The next sections present with further details the notion of musical memory. In Section 5, the case-based reasoning model is studied as the original inspiration of our idea of musical memory. Then, the main difficulties and specificities of applying this model to build a musical memory for musical domain are discussed. In Section 6, a model of reasoning is proposed which can deal with the use of the memory content.

5 Building a Musical Memory

5.1 The Notion of Memory in the Case-Based Reasoning

Our ideas about the use of a musical memory are related to Roger Schank's Case-Based Reasoning - CBR. He argues that the reasoning mechanism employed by people to understand situations, solve everyday problems and learn is not based on rules but on cases [Schank 90]. According to CBR's point of view, creativity and learning can be seen in a whole process tightly related to the capacity of inventing/adapting old solutions (or explanations) to new problems (or situations). When a new problem is presented to a case-based system, the relevant features of the problem are described (*i.e.*, the appropriate indexes are instantiated) in order to allow a search into the case-base for old case that is most similar the new one. The old solution associated to the old problem is adapted to the new one. The proposed solution is tested and if it works this solution and its associated problem are generalized and stored in a case-base so as they can be used in the future. If the proposed solution doesn't work, it must be repaired until it works and then stored. In this later case, the system revises its knowledge about how to adapt old solutions so as to avoid the same adaptation failure in the future [Slade 91]. The capacity of learning from its success and failures as well as the capacity of adapting and repairing old solutions to new problems show how flexible and powerful the CBR approach may be. However, an actual implementation of a case-based system has to deal with some very difficult problems related to the process of assign indexes to cases, retrieving similar cases and adapting old cases to new context.

5.2 Knowledge Acquisition Problems of Case-Based Systems

There are some differences between our point of view and Schank's [Ganascia 90]. Firstly, we don't state that memories (cases) play a unique role in composing. Musicians also do use rules learned at school or generalized from examples. We try to take into account this fact by proposing a formalism that incorporates both rules and musical memories as is briefly discussed in our model of musician reasoning (Section 6). Secondly, we don't think that cases can embody all knowledge. Indeed, in order to index, retrieve and adapt cases, a large amount of knowledge (probably expressed in terms of rules) is needed. Perhaps human beings can store cases in their memory without reference to any interpretation, but the representation of cases in computers is preceded by interpretation. Indeed, following the AI tradition, the representation of cases uses descriptors as, for example, slots identifiers that are a biased view of the raw cases. In this sense, finding relevant descriptors that allow the discrimination of cases and the manipulation of them is an actual knowledge elicitation problem. Furthermore, the construction of a musical memory (Case-Base) does not suffice for indicating how its content will be used. Nobody can learn to compose only by listening to existing music. Music theory and practice is also necessary. Our two visitors of Tzac Island are confronted with such a dichotomy. Thus, the knowledge used in the manipulation of pre-composed material in order to adapt it to different goals and needs must be acquired. In short, focusing on cases rather than rules, the CBR approach supposedly could solve one of the main problems of building intelligent systems, *i.e.*, the knowledge acquisition bottleneck. Nevertheless, instead of solving this problem, CBR approach only reformulates it.

5.3 The content of a musical memory

Music has highly implicit and multi-dimensional levels of description. This fact is the starting point of our solution to the indexing problem. A musical material can be described through different facets such as form, rhythm, plans, melodic contours, harmony and so on. In our case, the musical memory of a jazz trio may contain the multi-level representation going from the actual transcription (note-level) of the trio and the soloist performance to more abstract description concerning the above mentioned music facets. In order to exemplify what we mean by abstract description, it is showed on table 1 some descriptors used by David Baker [Baker 80] to provide guiding elements to his pupils to aid listening to Miles Davis' solos. The motivation of Baker's study lies on the wide spread jazz tradition of acquiring improvisation skills: listening to and imitating solos of the jazz great stars. A very interesting example of how to re-compose new material from stocked music is Simon Holland's work [Holland & Elson-Cook 90]. He has built a learning environment, called MC, that teaches composition of chord sequences and bass lines of western music. The songs are represented by different and redundant point of views or dimensions. The student investigates the role of each dimension in the song at hand by asking the system to re-compose it given a new value for one or more dimensions. For example, using a few number of descriptors (like chord vocabulary, number of notes in a chord, tonality, mode, etc.) the MC system is capable of producing appropriate chord replannings as, for example, the modal version of "All the Things You Are".

Attribute	Values
Title of composition	(Ex. Tune Up)
Instrument	trumpet
Tune type	blues, ballad, bebop, standard ...
Tempo	(Ex. half = 152)
Key	(Ex. D Major)
Tessitura	high, low, middle, middle to high, ...
Dramatic devices	vibrato, slurs, rips, glissandi, ...
Scale preferences	major, chromatic, diminished, ...
Developmental techniques	single climax vs. many climax simple to complex vs. complex to simple chord referential vs. thematic referential
Rhythmic practice	double time, half time, reiterative, ...
Melody	folk-like, riff-like, bebop, bluesy, ...
...	...
Note-level transcription	solo transcription + chord grid

Table 1: Examples of descriptors of Miles Davis' solos

¿From the above examples (from [Baker 80]), it can be inferred that descriptors of musical memories may play a twofold role. Firstly, they allow the comparison of musical events for the retrieval stage. In fact, based on these descriptors, the system can detect similarities and hierarchical dependencies between musical events and provide a means of retrieving them according to the stated goals. Secondly, the descriptors indicate the possible manipulations needed to adapt the retrieved material to the current situation. Thus, finding relevant descriptors and their relationship is the key for building a musical memory.

6 Using the Musical Memory

6.1 A model of musician's reasoning while performing

The construction of a rich and good indexed memory is the first step towards our system implementation. The following step is to define how this memory can be used, *i.e.*, how the information about musical context is employed to retrieve and adapt the content of musical memory. This problem is viewed by us as a typical knowledge engineering problem encountered in the building of knowledge-based systems[Wielinga B. & J. 92]. Taking as starting-point the Fran "strategy-based" representation of jazz knowledge [Pachet 91], we propose a reasoning model sketched in Figure 2. The proposed model of reasoning uses the notion of concurrent strategies to try to take into account a maximum amount of context elements related to the real condition of live performance in jazz. These context elements may include real-time constraints, mutual listening influences, grid harmonizations, arrangement references points, piece form, and so on. All the actions that musicians can take considering the above elements are represented by what we call strategies. For instance: "play an arpeggio", "create a rhythmic contrast with solo", "repeat melodic line played in the chorus", "play a lot of notes", "play with tensions in the introduction", "use dorian mode", etc. In the first step of the presented model the strategies are activated according to the context elements. For example, the strategy "play an arpeggio" may be activated when two chords have a long duration in time and a small intervalic distance between them. A context like "the soloist is using long rests" may activate the strategy "play a response to solo during its rests" [Pachet 91]. The second step is to eliminate conflicts between the activated strategies as well as reordering their priority. Strategies like "play loudly" and "play quietly" are not compatible while "use swing" and "use note chords" may remain together. The implementation step consists of finding a solution that closely satisfies the remaining strategies.

6.2 Strategies and the note-level

Depending on the type of active strategies, the solution can be implemented through rules or search in memory. Some strategies (what Pachet called low-level strategies) may determine directly the notes by applying simple musical knowledge. The above cited strategy "play an arpeggio" is an example of such a strategy because it suffices to determine the chord notes of the current chord. In the other cases, a solution will be found through a kind of pattern matching between the strategies and the memories' indexes. For example, the strategy "play a response to solo during its rests" is not directly implementable in terms of notes. Obviously, this later kind strategy cannot establish a direct connection with the note-level. This strategy is only one of the activated strategies that contribute to the global conditions imposed to the retrieval of a memory fragment. So, strategies can be seen as soft constraints with a sort of priority ordering organization because they don't impose a perfect matching. Among the strategies we stressed the real-time one which corresponds to the right-branch model path. If such a strategy is activated the system will play licks and other well known solutions (for example, the "tonic in first beat" rule cited by the bass player in Section 2). Time plays a very important role as a constraint

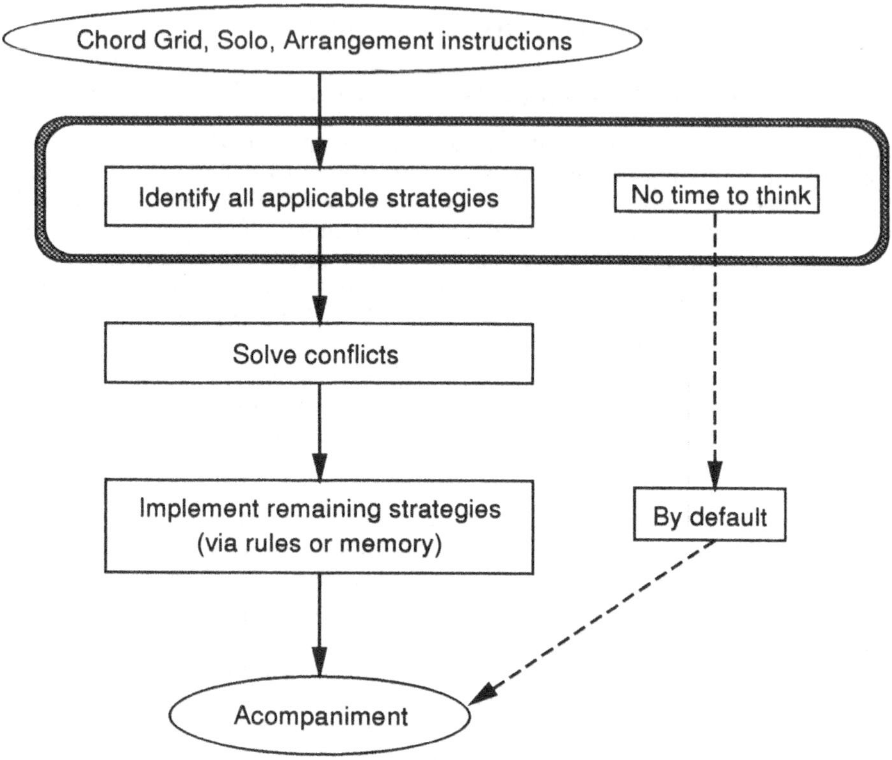

Figure 2: A model of musicians' reasoning while performing.

to human decision taking, particularly in the music performance. In spite of this, a little attention has been paid to time by knowledge-based systems. In various situations, humans, and specially musicians, don't seem to look for the best solution of a problem but mainly for a good solution that can be found in a limited period of time. It is important to stress out that the strategies configuration is quite dynamic because each strategy has a limited duration in time which can be, for example, a duration of a chord, bar, song, etc. This way of formalizing musical activity provides a good framework for the simulation of one of the creativity facets: musicians set and reconsider constraints during the composition process. The main difficult is to establish which criteria can be used to have a fine control of the interactions between strategies. In other words, express ongoing changes of mind in terms of reordering strategies priorities, supposes an a priori knowledge about the possible strategy combinations that might take place. In his work on formalizing jazz improvisation, David Levitt [Levitt 81] has proposed that human performance could be seen as process in which an initial set of defaults values for musical choices are changed gradually, *i.e.*, only one value is changed in turn. In fact, this corresponds to the preliminary results of our interviews with experts who say that there must be an equilibrium in musical dimensions. For example, when someone is producing music with a very complex rhythm, the harmony or melody must be simplified. This point of view raises two important consequences to our model. Firstly, the problem of ordering strategies can be naturally treated by the partial matching mechanism that is applied on the musical memory. An ordering of the all the activated strategies could be reduced to the choice of one or two main important ones. The rest of the strategies will be fully or partially taken into account by the matching process, depending on the richness of musical events stocked in the memory. The flexibility provided by the partial matching mechanism is a relevant advantage of the case-base approach. Secondly, as a variation of the first consequence, the efficiency of the retrieval stage could be improved because of the limitation of changes of directions in the search process. Since only few dimensions can change in turn, the search space is reduced.

7 Perspectives

We have presented in this paper some preliminary considerations relating to a particular approach to the simulation of a jazz trio behavior. As an alternative to most of current approaches ([Ames & Domino 92], [Giomi & Ligabue 92], [Vincinanza & Prietula 89], [Ebicioglu 92], [Lerdahl & Jackendoff 83], the proposed musical model explores the notions of a "musical memory" and "contextualized actions". This model potentially gives some insights for the formalization of the two first features of creativity proposed by Johnson-Laird [Johnson-Laird 92], *i.e.*, the non-determinism and the lack of well-defined and fixed goals. The former feature has been partially treated by the approaches cited above and by other knowledge representation techniques, such as genetic algorithms, heuristics coupled with meta-rules architectures, constraint satisfaction algorithms, etc. [Rowe & Partridge 93]. However, little work has been done on the modeling of the latter feature. A problem that has been left without any solution is what we call "the best-matching problem". Contrary to non-creative domains, the goal of the retrieval stage is not necessarily to achieve the "best matching". When musicians play the same chord grid twice, they don't play the same notes, even if the context elements have not enough changed. What do musicians remember and what do musicians forget? In other words, at which level of the memory description (from higher-levels to note-level) should we place ourselves in order to retrieve just slightly different memories? Another problem is related to the "temporal granularity". The question is to know what is the size of the memory events to be retrieved. May the system perform a search into memory for each chord, bar, turnaround or song's part? It seems that musicians access their memories at non-regular time intervals. So, the musical memory of our system might contain more than the simple transcriptions of the notes recorded from a performance. These note transcriptions could be broken into fragments such as typical phrases indexed by particular modulations, turnarounds, chord sequences, etc. Our current work is concerned with eliciting from experts (performers, teachers, arrangers, etc.) the implicit knowledge necessary to describe musical events as well as the strategic-level knowledge used to manipulate pre-composed material in order to achieve some given goals. From a methodological point of view, our work is divided into two fronts. On the one hand, we are interleaving sections of interview and record/transcription of musicians in action. We are also performing some analysis of "standard records" played by famous jazzmen. In particular, when different versions or *takes* of the same piece are available. On the other hand, our model is being confronted with some other interpretation models proposed in KADS [Wielinga B. & J. 92] and problem solving methods as the constraint-satisfaction one introduced in SALT [Marcus 88]. We have not treated explicitly here the machine learning issues related to our project. We think that effective learning is only possible when a great amount of domain knowledge is made available. So, we are waiting for the first practical knowledge acquisition results in order to begin machine learning experiments. Our research is not directly concerned with intelligent computer aided instruction (ICAI) but some points we raise in this paper may interest the developers of ICAI technology. These points are mainly related to the relevance of listening to and manipulating musical examples that belong to a particular cultural style. Another point, seem to be the role of time in musical problem solving. Finally, we hope that our approach may provide a better understanding of the concepts of experience and intuition in music as well as the pros and cons of the two following methods: "*going right away to one's room to start studying*" and "*spending the whole night listening to native musicians*".

8 Acknowledgments

We would like to thank some people that were involved in the discussion of the ideas presented in this paper: Fran from LAFORIA and Eriberto Paredes from IACP. We thank also the workshop participants for their comments, in special Simon Holland. This work has been partially supported by a grant from the Brazilian Education Ministry - CAPES.

References

[Ames & Domino 92] C. Ames and M. Domino. Cybernetic composer: an overview. In K. Ebicioglu M. Balaban and O. Laske, editors, *Understanding Music with AI: Perspectives on Music Cognition.* The AAAI Press, California, 1992.

[Baker 80] M. Baker. *Miles Davis Trumpet, Giants of Jazz Series.* Studio 224 Ed, Lebanon, 1980.

[Baudoin 90] P. Baudoin. *Jazz: mode d'emploi.* Editions Outre Msure, Paris, 1990.

[Ebicioglu 92] K. Ebicioglu. An expert system for harmonizing chorales in the style of j. s. bach. In K. Ebicioglu M. Balaban and O. Laske, editors, *Understanding Music with AI: Perspectives on Music Cognition.* The AAAI Press, California, 1992.

[Ganascia 90] J-.G. Ganascia. Commentary on schank's paper. In Y. Kodratoff and R. Michalski, editors, *Machine*

Learning: An Artificial Intelligence Approach Vol. III. Morgan Kaufman Pub., California, 1990.

[Giomi & Ligabue 92] F. Giomi and M. Ligabue. Computational generation and study of jazz music. *Interface*, 20, no. 1., 1992.

[Holland & Elson-Cook 90] S. Holland and M Elson-Cook. Architecture of a knowledge-based music tutor. In M. Elson-Cook, editor, *Guided Discovery Tutoring.* Paul Chapman Pub. London, 1990.

[Johnson-Laird 92] P. Johnson-Laird. *The Computer and the Mind.* Fontana, London, 1992.

[Laird J. & P. 87] Newell A. Laird J. and Rosembloom P. Soar: An architecture of general intelligence. *Artificial Intelligence*, 33:1–64, 1987.

[Lerdahl & Jackendoff 83] F. Lerdahl and R. Jackendoff. *A Generative Theory of Tonal Music.* The MIT Press, Massachusetts, 1983.

[Levitt 81] D. Levitt. A melody description system for jazz improvisation. Unpublished M.Sc. thesis, Department of Electrical Engineering and Computer Science, MIT, 1981.

[Marcus 88] S. Marcus. Salt: A knowledge acquisition tool for propose-and-revise systems. In S. Marcus, editor, *Automating Knowledge Acquisition for Expert Systems.* Kluwer Academic Pub., Boston, 1988.

[McAdams & Deliege 88] S. McAdams and I. Deliege. *La Musique et les Sciences Cognitives.* Pierre Mardaga Ed., Paris, 1988.

[Pachet 87] F. Pachet. Utilisation d'un syst me expert pour simuler les comportements d'un pianiste et d'un bassiste accompagnant un inprovisateur de jazz. Technical report, Rapport de DEA, LAFORIA, Universit Paris VI, 1987.

[Pachet 91] F. Pachet. Representing knowledge used by jazz musicians. In *Proceedings of the International Computer Music Conference, Montreal*, 1991.

[Rowe & Partridge 93] J. Rowe and D. Partridge. Creativity: a survey of ai approaches. *Artificial Intelligence Review*, 7:43–70, 1993.

[Schank 90] R. Schank. Explanations, machine learning and creativity. In Y. Kodratoff and R. Michalski, editors, *Machine Learning: An Artificial Intelligence*

Approach Vol. III. Morgan Kaufman Pub., California, 1990.

[Slade 91] S. Slade. Case-based reasoning: a research paradigm. *AI Magazine*, Spring 1991, 1991.

[Sloboda 85] J Sloboda. *The Musical Mind: The Cognitive Psychology of Music*. Oxford University Press, New York, 1985.

[Vincinanza & Prietula 89] S. Vincinanza and M. Prietula. A computational model of musical creativity. In *Proceedings of the Second Workshop on Artificial Intelligence and Music, Michigan*, 1989.

[Wielinga B. & J. 92] Schreiber T. Wielinga B. and Breuker J. Kads: a modeling approach to knowledge engineering. *Knowledge Acquisition*, 4, no. 1:1–64, 1992.

Automatic Characterisation of Musical Style

Martin D. Westhead & Alan Smaill
Department of Artificial Intelligence
University of Edinburgh
80 South Bridge, Edinburgh EH1 1HN, Scotland
martinwe@ai.ed.ac.uk; smaill@ai.ed.ac.uk

Abstract

This paper describes a system for automatically characterising musical style using motifs. Motifs are patterns of rhythms or pitches common to more than one piece of music in a style. The Style Analysis with Motifs (SAM) system uses an original classification technique and is able to learn to distinguish between different styles with a success rate of over 95%. It is suggested that since motifs can be used to automatically discriminate between different styles effectively, they may be very important in the way humans achieve the task.

This paper investigates how pitch patterns, or *motifs*, can be used for the characterisation of musical style. It is proposed that characterisation of a musical style can be demonstrated in one of three ways:

1. Composition of new music in the style.
2. Recognition of works in the style.
3. High level description of the style or of pieces of example works with respect to the style.

In this paper we concentrate on the second aspect, and describe how motifs can be used to construct a system that can learn to recognise examples of a musical style. We also demonstrate, using entropy, how effective the use of motifs is in characterising a style.

1 Background

The diversity of style across the breadth of musical history makes the concept difficult to encapsulate in an empirical definition. [Dickinson 65] describes style as

> "the individual essence of a work of art which gives it its identity. This identity is the result of a distinctive conjunction of components, coupled with distinctive emphasis among the components".

There are many similar intuitive definitions, for example:

> "Style is a replication or patterning, whether in human behaviour or in artifacts produced by human behaviour, that result from a series of choices made within some set of constraints." [Meyer 89]

Some authors, such as the composer Arnold Schönberg, are dubious about the possibility of ever defining style [Schönburg 75].

A starting point for this paper is the work of David Cope. Cope defines style as:

> "the identifiable characteristics of a composers music which are recognisably similar from one work to another."

In his book "Computers and Musical Style" [Cope 91], Cope describes a system he constructed for the automatic composition of works in a style. The system works using using *motifs*, or, as Cope calls them, *signatures*. These are patterns of pitch intervals or rhythmic ratios, which occur in more than one example work of a style. Other authors such as [Meyer 89] have talked about the use of such characteristic patterns. Meyer refers to it as *strategic play*. There are other authors who have used substrings for recognition and analysis (*e.g.*, [Kippen & Bel 89]. However the attention given this subject by theorists has been limited. Indeed, it has been authoritatively suggested that the main reason for the slow development of a serious theory of musical syntax is the refusal of music theorists to acknowledge the importance of repetition [Bernstein 76].

Cope's system for analysing musical style begins by collecting a number of motifs by matching two pieces of music and pulling out all the invariant substrings in the pitch intervals and rhythmic ratios. He uses the extracted motifs to automatically compose a new work in the style of the original two. The composition technique uses a grammar system derived by [Cope 87] inspired by the work of [Schenker 35], and the idea of *tonal function*. The grammar is used to produce a string of terminal symbols. Each symbol corresponds to a shift in the melody line by a particular number of semi-tones. Cope's system thus constructs a new melody line by replacing each symbol with a motif that shifts the melody the appropriate number of semitones up or down over its length.

This paper investigates the premise that motifs are indeed important in musical style and leads on from Cope's work by demonstrating how they can be used to construct a recognition system for classifying musical style.

2 The SAM system

2.1 Introduction

The recognition system Style Analysis with Motifs (SAM) reads in data from standard MIDI files and uses it to collect motifs which go into a style *dictionary*. The data is split into two *training sets*, positive examples (of pieces in the style) and negative examples (pieces not in the style). The dictionary contains two *style subsets* – one for each training set – which hold the motifs extracted from that set.

The motifs are extracted by taking pitch interval lists for each piece, and comparing each pair of lists for common substrings. An interval list simply consists of a list of integers corresponding to the intervals between consecutive notes in the melody. Each common substring represents a motif and is entered in the appropriate style subset in the dictionary. The frequency with which a motif is encountered is recorded.

When a test piece is presented to SAM, it attempts to classify the piece as being most similar, in terms of the motifs it contains, to either the positive or the negative training examples in the dictionary. This is done by first matching the test piece against the dictionary to extract a set S of all the motifs that have been encountered in the training phase. SAM then uses the relative frequency with which each of the motifs occur to calculate an estimate of which of the training sets S most resembles.

The estimate is made relative to the *dictionary mean*. Since the dictionary will invariably have different number of motifs of differing frequency in each style subset, it will display a bias towards one of the training sets. This can be seen in the dictionary mean which represents the expected value that would be returned for a piece constructed entirely from motifs selected at random from the dictionary. If the value obtained from the piece is higher than this then it is considered to be most similar to the positive examples. If lower, it is considered most similar to the negative examples.

Finally, using the concept of entropy from Shannon's information theory [Shannon & Weaver 49], we can produce some results to suggest empirically how well these motifs characterise musical style. The entropy of a note in a piece is the expected number of bits required to represent it. It is proposed by [Conklin & Witten 91] that a theory which minimises the entropy is one which most effectively characterises the style. Entropy estimates are made both with and without the use of motifs. The reduction in entropy which results from using motifs in the representation is then taken to suggest how well the style has been characterised.

2.2 Recognition

According to our earlier definition, recognition is one demonstrable aspect of musical style characterisation. The main thrust of this work is to develop a system for style recognition. We will consider this aspect first and, in the next section, go on to consider how the problem of characterisation can be addressed.

The recognition problem is essentially one of classification. We are given two sets of training data S_+ and S_- (say). The former represent the positive training examples, *i.e.* those in the style of music. The latter represent the negative training examples, *i.e.*, those not in the musical style. We are then given a new example M and the problem is to decide whether M should be in S_+ or S_-. The recognition process is illustrated in figure 1. The dictionary is shown containing two style subsets (S_+) and (S_-) constructed from the positive and negative training examples respectively. These style subsets are shown to overlap since there will be motifs that are present in both. The style subsets store the frequency of those motifs they contain. A new melody M is presented to the system and all the motifs present in M that are already in the dictionary are extracted to form the set $\rho(M)$. The frequencies with which these motifs occur in each style subset can then be used to classify M.

The way the problem has been tacked here is to search for common substrings or *motifs* in each of the data sets S_+ and S_-. Motifs are similar to

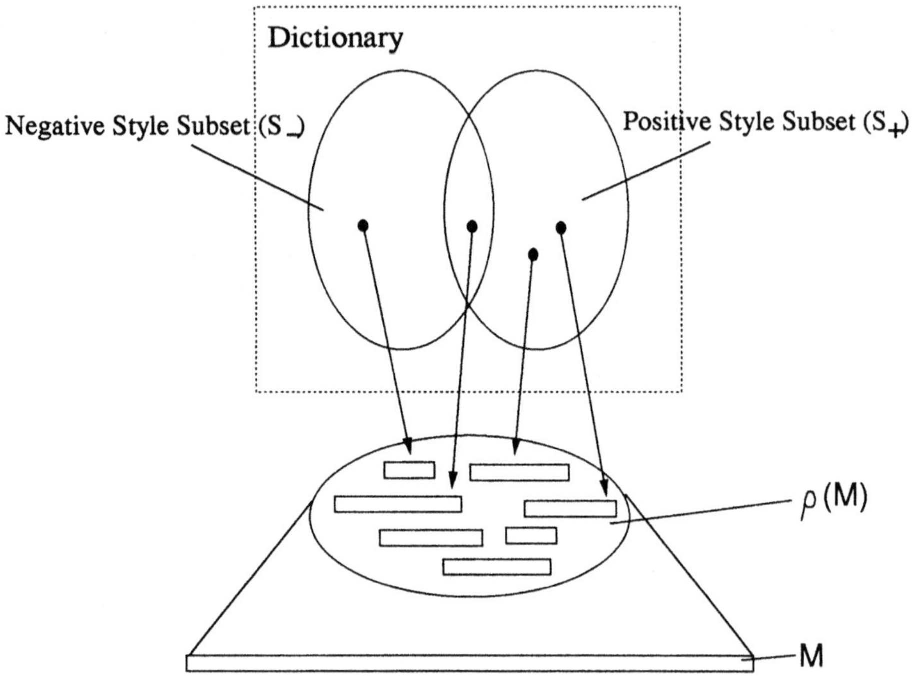

Figure 1: The Recognition Process

Cope's ***signatures***, except they are variable in length. The motifs are postulated to characterise the set, and their frequency of occurrence within each set is recorded in separate ***style subsets*** of the dictionary. An unseen test example is then presented to the system. It searches through to find all the motifs from the piece that are in the dictionary and, according to the relative frequencies of these motifs, produces an indicator as to whether the test example appears to be in the style or not.

We begin with a few definitions. Firstly for our purposes, a style is defined by those pieces which represent examples of it. So here a style S is a set of melodies M_i. A melody is a string of notes, each of which is specified by a pitch and a duration. No account is taken of harmonies. We can also define $\rho(M_i)$ and $\mu(S)$ the set of motifs drawn from M_i and S as follows:

$$\mu(S) = \{w : \exists M_i, M_j \in S; i \neq j; w \in C(M_i) \wedge w \in C(M_j)\}$$

where $C(M_i)$ is the set of all possible motifs (or substrings) of M_i.

$$\rho(M) = \{w : \exists \mu(S_i) \in D, w \in C(M) \wedge w \in \mu(S_i)\}$$

where D is a dictionary, *i.e.*, a set of sets of style specific motifs.

$\mu(S)$ represents the set of all motifs present in more than one melody in S, and $\rho(M)$ represents the set of all motifs present in the dictionary and in M.

Now the dictionary D is built up from style subsets each corresponding to a style, and constructed by pairwise matching of motifs across all example melodies in that style. A frequency count of motif occurrences is stored. For each match between two melodies, the motif frequency is incremented by one if that motif occurs at least once in both melodies. Notice that it is not incremented for each occurrence, the reason for this is because we are looking for motifs preserved over the style, and this could be biased by a motif that happened to occur a lot in just two examples of the style. Here we will only deal with the case where D comprises two styles that are constructed from the positive and negative training examples, $\mu(S_+)$ and $\mu(S_-)$ respectively.

So the problem is that we are given a new melody M and we want to calculate an estimate of the probability that M is a (possibly unseen) member of the style of positive examples rather than the negative examples. This is done by considering the set $\rho(M)$ as defined above – the set of motifs in the dictionary that could be found in M.

If we were to suppose that the set $\rho(M)$ were constructed by drawing random motifs from the $\mu(S_+)$ and $\mu(S_-)$, we could calculate a probability for each $w_i \in \rho(M)$ that it was taken from the set $\mu(S_+)$, *i.e.*, that it comes from the positive example set. Using "$\hookleftarrow$" to mean "drawn from", if the number of motifs in $\mu(S_+)$ were the same as in $\mu(S_-)$ we would get:

$$P(w_i \hookleftarrow \mu(S_+)) = \frac{q_i(\mu(S_+))}{q_i(\mu(S_+)) + q_i(\mu(S_-))}$$

where $q_i(\mu(S_k))$ is the number of occurrence of w_i in $\mu(S_k)$. We can then normalise this for different sized sets where $|\mu(S_k)|$ is the size of $\mu(S_k)$. This gives us:

$$P(w_i \hookleftarrow \mu(S_+)) = \frac{\frac{q_i(\mu(S_+))}{|\mu(S_+)|}}{\frac{q_i(\mu(S_+))}{|\mu(S_+)|} + \frac{q_i(\mu(S_-))}{|\mu(S_-)|}}.$$

We use these values to give an indication of how likely M is to be in the style by taking the arithmetic mean of these values, which we call z:

$$z = \frac{\sum_{i=1}^{|\rho(M)|} P(w_i \hookleftarrow \mu(S_+))}{|\rho(M)|}.$$

If $\rho(M)$ contains motifs that are predominantly in $\mu(S_+)$ then this value should be close to 1. Conversely if $\rho(M)$ contains motifs predominantly from $\mu(S_-)$ then this value will be closer to zero. However the figure is biased by the relative size of the style subsets. To allow for this bias z is compared to the dictionary mean μ which is the mean probability over all the motifs in the dictionary. It represents the expected value of z for a piece composed entirely from motifs selected entirely at random from the dictionary. The value μ is defined as follows

$$\mu = \frac{\sum_{i=1}^{(|\mu(S_+)|+|\mu(S_-)|)} P(w_i \hookleftarrow \mu(S_+))}{(|\mu(S_+)| + |\mu(S_-)|)}.$$

Furthermore we can estimate the significance of this result if we make the assumption that these probabilities are normally distributed. The variance of this mean, which we call σ^2, is just:

$$\sigma^2 = Var[P(w_i \hookleftarrow \mu(S))]/n.$$

So using our assumption of a normal distribution, the probability of obtaining a value z is:

$$P(Z = z) = \frac{1}{\sqrt{2\pi}} e^{-\frac{1}{2}x^2}.$$

with x:

$$x = \frac{z - \mu}{\sigma^2}.$$

The dictionary mean represents the expected value of $P(w_i \hookleftarrow \mu(S_+))$ for some w_i drawn at random from the dictionary. If this differs significantly from 0.5 then the results from the dictionary may reflect this bias.

2.3 Characterisation

The intention of this paper is not to produce a complete theory of musical style. Rather, it is to investigate the extent to which motifs alone can be used to characterise a style. The previous section describes how style can be recognised; here, we investigate how we can estimate how well the motifs characterise the style, in terms of synthesis of new works. The system does not actually generate new works, because it would be very difficult to assess the style of such computer generated material. Instead we use the assumption made by [Conklin & Witten 91] that "the predictive theory which minimises the entropy estimate will also generate original, acceptable works." Entropy here refers to the concept defined by [Shannon & Weaver 49], the expected information required to represent a concept. The entropy estimate in question is the entropy of the "next event in a piece".

The entropy of a concept, $H(X)$, is defined as:

$$H(X) = -\sum_{x \in X} p(x) log_2 p(x)$$

where the concept is viewed as a set with a probability function represented by the random variable X such that $p(x) = P(X = x)$. The entropy represents the minimal expected number of bits required to specify an element of X. Hence minimising description length is achieved by minimising the entropy. According to Conklin and Witten there are three techniques which can be used to estimate entropy; these are:

1. **Hypothesis Testing**, also known as the non-Bayesian approach. Here the examples E are divided into a randomly chosen training set E_{tr} and a disjoint test set E_{te}. Our estimate of entropy is then $\frac{L(E_{te}|T)}{|E_{te}|}$, where $L(E|T)$ means the length (in bits) of an encoding of the data E in the representation T, and $L(T)$ is the length of the encoding of the representation T. E_{te} should be large enough to ensure statistical significance, E must also be large, or else the estimate may be too high.

2. **Complexity-based** estimate, also known as a non-Bayesian estimate. Using the same notation as above, the estimate here is $\frac{L(T)+L(E|T)}{|E|}$.

3. **Knowledge Engineering** estimate. Here probabilities are elicited from a human expert by putting him or her in a gambling situation.

We employed the first technique to estimate the entropy. The process works by splitting the test pieces into a concatenation of motifs selected from the dictionary. The longest motifs that represented the piece were selected. This sequence forms the basic representation, however certain modifications are necessary to complete the representation. Any gaps between recognised sequences are represented using single interval values or durations. Since the motifs are represented as pitch intervals and duration ratios these also need to be given a value to make them absolute values. The probabilities of these motifs, single events and values are can be calculated, and so can be used to calculate an estimate.

3 Results

3.1 Introduction

SAM compares two style subsets and attempts to classify pieces into one or the other. It was decided that the most appropriate way to organise the tests was to consider first the case of comparing dictionaries of a single homogeneous style with one another *e.g.* Bach inventions versus Nutcracker Suite. We then went on to consider more general style subsets *e.g.* a collection of Bach, or even just a collection of different composers from the Baroque, Classical and Romantic periods, and to see how these compared to each other, and to the single style dictionaries. For each dictionary constructed in this way, test data consisted of positive examples, negative examples, examples in styles that were obviously related to either positive or negative styles, and finally orthogonal examples which are not so obviously related.

The scope of the experiments was limited to a certain extent by the MIDI files which were available on ftp-sites on the Internet; over 300 MIDI files were collected. However, documentation on the majority of them was poor or nonexistent and it is important to be sure about the composer of the work if it is to be included in a homogeneous style subset. Consequently the homogeneous style subsets were limited to Bach pieces of differing forms (chorales, inventions, fugues and preludes), and a style subset made up from pieces from Tchaikovsky's Nutcracker Suite. We begin by looking briefly at the data produced by SAM.

3.2 System Output

The numbers which the SAM system produces fall into two categories, information about the dictionary and information about the melody under test:

Dictionary Data

- Mean - The mean probability over all motifs in the dictionary that a motif was drawn from the positive style subset.

- Variance - The variance of these same probabilities.

- Number of positive style motifs - Simply the total number of motifs collected from the positive training set.
- Number of negative style motifs - Similarly for negative style motifs.

Melody Data

- Length - The number of pitch intervals in the melody.
- Mean - The mean probability over all the motifs matched in the melody that the motif comes from the positive style style subset.
- Variance - The variance of the above probabilities.
- Number of matched positive motifs - The number of motifs in the melody that match only with motifs in the positive style subset.
- Number of matched negative motifs - The number of motifs in the melody that match only with motifs in the negative style subset.
- Significance - The probability that the melody's mean value was arrived at by chance.

The most important information here are the two means. The null hypothesis is that the motifs taken from the piece are drawn from the dictionary entirely at random. The dictionary mean corresponds to the expected value that would be obtained if this were the case. The melody mean corresponds to the mean value of the motifs contained in the melody. The difference between these two corresponds to a stylistic bias in the music towards one or other of the style style subsets. This gives us a two-tailed experimental hypothesis. If the melody mean is greater than the dictionary mean then this shows a bias towards the positive set. If it is smaller then the bias is towards the negative set. If we assume these values are normally distributed, then we can use the dictionary variance and mean to calculate the probability that these results are due to chance. In practice, it turns out that all the pieces presented to the dictionary were so unlikely to have motif sets occurring by chance that this significance value was very close to zero. Therefore, unfortunately, it provides little information. The reason that the results seem so significant is probably due to the high degree of dependency between the occurrence of different motifs. In order to derive the figure, independence had to be assumed and it may be the case that violating this assumption leads to such low probability values.

The dictionary variance gives an indication of the similarity between the two style subsets in the dictionary. The more motifs they have in common, the smaller the variance. For example, the dictionary variance of a dictionary containing Bach preludes and inventions is 0.187. These two classes are obviously very similar, and hence difficult to distinguish. On the other hand, the variance of a dictionary containing Bach chorales and parts of Tchaikovsky's Nutcracker suite was 0.245. There is also a tendency for the dictionary variance to decrease with the size of the dictionary (in accordance with the central limit theorem). For instance, the variance of a dictionary comparing 3 inventions with 3 Nutcracker suite movements is 0.236 compared with the slightly smaller value of 0.230 when five of each are used.

The melody variance should give an indication of the motif homogeneity within a piece with respect to the two styles in the dictionary. A piece containing a large number of motifs from both positive and negative styles will have a high variance, whereas a piece with a motifs principally from one style will have a lower variance.

3.3 Single Style Subsets

3.3.1 Introduction

In this section we consider the results of classification of pieces using dictionaries composed of homogeneous style subsets. In each case there are 4 sets of test examples: those from the same style as the positive set, the negative set, related examples (in this case examples of some Bach form other than that in the style subset) and orthogonal examples from unrelated styles. In all cases the test examples were different from those used to build the dictionaries.

3.3.2 Bach versus Tchaikovsky

Dictionary Size	N° of tests	Correct	Incorrect	%age
Chorales v. Nutcracker				
Small	11	11	0	100
Fugues v. Nutcracker				
Small	21	20	1	95
Medium	19	19	0	100
Inventions v. Nutcracker				
Small	15	14	1	93
Medium	11	11	0	100
Preludes v. Nutcracker				
Small	21	18	3	85
Medium	18	16	2	100

Each of the Bach forms was tried in a style subset against a style subset of Tchaikovsky motifs taken from the Nutcracker suite. In total seven dictionaries were constructed: the small ones used three pieces from each style; the medium ones used 5.

Chorales Since there was a limited number of chorales this group of runs only featured a single positive example of an unseen chorale. However a number of Bach inventions were tested against the dictionary (as related works), and, as hoped, they were classified as being more like Bach chorales than Nutcracker movements.

Fugues In the case of the small dictionary there is one misclassified piece, which is actually the waltz from the Nutcracker Suite. This piece seems to match better with the Bach invention motifs than with the rest of the Nutcracker Suite. This may be due to the fact that the different movements of Nutcracker Suite involve quite diverse musical styles and that the three pieces that were used to make up the style subset were insufficient to capture the style. Increasing the number of training examples seems to solve this problem effectively, and raises the success rate to 100%.

Inventions This misclassified piece was, again, the Waltz from the Nutcracker. The discrepancy here was slightly smaller than it was with the Fugues but nonetheless the melody mean was significantly smaller than the dictionary mean. Increasing the number of test examples seems to solve the problem. This suggests, as one would expect, that the more pieces used in training, the better the system is at classification – because it contains a richer selection of motifs from the style.

Preludes In this case, there are more errors. The preludes seem to cause more classification problems than any of the other styles. The three misclassified pieces in the first set of runs are the Waltz (again), a B minor prelude, and a chorale (No. 197) – which is included as an example of a Bach piece (related example) and would be expected to be classified as being more like a prelude. Interestingly, the same chorale was successfully classified when the Nutcracker examples were compared to inventions and fugues. Furthermore, increasing the dictionary size only results in rectifying the classification of the Waltz; the other two pieces remain wrongly classified.

The orthogonal examples – in this case, movements of a Beethoven piano piece – are not included in the summary above, since it is not clear whether they were correctly classified or not. They are considered in section 3.5.

3.3.3 Bach versus Bach

Dictionary Composition	N° of tests	Correct	Incorrect	%age
Inventions v Chorales	6	6	0	100
Fugues v Inventions	16	10	6	63
Preludes v Inventions	16	4	12	25
Overall	38	20	18	53

This table shows results collected by comparing examples of the different Bach forms against one another. The use of motifs in style analysis was proposed by Cope as being composer specific, not form specific. The motifs themselves are only taken from pitch intervals in the melody line, and the system has no representation of their rhythms, nor of the structure of the piece. It is not surprising therefore that attempting to classify examples on this basis is rather unsuccessful. It seems to have some success in differentiating Inventions and Chorales, although this may well be due simply to the small number of test examples that were available for these sets.

3.4 Mixed Style Subsets

In this section we look at results obtained with tests on dictionaries composed of mixtures of styles. Two such dictionaries were constructed. The first was built of different examples of Bach, one example of each form. The second was more general and incorporated works from Mozart, Beethoven, Chopin, Rimsky-Korsakov and Brahms.

Dictionary Composition	N° of tests	Correct	Incorrect	%age
Bach v General	10	10	0	100
Bach v Nutcracker	14	12	2	86
Nutcracker v General	5	5	0	100

Bach In the first run, Bach is paired with the general mix style subset and in the second with the Nutcracker style subset. Most of the Bach pieces seemed to classify very strongly as Bach against the general style subset, except for one prelude which only just made it. The second set of runs, against the Nutcracker style subset, gives two incorrect classifications. Predictably these are the Waltz, and one of the preludes.

General Here, again, negative set tests were not counted. All the Nutcracker examples seemed to be comfortably classified correctly. Again, the closest case was that of the Waltz, but even this looked fairly safe.

3.5 Orthogonal Tests

The orthogonal test results have not been scored since it is not clear whether any given result is correctly or incorrectly classified. However there are some interesting patterns in the data. Throughout the inter-Bach comparisons, Händel's "Hallelujah" Chorus, and Telemann's Passepied were considered more like inventions than any other style. Similarly the two movements of a Beethoven piano piece which were used as orthogonal test examples tended to be classified as being more like the Nutcracker suite than like any of the Bach forms. The exception is the case where the Nutcracker is paired with the preludes style subset. In this case the results differed with different dictionary sizes. With the small dictionary the first movement of the Beethoven was classified as being closest to the Nutcracker, whereas the second movement was just classified as being closest to the preludes. Curiously, with the larger dictionary, the situation was reversed.

3.6 Entropy Reduction

The entropy reduction tests were based on the assumption made by [Conklin & Witten 91], that a theory capable of minimising an entropy estimate will also generate original, acceptable works. In other words we may take the reduction in entropy estimates that results from applying the theory as a measure of how well a technique characterises a musical style. Here we used the technique described earlier to estimate the entropy of a representation that employed the motif dictionary. This value was compared to the raw entropy of each piece. The results were averaged over a number of pieces. In all cases the training and test sets were disjoint. Three different style subsets were used to build the representations. These were:

1. A single Bach style – Fugues,
2. A mixture of Bach styles,
3. The Nutcracker style subset.

Style	Entropy	Motif-Entropy	Difference	% Difference
Bach Style Subset				
Nutcracker	6.301	5.203	1.098	17.4
Fugues	5.141	3.700	1.441	28.0
Inventions	4.882	4.005	0.877	18.0
Mixed Bach Style Subset				
Nutcracker	6.301	5.267	1.034	16.4
Fugues	5.141	3.705	1.436	27.9
Nutcracker Style Subset				
Nutcracker	6.301	4.273	2.028	32.2
Fugues	5.141	4.357	0.784	15.3
Mixed Bach	4.556	4.342	0.213	4.7

Bach Style Subset Encoding these styles against a dictionary style subset of Fugues gives the above results. Clearly the Fugues are better represented by the style subset than the Nutcracker examples are, as we would have hoped. The inventions do not achieve as good a reduction in entropy as the fugues do. This is to be expected since they have a much lower raw entropy to begin with. It can be seen that the percentage reduction in entropy is marginally better than that of the Nutcracker style, again as would be expected.

Mixed Bach Style Subset Here we see, as expected, that when the same pieces from the Nutcracker and fugues are represented using a style subset of mixed Bach styles, the reduction in entropy is smaller. However the fugues are still considerably better represented.

Nutcracker Style Subset These results show the reduction in entropy for pieces represented using a style subset constructed from the Nutcracker suite. As we would hope the reduction in entropy of other examples of the suite is significantly greater than the reduction in entropy of the fugues. The mixed Bach style trails very much behind, although this had a much lower raw entropy to begin with, and so less improvement might be expected.

3.7 Summary

Overall, providing the dictionary is large enough (at least 5 examples), these results show successful classification on 95% of the 88 scorable runs. Furthermore the misclassifications seem to result from the same pieces. It would seem that the Waltz movement of the Nutcracker suite contains a number of motifs reminiscent of Bach, and that the preludes have surprising variation in style. Though the training data is not as wide ranging as it could be, these results would suggest that the basic technique is quite successful as a classification algorithm and therefore pitch motifs do indeed capture a great deal of stylistic information.

This conclusion is strengthened by the results from entropy tests which show a significant reduction in the entropy of a piece when motifs extracted from pieces of the same style are used to represent it.

4 Conclusion

This paper began with the intention of investigating the proposition made by Cope that musical style can be characterised by patterns of pitch intervals and duration ratios which recur in distinct works by the same composer. Using this premise as a starting point the SAM system was constructed to learn style classifications. The system extracted motifs from positive and negative example sets and stored their frequencies in two separate style subsets in the style dictionary. When a test piece was presented to the system it extracts all known motifs, and using the relative frequencies of these motifs in each dictionary, calculates an estimate as to which style subset it most resembles.

The results demonstrated that providing the test sets were large enough (at least 5 pieces), the system was able to correctly classify pieces from two different composers over 95% of the time. The results could be criticised for the small number of styles tested. Nonetheless they strongly support Cope's idea that style is characterised by motifs.

This idea is further supported by the results from the entropy tests which demonstrate that a greater reduction in entropy is achieved when a piece is represented using motifs from its style than using motifs from elsewhere.

The definition of motif used here is different from that of Cope's signatures in that they can be of any length and can occur at any point in the music. Like a signature, they need only occur in at least two examples of a style to be considered motifs. However there are many other possible definitions. Motifs could be defined as substrings that must occur in all examples of the style, or some fixed percentage of them. The motifs that are used here are in pitch only. However, rhythm could be employed to define independent rhythmic motifs, or motifs which might incorporate both pitch and rhythm. Matches for Cope's signatures allow variations between the two patterns within certain constraints. This is something else that could be incorporated into our motif definition.

The use of motifs in the analysis of musical style is a new area of research. These results show that motifs provide a way of successfully discriminating between styles. Therefore, they may play a significant part in our own ability to recognise and distinguish musical style. There is a great deal more research that could be carried out to investigate whether the conclusions reached here about motifs (using this, or another, definition) can be applied to other musical styles.

References

[Bernstein 76] Leonard Bernstein. *The Unanswered Question – Six Talks at Harvard.* Harvard University Press, 1976.

[Conklin & Witten 91] D. Conklin and I. H. Witten. Prediction and entropy of music. Technical Report 91/457/41, Department of Computer Science, University of Calgary, Alberta, Canada, December 1991.

[Cope 87] D. Cope. Experiments in musical intelligence. In *Proceedings of the International Computer Music Conference*, San Francisco, 1987.

[Cope 91] D. Cope. *Computers and Musical Style.* Oxford University Press, 1991.

[Dickinson 65] S. Dickinson. *A Handbook of Style in Music.* Vassar College, Ploughkeepsie, N.Y., 1965.

[Kippen & Bel 89] J. Kippen and B. Bel. The identification and modelling of a percussion 'language', and the emergence of musical concepts in a machine-learning experimental set-up. *Computers and the Humanities*, 23(3):199–214, 1989.

[Meyer 89] L. Meyer. *Style and Music.* University of Pennsylvania Press, Philadelphia, 1989.

[Schenker 35] H. Schenker. *Free Composition.* Schirmer, 1935. Original German title: "Der Freie Satz"; Translated and edited by E. Oster.

[Schönburg 75] A. Schönburg. *Style and Idea.* University of California Press, Berkeley, 1975. Editor: L. Stein.

[Shannon & Weaver 49] C. E. Shannon and W. Weaver. *The Mathematical Theory of Communication.* The University of Illinois Press, 1949.

Author Index

Published in 1990–92

AI and Cognitive Science '89, Dublin City University, Eire, 14–15 September 1989
Alan F. Smeaton and Gabriel McDermott (Eds.)

Specification and Verification of Concurrent Systems, University of Stirling, Scotland, 6–8 July 1988
C. Rattray (Ed.)

Semantics for Concurrency, Proceedings of the International BCS-FACS Workshop, Sponsored by Logic for IT (S.E.R.C.), University of Leicester, UK, 23–25 July 1990
M. Z. Kwiatkowska, M. W. Shields and R. M. Thomas (Eds.)

Functional Programming, Glasgow 1989
Proceedings of the 1989 Glasgow Workshop, Fraserburgh, Scotland, 21–23 August 1989
Kei Davis and John Hughes (Eds.)

Persistent Object Systems, Proceedings of the Third International Workshop, Newcastle, Australia, 10–13 January 1989
John Rosenberg and David Koch (Eds.)

Z User Workshop, Oxford 1989, Proceedings of the Fourth Annual Z User Meeting, Oxford, 15 December 1989
J. E. Nicholls (Ed.)

Formal Methods for Trustworthy Computer Systems (FM89), Halifax, Canada, 23–27 July 1989
Dan Craigen (Editor) and Karen Summerskill (Assistant Editor)

Security and Persistence, Proceedings of the International Workshop on Computer Architectures to Support Security and Persistence of Information, Bremen, West Germany, 8–11 May 1990
John Rosenberg and J. Leslie Keedy (Eds.)

Women into Computing: Selected Papers 1988–1990
Gillian Lovegrove and Barbara Segal (Eds.)

3rd Refinement Workshop (organised by BCS-FACS, and sponsored by IBM UK Laboratories, Hursley Park and the Programming Research Group, University of Oxford), Hursley Park, 9–11 January 1990
Carroll Morgan and J. C. P. Woodcock (Eds.)

Designing Correct Circuits, Workshop jointly organised by the Universities of Oxford and Glasgow, Oxford, 26–28 September 1990
Geraint Jones and Mary Sheeran (Eds.)

Functional Programming, Glasgow 1990
Proceedings of the 1990 Glasgow Workshop on Functional Programming, Ullapool, Scotland, 13–15 August 1990
Simon L. Peyton Jones, Graham Hutton and Carsten Kehler Holst (Eds.)

4th Refinement Workshop, Proceedings of the 4th Refinement Workshop, organised by BCS-FACS, Cambridge, 9–11 January 1991
Joseph M. Morris and Roger C. Shaw (Eds.)

AI and Cognitive Science '90, University of Ulster at Jordanstown, 20–21 September 1990
Michael F. McTear and Norman Creaney (Eds.)

Software Re-use, Utrecht 1989, Proceedings of the Software Re-use Workshop, Utrecht, The Netherlands, 23–24 November 1989
Liesbeth Dusink and Patrick Hall (Eds.)

Z User Workshop, 1990, Proceedings of the Fifth Annual Z User Meeting, Oxford, 17–18 December 1990
J.E. Nicholls (Ed.)

IV Higher Order Workshop, Banff 1990
Proceedings of the IV Higher Order Workshop, Banff, Alberta, Canada, 10–14 September 1990
Graham Birtwistle (Ed.)

ALPUK91, Proceedings of the 3rd UK Annual Conference on Logic Programming, Edinburgh, 10–12 April 1991
Geraint A.Wiggins, Chris Mellish and Tim Duncan (Eds.)

Specifications of Database Systems
International Workshop on Specifications of Database Systems, Glasgow, 3–5 July 1991
David J. Harper and Moira C. Norrie (Eds.)

7th UK Computer and Telecommunications Performance Engineering Workshop
Edinburgh, 22–23 July 1991
J. Hillston, P.J.B. King and R.J. Pooley (Eds.)

Logic Program Synthesis and Transformation
Proceedings of LOPSTR 91, International Workshop on Logic Program Synthesis and Transformation, University of Manchester, 4–5 July 1991
T.P. Clement and K.-K. Lau (Eds.)

Declarative Programming, Sasbachwalden 1991
PHOENIX Seminar and Workshop on Declarative Programming, Sasbachwalden, Black Forest, Germany, 18–22 November 1991
John Darlington and Roland Dietrich (Eds.)

Building Interactive Systems: Architectures and Tools
Philip Gray and Roger Took (Eds.)

Functional Programming, Glasgow 1991
Proceedings of the 1991 Glasgow Workshop on Functional Programming, Portree, Isle of Skye, 12–14 August 1991
Rogardt Heldal, Carsten Kehler Holst and Philip Wadler (Eds.)

Object Orientation in Z
Susan Stepney, Rosalind Barden and David Cooper (Eds.)

Code Generation – Concepts, Tools, Techniques
Proceedings of the International Workshop on Code Generation, Dagstuhl, Germany, 20–24 May 1991
Robert Giegerich and Susan L. Graham (Eds.)

Z User Workshop, York 1991, Proceedings of the Sixth Annual Z User Meeting, York, 16–17 December 1991
J.E. Nicholls (Ed.)

Formal Aspects of Measurement
Proceedings of the BCS-FACS Workshop on Formal Aspects of Measurement, South Bank University, London, 5 May 1991
Tim Denvir, Ros Herman and R.W. Whitty (Eds.)

AI and Cognitive Science '91
University College, Cork, 19–20 September 1991
Humphrey Sorensen (Ed.)

GPSR Compliance

The European Union's (EU) General Product Safety Regulation (GPSR) is a set of rules that requires consumer products to be safe and our obligations to ensure this.

If you have any concerns about our products, you can contact us on ProductSafety@springernature.com

In case Publisher is established outside the EU, the EU authorized representative is:

Springer Nature Customer Service Center GmbH
Europaplatz 3
69115 Heidelberg, Germany

Batch number: 10844675

Printed by Printforce, the Netherlands